Discovery

Christianity & Islam

PHILOSOPHY & ETHICS FOR OCR GCSE RELIGIOUS STUDIES

Jon Mayled

Nelson Thornes

a Wolters Kluwer business

Published in 2007 by:
Nelson Thornes Ltd
Delta Place
27 Bath Road
CHELTENHAM
GL53 7TH
United Kingdom

07 08 09 10 11 / 10 9 8 7 6 5 4 3 2 1

A catalogue record for this book is available from the British Library

ISBN 978 0 7487 8132 4

Page make-up by Thomson Digital
Printed in Croatia by Zrinski

Contents

Acknowledgements

The publishers are grateful to the following for permission to reproduce photographs and other material:

Page 2: watch © Ellen Richards (NT); page 3: Painting of 'Ancient of Days by William Blake (DS001502) © Leonardo de Delva / CORBIS; page 4: scientist performing an experiment (169NTRF) Photodisc 72 (NT); page 6: The Trinity artwork © Anglican Missal, Society of SS Peter & Paul; page 6/7: 'The ascension of Jesus Christ' wall illustration (AYMMG5) © ReligiousStock / Alamy; page 8/9: reading a bible (054NTRF) Digital Stock 11 (NT); page 11: Muslims praying (077NTRF) Digital Stock 11 (NT); page 14: cave on Mount Nur (10409268) © ArkReligion.com; page 19: The Judgement detail from the 'Table of the Seven Deadly Sins and the Four Last Things' c1480 oil panel (A9MXX8) © Visual Arts Library (London) / Alamy; page 20: 'John Baptises Jesus in the River Jordan' painting by Henry Coller (AH0W08) © ArkReligion.com / Alamy; page 21: set of rosary beads (051NTRF) Digital Stock 11 (NT); page 24: sharing bread and wine (CO584096NTRF) Corel (NT); page 27: an eagle lectern at Bath Abbey (A43X25) © Ian M Butterfield / Alamy; page 28: icon (037A) Digital Stock DS11 (NT); page 29: ICTHUS fish symbol (183NTRF) Photodisc 32 (NT); page 32: Muslim women perform Wudu (A5B10G) © Sally and Richard Greenhill / Alamy; page 36: Mosque Haifa Israel Middle East (ATYCXB) © CuboImages srl / Alamy; page 41: battery chickens (118028NTRF) Digital Vision (NT); page 43: The Creation of the World closed doors of the triptych the Garden of Earthly Delights c1500 (A4JX2Y) © The Print Collector/ Alamy; page 48/49: Brazil South of State of Maranhao Forest burnt to fertilize the soil (ANC6A4) © Mireille Vautier / Alamy; page 50: light of the earth (0301315NTRF) Digital Vision (NT); page 57: Overgrown graves (AJMP3D) © Spencer Dare / Alamy; page 59: The Last Judgement by Michelangelo on the wall of the Sistine Chapel (A0BFGP) © Alex Segre / Alamy; page 62: grave covered in fresh wreaths and flowers after a funeral (AP9N05) © Kathy deWitt / Alamy; page 64 (top): man being prepared for burial (TL008204) © David Turnely / CORBIS; page 64 (bottom): Muslim community at the funeral of a young man UK (ATDKD5) © by Ian Miles-Flashpoint Pictures / Alamy; page 71: Mother Theresa (785054) Corel 654 (NT); Adolph Hitler (ILN VI 118) (NT) page 74: gargoyle © Ellen Richards (NT) page 77: Jesus carrying cross (BXRW.25568NTRF) (NT); page 88: Same sex partnership (075NTRF) Photodisc 45 (NT); page 90: modern family (136NTRF) Photodisc 79 (NT); page 97: three young muslim women wearing headscarves (AR76G7) © Stephen Bisgrove / Alamy; Muslim women traditional dress (UT0051205) © Reuters / CORBIS; page 99: a Muslim wedding in Pakistan (CJ004996) © Charles & Josette Lenars / CORBIS; page 106: mouse growing human ear (EMP-2743648) © PA Photos; page 108 anti-abortion demonstration (EMP-1954947) PA Photos; page 116: a concerned man watches over his wife in an intensive care unit (A68KKN) © Mira / Alamy; page 121: Eleanor Roosevelt (518030) Corel 588 (NT); page 125: Archbishop Desmond Tutu (AXW6TD) © David Pearson / Alamy; Father Trevor Huddleston (A8320E) © POPPERTFOTO / Alamy; page 127: Female vicar performing Eucharist in church UK (ARX94B) © Photofusion Picture Library/ Alamy; page 132: Shabina Begum (DW15-1192533) © Toby Melville/ Reuters/ CORBIS; page 134: Iran Police Trial (EMP4977851) © Kamran Jebreili/ AP/PA Photos; page 137: Bill Gates (DWF15-609236) © Rick Friedman / CORBIS; page 144: Oscar Romero (EF001338) © Leif Skoogfors / CORBIS; page 146: Islamic Aid at work reproduced with permission; page 152: soldier shooting (42-17094782) © Sgt. Roe F. Seigle/ ZUMA/ CORBIS; page 154: School students protest in Parliament Square against the invasion of Iraq (A7F937) © Philip Wolmuth / Alamy; page 157: Death chamber (IK001179) © Mark Jenkinson / CORBIS; page 160: Soldier outside mosque in Iraq (42-15854993) © Hassan Ali/ epa/ CORBIS; page 162: portrait of Asian elderly man (A5XC94) © Photofusion Picture Library / Alamy.

Introduction

This book has been written especially to cover the content and skill of the OCR GCSE Religious Studies specifications B 1931 (full course) and 1031 (short course) Philosophy and Ethics in relation to Christianity and Islam. However, it is also suitable for use with some of the specifications of other awarding bodies.

The entire content of the course for each of the ten units for Christianity and Islam is covered by the text.

Each unit has an introductory section containing general background information before the religion-specific content.

A number of conventions have been adopted in this text. All spellings conform to the SCAA Glossary of Religious Terms 1994. The sacred texts used for quotations are those used by OCR in examination papers:

Holy Bible New International Version, International Bible Society, Colorado, 0-340-56782-1

The Meaning of the Holy Qur'an, Ali, Amana Publications, 0951595755-8

In Islam Muslims use the words '**Salla-llahu alaihi wa sallam**'– peace and blessings of Allah upon him, every time the Prophet Muhammad ﷺ is mentioned. Similar respect is accorded to the other prophets. The Arabic colophon ﷺ in the text represents these words.

The transliteration of Arabic words in the text is based on the SCAA Glossary 1994 and 'A Popular Dictionary of Islam', I R Netton, Curzon Press, London, 1992, 0 7007 0233 4. The Arabic letters 'ayn and hamza are transliterated throughout as ' and ' respectively.

Throughout this book dates are given as CE (Common Era) or BCE (Before Common Era). These replace the traditional AD (Anno Domini) and BC (Before Christ).

Introduction

What is 'God'?
- Is there a thing we call God?
- If there is a God, what is it?
- Is God a person or a thing?
- If God is a person, is this person male or female?

These questions cannot be answered in any 'scientific' manner. A scientific proof to a question relies on being able to carry out an experiment again and again and reaching the same result. Here, there is no experiment to carry out – so there are no results.

Most religious people see 'God' as a divine and supreme being who is totally good and who is so far beyond our experience and our thoughts that we cannot find any way to describe him/her. In fact, Christianity and Islam both represent God as male, though some followers of Christianity suggest that this may leave out some of the aspects of God which perhaps we would normally think of as female, such as nurturing and life giving. They claim that the only reason God is thought to be male is because it was men who founded these religions.

We may ask questions such as:
- If there is a God, would he/she let this happen?
- If there is a God, then why am I so unhappy, unlucky, etc?
- There must be a God because otherwise how did we get here?
- There must be a God because otherwise what would happen to us after we die?
- There must be a God because otherwise why do so many people believe in religion?

We could say that religion exists to answer these questions, but the existence of so many different religions in the world, and even different groups within religions, shows that we have not managed to come up with 'the' answer to these questions, only suggestions.

For centuries, people have tried to find answers to these questions and there are several arguments which have been produced in an attempt to prove that God does exist:

Ontological argument

Anselm (1033–1109) said that people described God as 'that than which nothing greater can be conceived', therefore, God must exist otherwise we could not produce this description.

Cosmological argument

Thomas Aquinas (1225–1274) argued that something cannot come from nothing. Therefore, because there is a universe, someone or something has brought it into existence. He said that this 'first cause' of the universe was God.

Teleological argument (Design argument)

William Paley (1734–1805) produced a theory which has become known as the Divine Watchmaker. He said that if you were walking across a field and saw a large rock, you would just assume that it had always been there. However, if you also found a watch there you would assume that its parts had not come together by chance but that someone had designed it. He then applied this argument to the world and God by saying that the world was so complicated that it could not have come into existence by chance. If the world did not appear by chance, then it must have been designed and that designer must have been God.

If you stumbled upon this watch, you would not assume that its parts had come together by chance but that someone had designed it.

More modern arguments:

Argument from experience

Some people have argued that God can be experienced. This may be through incidents such as answers to prayers or the experience of miracles. Because people have experienced these things, they argue that God must exist.

Moral argument

This argument says that all people have a basic understanding of what is 'right' and 'wrong'. If this is the case, then where did this knowledge come from? The only answer to this must be from God.

All of these arguments have people who support them and people who disagree with them but they are still only arguments. None of them can actually 'prove' the existence of God in any way which would be acceptable as proof to a scientist.

As well as those who do believe in God, there are many people who do not believe. These people are usually divided into two groups: agnostics, who say that they do not know whether there is a God or not; and atheists who say that they are sure that there is not a God.

Another difficulty which many religions face is:

How can God be described? If you had to sit down now and write a description of God, what would it be?

The ways in which different religions have described God, and also the way in which some of them have drawn pictures or made statues of God, are very different. They are different because, as we cannot prove whether or not God exists, we have no real idea what he or she looks like. Some religions, such as Islam and Judaism, forbid their followers to attempt to make a picture or statue of God because this would be disrespectful.

We must also remember that if we could truly describe God, then we would have somehow limited God to something which is within our human experience. God becomes no more than human if humans can describe what God is.

If you try to think of the universe being infinite, going on for ever, and then you imagine travelling beyond every part of it which we can see with even the strongest and most sophisticated scientific equipment, you soon reach a point where you really cannot think any more, the idea is so vast that your brain begins to 'hurt' just trying to imagine it. Yet, if what religions say about God is true, then this being, or force, must be infinitely larger and more difficult to think about than something which he or she created.

It is because of this that people use words or qualities to describe God which are often not very definite:
● Some people think of God as a father, a ruler, a king or a friend.

Others may say that God is **omnipotent** (all-powerful), **omniscient** (all-knowing), **omnibenevolent** (all-loving) and **omnipresent** (everywhere at the same time).

All these words may help us to think about God but they do not really help us to understand what this thing, which some people believe in, called 'God', is.

What is truth?

It is sometimes very difficult to know what we mean by 'truth'.

The truth is usually something which we definitely know to be a fact. People say 'I want the truth' or 'I want to get to the truth', and this suggests that when they hear or find the truth they will recognise it.

On the other hand, some people say that for something to be true we must have evidence which proves that truth.

However, we do not have evidence for religions which we can test scientifically. People usually do not say things like, 'Whenever I'm short of money I pray to God and he or she gives me some'. Even if they did say this we would probably not believe them, at the most we would say that it was a coincidence because this is not how experience might suggest God works.

There are various types of truth:
- Scientific truth is perhaps the easiest sort of truth. When a scientist conducts an experiment which can be repeated over and over again with the same results, this establishes a truth, for example, the way in which two chemicals will react if you mix them together. This is sometimes called 'empirical truth'.
- Historical truth is found when, perhaps, evidence about a king is discovered which proves that a particular event took place in the past.
- Moral truth is a suggestion that we might 'know' what is actually right or wrong without necessarily being able to prove it.
- Aesthetic or artistic truth can be found in novels, pictures, films and even, perhaps, music. It is the idea that, for example, although what we are reading or watching may be a work of fiction which a person created, the way in which the people involved behave is 'true to human nature'.
- Spiritual truth is the type of truth which we find in religion. This is the idea that people believe in a religion and follow it in order to discover the 'real truth', the truth which comes from God.
- Religious people often say that there is an 'absolute truth' because they believe in the teachings of their religion. If we belong to one religion and accept its claims to truth, we may, therefore, be in a position were we feel we can say that all other religions are wrong and do not have the truth.

Symbols and language

Because it is so difficult to find words to use to describe God, people sometimes use particular types of language:

Allegory – a symbolic way of using words so that they may have a deeper meaning. An example is calling God 'Father'. People do not mean that God is their natural, physical father but they are using the word to show the sort of relationship which they have with God.

Analogy – a comparison between two things. In the Bible there is a passage where God is described as being like a mother hen looking after her chickens. This helps to show how God cares for creation.

Myth – a story which may not be literally true but which contains important spiritual or moral truths. Some people think that the Jewish Creation stories in Genesis 1–3 are myths. Perhaps they were not intended to be taken as literal truth but they explain God's relationship with the world and with humanity.

Symbol – something which represents something else. For example, Christians often use the symbol of a dove to represent the Holy Spirit.

Activity

Read the arguments for the existence of God. Which do you think are the most convincing arguments and which are the least? Why?

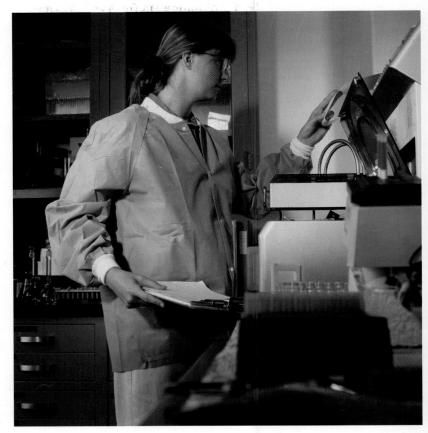

Scientific truths can be proven because experiments can be repeated again and again with the same results.

Christianity

This topic looks at the idea of belief in a god or a divine being:

- What do Christians believe about the nature of God?
- What reasons do Christians give to support their belief in God?
- What do Christians believe about Jesus?
- Why is the Bible so important to Christians?
- What do Christians believe about miracles?

Christian beliefs about the nature of God

Christianity is a **monotheistic** religion. This means that Christians believe there is only one God. God is so different from anything else that it is difficult to describe him in any way. Sometimes God is simply described as 'holy'.

Christians believe that God has certain attributes or characteristics:

- God is eternal.
- God is omnipresent (everywhere) and has no physical body.
- God created the world for a purpose.
- God is omnibenevolent (all-loving).
- God wishes people to live morally.
- God is omnipotent and omniscient (all-powerful and all-knowing).
- God will judge everyone.

Beliefs about God

Christians believe that the God of the Jews found in the Jewish Scriptures (**Old Testament**) and the God of the **New Testament** is one God.

This God is sometimes described as God the Father, the creator of all life, this is the God to whom Jesus was praying in the Lord's Prayer:

> **Our Father in heaven,**
> **hallowed be your name,**
> **your kingdom come,**
> **your will be done,**
> **on earth as it is in heaven.**

> **Give us today our daily bread.**
> **Forgive us our sins as we forgive those who sin against us.**
> **Lead us not into temptation but deliver us from evil.**

The title 'Father' also expresses a close family relationship with God, as a father may care for and look after his children.

Sometimes God is described as God the Son, Jesus Christ or Jesus of Nazareth. God chose to come to earth as a human. This belief is called the Incarnation when Jesus was born by Mary.

He came to teach people God's will and to show them what life would be like in the future in the **kingdom of God**.

Jesus of Nazareth, the Messiah of Christianity, is particularly important because, although he was innocent, he willingly died on the cross to save people from their sins. This was the crucifixion.

Christianity teaches that because Jesus, and so God, chose to die because he loved humanity and wanted to save them, all people are forgiven their sins and so have a chance, when they die, to go to heaven. By dying, Jesus atoned for the sins of the world.

When Jesus rose from the dead, three days after he was killed, (the **resurrection**) he showed that death was not the end and that God had power over death:

> **Here is a trustworthy saying that deserves full acceptance: Christ Jesus came into the world to save sinners – of whom I am the worst. But for that very reason I was shown mercy so that in me, the worst of sinners, Christ Jesus might display his unlimited patience as an example for those who would believe in him and receive eternal life. Now to the King eternal, immortal, invisible, the only God, be honour and glory for ever and ever. Amen.**
> (1 Timothy 1:15–17)

Sometimes God is seen as God the Holy Spirit who inspires people and gives them strength.

Clearly the God who appears in the Old Testament seems to be different from the God whom Jesus speaks of as 'Father', but Christians believe that the whole Bible is the revealed Word of God and that these differences show the changing relationship between God and humanity over thousands of years.

> **All Scripture is God-breathed and is useful for teaching, rebuking, correcting and training in righteousness, so that the man of God may be thoroughly equipped for every good work.**
>
> (2 Timothy 3:16–17)

This belief that God is made up of three different parts: the Father; the Son; and the Holy Spirit is called the **doctrine of the Trinity** and it is this teaching which makes Christian beliefs about God different from all other religions. The Trinity is the three 'persons' or 'natures' of God. This can be very difficult to understand: the Creed of St Athanasius says:

> **So the Father is God, the Son is God: and the Holy Spirit is God. So likewise the Father is Lord, the Son Lord: and the Holy Spirit Lord. And yet not three Lords: but one Lord.**

Other statements about the Trinity are found in the Nicene Creed:

> **We believe in one God, the Father, the almighty, maker of heaven and earth...**
>
> **We believe in one Lord, Jesus Christ, the only Son of God, eternally begotten of the Father, true God from true God, begotten not made, of one Being with the Father...**
>
> **We believe in the Holy Spirit, the Lord, the giver of life, who proceeds from the Father and the Son. With the Father and the Son he is worshipped and glorified. He has spoken through the Prophets.**

Many people have tried to represent the Trinity to show the relationship between these three 'Persons': God the Father; God the Son; and God the Holy Spirit, and to show that they are parts of the one God.

Some people have said that the Trinity can be represented by water: it can be a fluid; it can be frozen and become solid; or it can be heated and become steam, but all the time it still has the same chemical formula (H_2O).

Discussion

Do you think that Christianity provides convincing reasons for belief in God? Explain why.

Activity

1 Make a list of the characteristics of God, explaining what each of them means.

2 To what extent do you think that people's beliefs are influenced by their families and their friends?

Christian beliefs about Jesus

In the Bible God and God's teachings are revealed through the prophets such as Isaiah, Jeremiah and John the Baptist. In the Old Testament there are references to a Messiah who will come from God to lead the people:

> **For to us a child is born, to us a son is given, and the government will be on his shoulders. And he will be called Wonderful Counsellor, Mighty God, Everlasting Father, Prince of Peace. Of the increase of his government and peace there will be no end. He will reign on David's throne and over his kingdom, establishing and upholding it with justice and righteousness from that time on and for ever.** (Isaiah 9:6–7)

This is a mediaeval drawing which tries to show the Trinity. In the three corner circles are the words (in Latin) Pater (Father), Filius (Son) and Sanctus Spiritus (Holy Spirit). In the centre is Deus (God). The words around the outside show that the Father non est (is not) the Son, the Son is not the Spirit and the Spirit is not the Father. The other lines show that the Father est (is) God, the Son is God and the Spirit is God.

In the New Testament Jesus is seen as this Messiah, the Son of God:

> **Today in the town of David a Saviour has been born to you; he is Christ the Lord.**
>
> (Luke 2:11)

Following the resurrection, Jesus told his disciples that after he had left them he would send the Holy Spirit to them. At the **ascension** Jesus rose into heaven:

> **He said to them: 'It is not for you to know the times or dates the Father has set by his own authority. But you will receive power when the Holy Spirit comes on you; and you will be my witnesses in Jerusalem, and in all Judea and Samaria, and to the ends of the earth.'**
>
> **After he said this, he was taken up before their very eyes, and a cloud hid him from their sight.**
>
> **They were looking intently up into the sky as he was going, when suddenly two men dressed in white stood beside them. 'Men of Galilee,' they said, 'Why do you stand here looking into the sky? This same Jesus, who has been taken from you into heaven, will come back in the same way you have seen him go into heaven.'**
>
> (Acts 1:7–10)

This coming of the Holy Spirit is first shown in the Bible when the disciples are gathered together on what became known as the Day of Pentecost:

> **Suddenly a sound like the blowing of a violent wind came from heaven and filled the whole house where they were sitting. They saw what seemed to be tongues of fire that separated and came to rest on each of them. All of them were filled with the Holy Spirit and began to speak in other tongues as the Spirit enabled them.**
>
> (Acts 2:2–4)

So, although God is described in many different ways: as a judge and ruler; as a father; as a great and mysterious power; as a friend and saviour and particularly as love; all these are aspects of the Christian God and, rather than showing that this God is inconsistent or changeable, they indicate that he is so much beyond the understanding of humanity that it is impossible for people really to know how to describe him.

Activity

1 Explain what is meant by Jesus being described as the Son of God?

The importance of the Bible

The Bible is in two parts: the Old Testament (Jewish Scriptures); and the New Testament.

The Old Testament has 39 books which contain the law, history, poetry, prophecy and stories.

The New Testament has 27 books. The four **gospels**, Matthew, Mark, Luke and John give accounts of the life and teaching of Jesus. The Acts of the Apostles tells the story of the Early Church. There are 21 letters (epistles) and the book of Revelation which is one early Christian's idea of what the Day of Judgement might be like.

The ascension of Jesus into heaven.

The Bible is seen as different from any other book because it contains God's word and therefore is believed to be true.

Christians believe that the Bible is the revealed Word of God. However, they may think about the Bible in different ways:

- *Inerrancy* – this is a belief that every word of the Bible is absolutely true and that it is free from any kind of error or mistake.
- *Typology* – this view looks at the stories in the Bible as being symbolic. There is truth found in the stories but the stories themselves may not be true.
- *Allegory* – it has been suggested by some people that it is possible to read the Bible literally as well as to see it as a series of stories which contain the truth about God.

If the Bible is really the word of God, then probably Christians ought to obey it. However, there are often cases where people say, 'Oh, but the Bible is very old, we need to interpret it for today.' If people look to the clergy or to theologians to explain what the Bible 'really' means about how they should live, then perhaps they are placing human beings in a higher position of authority than the Bible itself.

Christians disagree about this. Some will say that the Bible is, indeed, completely free from any mistakes or errors at all. When they find something in the Bible which they cannot understand or where one verse seems to disagree with another one, they will say that this is simply because it is the word of God and they are not intelligent enough, or good enough Christians, to understand it. These sorts of problems arise when people look, for example at the account of Jesus' last days in Jerusalem in the four gospels and it appears that the dates and events are different.

Other Christians are quite happy to say that although the Bible is the word of God, it was written down by human beings and so, naturally, there may be mistakes and errors in it. They are not saying that the Bible is, therefore, any less important but they believe that people should read it

carefully in order to understand what it is saying rather than attempting to take every word literally. They also point out that the version of the Bible which most people read is a translation from several ancient languages such as Hebrew, Aramaic and Greek and that scholars are still uncertain as to what some of the words originally meant. The Hebrew Bible also has no punctuation or vowels in it so it is possible that there may be some sections which are not translated in a way which exactly explains the original meaning.

In the last 200 years, many scholars have read the Bible very closely and they say that they can see evidence of the writing of different people working at different times. Whilst this has upset some Christians who take the text very literally, others say that this does not matter. If these people were inspired by God, then the teachings of the Bible are still true.

Christians may say, therefore, that the Bible has moral truth and spiritual truth. It is possible that some of the stories in it, even if they are not literally true, still have aesthetic truth. What has always been very difficult is to prove historically that the things written down in the Bible actually happened.

Another very important part of the truth, for Christians, is the way in which they lead their lives. A life of a Christian, and in particular the way in which they treat other people, is an expression of their belief in God and in Jesus. By following the teachings of Jesus written in the New Testament, Christians are living according to God's will and so they are showing their belief in him.

The Bible is used in church services every day and at ceremonies such as the Eucharist, weddings and funerals. Passages are often chosen which have some special significance to the day or to the ceremony which is taking place. Many Christians also read the Bible privately at home. They may use the Bible to seek advice in difficult situations or they may read and perhaps re-read certain passages which help them and give them support in their lives.

Discussion

Do you think that something like the revelation of the Bible could happen today? Give reasons to support your answer.

Activity

1 Explain what Christians mean when they say that the Bible is revealed.

2 Describe how Christians might use the Bible in their daily lives.

3 Read Genesis 11:1–11 and consider whether or not this story might be a myth. What truth was it trying to teach?

Christian beliefs about miracles

A miracle is a marvellous event which cannot have been brought about by humans or by nature, and so is said to be performed by God. Usually a miracle shows control over the laws of nature.

There are many examples in the New Testament of Jesus performing miracles: he turned water into wine; walked on the sea; he healed the sick; raised the dead; calmed a storm and exorcised demons.

> **That day when evening came, he said to his disciples, 'Let us go over to the other side.' Leaving the crowd behind, they took him along, just as he was, in the boat. There were also other boats with him. A furious squall came up, and the waves broke over the boat, so that it was nearly swamped. Jesus was in the stern, sleeping on a cushion. The disciples woke him and said to him, 'Teacher, don't you care if we drown?'**
>
> **He got up, rebuked the wind and said to the waves, 'Quiet! Be still!' Then the wind died down and it was completely calm.**
>
> **He said to his disciples, 'Why are you so afraid? Do you still have no faith?'**
>
> **They were terrified and asked each other, 'Who is this? Even the wind and the waves obey him!'**
> (Mark 4:35–41)

It may also be described as miraculous that Jesus was born of a virgin and himself came back from the dead.

> **The Word became flesh and made his dwelling among us. We have seen his glory, the glory of the One and Only, who came from the Father, full of grace and truth.**
> (John 1:14)

The question is whether God would be willing to break the natural laws of the universe which he created. While it could be said that God would of course break the laws if there was sufficient reason, it is difficult to say that events such as turning water into wine were important enough for this to happen.

Some Christians have argued that it does not matter whether the miracles of the New Testament really happened or not. What is important is the spiritual messages about God's love for humanity which lie behind these miracles.

Many Christians believe that the Holy Spirit continues to work miracles today. All miracles are seen as the work of the Holy Spirit. Some people believe that there are Christian faith healers who can use the power of the Holy Spirit to heal people of illnesses.

Lourdes is a town in south-western France. In 1858, a 14-year-old girl called Bernadette Soubirous had a series of visions of the Virgin Mary. These took place on the bank of a stream in Lourdes. In 1862, Pope Pius IX ruled that the visions were genuine. More than five million pilgrims visit Lourdes every year in the hope of a cure for themselves or someone close to them.

Many people are said to have recovered from illnesses after visiting Lourdes, but the Roman Catholic Church has only accepted 66 cases as miracles.

Activity

Read these statements:

- Five million pilgrims go to Lourdes each year.

- People have been visiting Lourdes for over 100 years hoping for a cure for their illnesses.

- Only 66 cases of healing have been recognised as miracles.

1 What do you think people might believe about these statements?

2 Do these statements suggest that there are very few people who God chooses to heal?

3 If this is true, then why does God not heal everyone who goes to Lourdes?

Islam

This topic looks at the idea of belief in a god or a divine being:

- What do Muslims believe about the nature of Allah?
- What reasons do Muslims give to support their belief in Allah?
- Why is the Qur'an so important to Muslims?
- What do Muslims believe about Allah intervening in the world through miracles and through the teaching of Muhammad ﷺ?

Muslim beliefs about the nature of Allah

Muslims are **monotheists**. This means that they believe there is only one God – Allah. According to Islam, Allah is unlike anything else that exists and no attempt is made to describe him.

Muslims believe:

- Allah is eternal, beyond time and space
- Allah is not limited by having a physical body, and is everywhere at all times
- Allah is the creator of the world and everything in it, and has a purpose for the world
- Allah is perfectly good and perfectly loving
- Allah is interested in how people behave, and wants them to treat each other properly
- Allah is all-powerful (omnipotent) and all-knowing (omniscient)
- Allah will judge each individual.

Prayer five times a day is an essential part of Muslim life.

Muslim life is an expression of **Islam** (submission) to the will of Allah and is lived according to the words of the **Qur'an** and following the teaching and example of Muhammad ﷺ.

The importance of Allah to Muslim life is stressed in the first **Surah** of the Qur'an:

> **In the name of Allah, Most Gracious, Most Merciful. Praise be to Allah, the Cherisher and Sustainer of the Worlds.**

At the centre of Muslim belief in Allah are the **Shahadah** and the Qur'an.

The Shahadah is the first pillar of Islam and the central statement of belief. It states the importance of Allah:

> **La ilaha illal lahu Muhammad ﷺ Dur rasulul lah There is no god but Allah, Muhammad ﷺ is the messenger of Allah.**

This importance is stressed in **salah**, daily prayers.

The **adhan**, or call to prayer, has the following statements:

> **Allah is the Greatest (x4) I bear witness that there is no god but Allah (x2) I bear witness that Muhammad ﷺ is Allah's messenger (x2) Rush to prayer (x2) Rush to success (x2) Allah is the Greatest (x2) There is no god but Allah**

A statement of the seven basic beliefs of Islam is contained in **Al-Imanul Mufassal:**

> **I believe in Allah, in His angels, in His books, in His messengers, in the Last Day and in the fact that everything good or bad is decided by Allah, the Almighty, and in the Life after Death.**

Tawhid – the 'oneness' of Allah – is clearly expressed in the Qur'an and is the most important aspect of Islamic belief:

> Say: He is Allah, the One and Only; Allah, the Eternal, Absolute; He begetteth not, nor is He begotten; and there is none like unto Him.   (Surah 112:1–4)

Muslims say that they must let Tawhid grow in their heart, and shape and control the whole of their lives. By following Tawhid, Muslims become contented, trusting in Allah, and dedicate their lives to seeking his pleasure.

From the Qur'an and the **Hadith**, Muslims have collected the 99 'most beautiful names' of God, and these are often used in meditation. Tradition says that the hundredth name is a secret, known only to the camel. Muhammad ﷺ taught that:

> There are ninety-nine names that are Allah's alone. Whoever learns, understands and enumerates them enters Paradise and achieves eternal salvation.

These principles of Muslim belief can all be found, with many other Muslim teachings, in the last sermon which Muhammad ﷺ preached on Mount Arafat at the end of the Hajj:

> O People, just as you regard this month, this day, this city as Sacred, so regard the life and property of every Muslim as a sacred trust. Return the goods entrusted to you to their rightful owners. Hurt no one so that no one may hurt you. Remember that you will indeed meet your Lord, and that he will indeed reckon your deeds...

> All mankind is from Adam and Eve, an Arab has no superiority over a non-Arab nor a non-Arab has any superiority over an Arab; also a white has no superiority over a black nor a black has any superiority over a white—except by piety and good action.

> O People, no prophet or apostle will come after me, and no new faith will be born. Reason well, therefore, O People, and understand my words which I convey to you. I leave behind me two things, the Qur'an and my Sunnah (the customs and traditions of the Prophet) and if you follow these you will never go astray.

> All those who listen to me shall pass on my words to others and those to others again... (Hadith)

These beliefs about Allah are often presented as the Kalam argument for the existence of God.

> Everything that has a beginning of its existence has a cause of its existence.
> The universe has a beginning of its existence.
>
> Therefore:
> The universe has a cause of its existence.
> If the universe has a cause of its existence then that cause is God.
>
> Therefore:
> God exists.

Activity

Compare the Kalam argument with the arguments given in the introduction of this unit. Which of these does it most closely resemble?

Beliefs about Allah

Muslims believe in Allah because of the evidence of his goodness which they see in their daily lives and in creation and also because of his revelation of the Qur'an to Muhammad ﷺ.

In their daily lives, Muslims see the influence of Allah through their belief in **Al-Qadr**: belief that Allah has laid down a pre-determined course for the world and knows the destiny of every living creature. However, this does not mean that people do not have free will. Allah made humans his **khalifahs**, or agents, on earth. People are not forced to obey Allah's will and may choose to disobey him but he knows what decisions people will make. Humans are judged on these decisions at **Akirah**, the Day of Judgement (see Unit 4, page 64).

Allah communicates with humanity by **Risalah** – the prophets. According to Muhammad ﷺ there are 124,000 prophets but only 25 are mentioned in the Qur'an. Many of these prophets are the same people as are found in the Jewish and Christian scriptures, showing part of the common origins of these three religions.

The main prophets are Nuh (Noah), Ibrahim (Abraham), Musa (Moses), Dawud (David) and 'Isa (Jesus), peace be unto them.	
Adam	Adam
Idris	Enoch
Nuh	Noah
Hud	
Salih	Salih
Ibrahim	Abraham
Isma'il	Ishmael
Ishaq	Isaac
Lut	Lot
Ya'qub	Jacob
Yusuf	Joseph
Shu'aib	
Ayyub	Job
Musa	Moses
Harun	Aaron
Dhu'l-kifl	Ezekiel
Dawud	David
Sulamain	Solomon
Ilas	Elias
Al-Yasa'	Elisha
Yunus	Jonah
Zakariyya	Zechariah
Yahya	John
'Isa	Jesus
Muhammad ﷺ	

Muhammad ﷺ was the last prophet and received the final revelation from Allah. He is sometimes called the 'Seal of the Prophets'.

Discussion

How do you think Muslim beliefs about Allah might affect the life of a believer?

Activity

1 Choose one of the prophets who appears in both the Qur'an and the Christian Bible and compare the stories about them.

2 Look again at the prophet's Last Sermon. What key Muslim beliefs does this contain?

The importance of the Qur'an

The Qur'an is the holy book of Islam but other books are mentioned in it as having being revealed by God: *Zabur* Psalms of David, *Tawrat* Torah of Moses, *Injil* Gospels of the New Testament, *Suhuf-i-Ibrahim* Scrolls of Abraham. Islam teaches that only the Qur'an still exists in its original form and that these other revealed books have been changed from the true words of God.

The Qur'an is, in some ways, very different from the holy books of Judaism and Christianity.

Muslims say that the Qur'an was revealed to Muhammad ﷺ by the angel Jibril and is the actual words of Allah.

In 611 CE, Muhammad ﷺ, then aged 40, was meditating in a cave. Jibril appeared to him and ordered him to read. Muhammad ﷺ said that he could not read. This happened three times and eventually the angel said:

> **Proclaim! (or read) in the name of thy Lord and Cherisher, Who created —created man, out of a (mere) clot of congealed blood. Proclaim! And thy Lord is Most Bountiful—He Who has taught (the use of) the Pen— taught man that which he knew not.**
>
> (Surah 96:1–5)

Muhammad ﷺ recited these words and then the angel said, 'O Muhammad ﷺ, you are the messenger of Allah and I am Jibril', and left.

Muhammad ﷺ continued to receive visits from Jibril over the next 23 years. Finally, just before his death, he received the final verse:

> **This day have I perfected your religion for your benefit,**

completed My favour upon you, and have chosen for you Islam as your religion. (Surah 5:3)

Because Muhammad ﷺ could not read or write, he memorised the Qur'an as he heard it and then dictated it to his secretary, Zaid Bin Thabit. It was not compiled as one book until after his death.

Every copy of the Qur'an records the words of Allah completely unchanged from the manner in which they were received by Muhammad ﷺ. For this reason, versions of the Qur'an in languages other than Arabic are not called translations. Muslims say that it is not possible to translate God's words successfully into any other language without changing them.

The Qur'an is not written in chronological order, but in the order Muhammad ﷺ was told to place the words by Jibril. Surah 1 is the shortest and is then followed by Surah 2, the longest Surah. The Surahs then grow progressively shorter until the last which is 114.

No form of critical study of the Qur'an is undertaken because it is the word of Allah. Because every word is seen as a direct revelation, there is no idea of discussing who wrote it and why. Islam does not consider these ideas as they would be irrelevant and disrespectful.

The Qur'an is seen as unchanging, unchangeable and untranslatable **iman** (faith), and is regarded as the complete and final book of guidance from Allah for the whole of humanity forever.

In this way the Qur'an and the teachings of Islam are regarded as absolute truth. It can be said that Muslims do not therefore have to believe because they actually know these teachings to be true.

Muslims use the Qur'an in worship when a passage may be explained or discussed in the mosque. They also study the Qur'an. People may read the Qur'an privately or with others. Some people may use the Qur'an for guidance when they are faced with a difficult decision or a problem and they do not know how to solve it.

The cave on Mount Nur where Jibril spoke to Muhammad ﷺ.

Discussion

Do you think that an event like the revelation of the Qur'an could still happen today? Give reasons to support your answer.

Activity

1 Explain what Muslims mean when they say that the Qur'an is revealed.

2 Describe how Muslims might use the Qur'an in their daily lives and how it might help them.

Muslim beliefs about miracles

Miracles do not play a particularly important part in Islam. Because Muhammad ﷺ was a prophet and was in no way seen as a god, there is no reason why he should have performed miracles.

Allah, of course, can perform miracles and the revelation of the Qur'an to Muhammad ﷺ is often viewed as a living miracle.

It can be seen that, in order to protect the message of the Qur'an and the religion of Islam, there are many instances in the life of Muhammad ﷺ when Allah intervened.

One story relates to Muhammad's ﷺ birth. On the night that he was born a great star appeared in the sky. His grandfather Abd al-Muttalib prayed for six days to decide on a name for the child. On the seventh day both he and Muhammad's ﷺ mother dreamt that he should be called Muhammad ﷺ the 'Praised One'.

The most important miraculous event in the life of the Prophet was Al-Mi'raj – the Ascent. Muslims believe that Muhammad ﷺ was woken by Jibril who took him to Jerusalem, riding on an animal with wings, called Buraq. As he rode through Jerusalem, Muhammad ﷺ met the prophets Adam, Ibrahim, Musa, 'Isa and Harun and he then travelled through the heavens until he came into the presence of Allah.

By choosing Muhammad ﷺ as his messenger and by revealing the Qur'an to him, Allah ensured the protection and preservation of Islam. It is this revelation which can be viewed as the greatest intervention of Allah in the world.

Muslims believe that, although Allah has performed miracles these take place when he decides. Therefore, Muslims might pray to Allah and ask for his help and guidance but they are not expecting a miracle to happen.

Activity

1 Explain why Muhammad ﷺ could not perform miracles.

2 Why do Muslims believe that the revelation of the Qur'an was a living miracle?

Summary

Perhaps, at the end of this unit, you are no clearer than you were before about 'What is God' or 'What God is' but you have now seen some of the arguments which people have used to 'prove' that there is, or is not, a God.

This unit is particularly important because without some sort of belief in God there would probably be no religion. What is certain is that until someone can prove that God does, or does not, exist (if this is ever possible), then it will be a matter of faith and belief for religious people and the arguments will continue.

Questions

1 What do you understand by:
   (a) revelation
   (b) the ontological, cosmological and teleological arguments
   (c) arguments from experience and morality
   (d) scientific proof
   (e) infinity and eternity
   (f) analogy, metaphor and symbol
   (g) atheist and agnostic?

2 Look at the arguments for the existence of God. Which do you think are the most convincing and the least convincing arguments? Why?

3 Make a list of some of the different ways in which God is described and explain why these are used.

4 Try to write a description of God. You may decide to write a physical description, to use symbolic language or to describe the characteristics of God.

5 Explain why some religious people may say that they 'know' God exists.

6 Do you think it would matter if people discovered that God was actually female? Why?

Practice GCSE questions

Christianity

1 (a) Describe the reasons why Christians believe in God. [8 marks]

(b) Explain why believing that the Bible is the word of God is important for Christians. [7 marks]

(c) 'There is no way of knowing what God is like.'
Do you agree? Give reasons to support your answer, and show that you have thought about different points of view. You must refer to Christianity in your answer. [5 marks]

2 (a) Describe what Christians believe about miracles. [8 marks]

(b) Explain how believing in miracles might help a Christian. [7 marks]

(c) 'If miracles were true, they would happen all the time.'
Do you agree? Give reasons to support your answer, and show that you have thought about different points of view. You must refer to Christianity in your answer. [5 marks]

Tips

There is a lot of material to write for this answer. You might use the classical arguments or the more modern ones such as the moral argument or the argument from experience. You might also talk about people having personal experiences of God or of events which the person relates to God: visions; miracles; examples of others; reading the Bible; or prayers which are answered.

You might explain that belief in the divine inspiration of the Bible might mean that Christians would try to live completely in accordance with its teachings, and so lead more prayerful and holy lives. You could explain that, in doing so, people might refer to the Bible and its teachings in order to ensure that they are doing God's will. People might try to find an answer to any problem or argument in the biblical teachings.

You could say that some people believe that the Bible makes it clear what God is like. However, you could also consider whether the Bible really says anything other than that God is a judge and loves creation. Some people might say that God is a father-figure or perhaps, as is often suggested, a sort of divine moral policeman.

You may want to talk about what a miracle is and how Christians have understood them. You could write about particular biblical miracles, as well as miracles which happen today such as those at Lourdes. You could also write about whether all Christians believe in miracles in the same way.

You might argue that the existence of biblical miracles would help a Christian. You may also say that experiencing a miracle or knowing about one might strengthen a Christian's faith. On the other hand, you might consider whether a prayed for miracle that does not happen damages faith.

You might consider that if miracles happened all the time then perhaps they would not be miracles but normal events. Another view may be that miracles happen when God chooses and that their frequency does not affect whether or not they are true.

Islam

1 **(a)** Describe the reasons why Muslims believe in Allah. [8 marks]

(b) Explain why believing that the Qur'an is the word of Allah is important for Muslims. [7 marks]

(c) 'There is no way of knowing what Allah is like.'
Do you agree? Give reasons to support your answer, and show that you have thought about different points of view.
You must refer to Islam in your answer. [5 marks]

2 **(a)** Describe what Muslims believe about miracles. [8 marks]

(b) Explain how believing in miracles might help a Muslim. [7 marks]

(c) 'If miracles were true, they would happen all the time.'
Do you agree? Give reasons to support your answer, and show that you have thought about different points of view.
You must refer to Islam in your answer. [5 marks]

Tips

There is a lot of material to write for this answer. You might use the classical arguments or the more modern ones such as the moral argument or the argument from experience. You could also use the Kalam argument. You might also talk about people having personal experiences of Allah, or of events which the person relates to Allah: miracles; examples of others; reading the Qur'an; or prayers which are answered.

You might explain that belief in the divine inspiration of the Qur'an might mean that Muslims would try to live completely in accordance with its teachings, and so lead more prayerful and holy lives. You could explain that, in doing so, people might refer to the Qur'an and its teachings in order to ensure that they are doing the will of Allah. People might try to find an answer to any problem or argument in the Qur'anic teachings.

You could say that some people believe that the Qur'an makes it clear what Allah is like. However, you could also consider whether the Qur'an really says anything other than that Allah is a judge and loves creation. Some people might say that Allah is a father-figure or perhaps, as is often suggested, a sort of divine moral policeman.

You may want to talk about what a miracle is and how Muslims have understood them. You could write about particular miracles in the life of Muhammad ﷺ, as well as miracles which may happen today. You could also write about whether all Muslims believe in miracles in the same way.

You might argue that the existence of Qur'anic miracles would help a Muslim. You may also say that experiencing a miracle or knowing about one might strengthen a Muslim's faith. On the other hand, you might consider whether a prayed for miracle that does not happen damages faith.

You might consider that if miracles happened all the time then perhaps they would not be miracles but normal events. Another view may be that miracles happen when Allah chooses and that their frequency does not affect whether or not they are true.

Introduction

Belief is said to be the acceptance of the truth of something, often supported by an emotional or spiritual sense of certainty. This is clearly something different from 'knowledge'.

Religious believers may say that they know that their faith is true, or the truth, but it is not the same as knowing about a scientific truth.

Believers would be offended if someone said that their religion was 'untrue'. It is as impossible to prove that religious truth is untrue as it is to prove that it is true.

Belief is therefore different from knowing something based on scientific evidence but it is just as real to the believer.

Prayer, worship and the 'wholly other'

Spirituality is a difficult word to explain and can be a difficult idea to understand.

The dictionary says that spirituality means:

> **The quality or condition of being spiritual; attachment to or regard for things of the spirit as opposed to material or worldly interests.**

In fact, it deals with ideas and feelings which some people have and which cannot be described in a 'normal' way.

You might be standing on a cliff by the sea in a strong wind and feel a sense of excitement. You might get a special feeling when you hear a particular piece of music. You might get a particular feeling when you walk into a big sports arena or into a religious building.

However, it is difficult to put these feelings into words. We might try by using an expression such as 'a sense of awe' or 'a sense of wonder'.

We are experiencing something which we cannot explain because often we do not have the words which really mean what we feel.

A lot of religious people might say that we are having a religious experience – we are feeling something which is different from the ordinary feelings or sensations which we have every day.

A man called Rudolf Otto (1869–1837) said that in these circumstances we were experiencing God and he used the word 'numinous' (the presence of God which inspires awe and reverence), calling this feeling the 'wholly other': something which was totally different from any other experience.

For some people, this spiritual feeling gives them certainty in their belief – they feel that they 'know' God exists because of this spiritual feeling.

People express their spiritual feelings in different ways:

- Some may pray. This does not necessarily mean asking for anything for themselves (petitionary prayer), it could be asking God to intervene in the world and, perhaps, help someone who is ill (intercessory prayer). Or it could simply be thanking God for what has happened or for life and existence in general.
- Others may meditate. They sit quietly, try to empty their minds of ordinary thought and, they would say, listen to their spiritual feelings.
- Others may express spirituality by attending religious services, while some people will see their whole life and their relationships with other people as a spiritual experience.

There are also different ways in which spirituality can be expressed: through art; religious buildings; music; and in the religious ceremonies and liturgy – the way in which people worship.

As well as these ways of expressing spirituality, these beliefs and feelings are also expressed in the sacred writings of religions and the ways in which these are regarded and treated.

The ways in which spirituality is expressed varies between religions.

Activity

1 Try to explain a particular event in your life when something gave you a feeling of the 'wholly other'.

2 Explain how the use of a particular type of prayer might help a believer.

The dead rising from their graves on the Day of Judgement.

Christianity

This topic looks at:
- private and public worship – prayer and contemplation
- church services
- food and fasting
- the architecture of Christian places of worship
- the use of music and art in Christian worship
- the ways in which symbols are used in Christianity.

For many Christians, their worship and spirituality is centred on the church. This does not necessarily mean a church building but also refers to the group of people who form the local Christian community.

This idea of the church and its members is shown in the Apostles' Creed:

> I believe in... the holy catholic Church, the communion of saints...

The phrase 'holy catholic Church' is not just about the Roman Catholic Church but means the 'universal' Christian Church all over the world.

Christians believe that the church is guided in its way by the Holy Spirit. The Holy Spirit is the third person or part of the Christian Trinity and came to the first disciples on the Festival of Pentecost, just after Jesus' ascension into heaven.

> When the day of Pentecost came, they were all together in one place. Suddenly a sound like the blowing of a violent wind came from heaven and filled the whole house where they were sitting. They saw what seemed to be tongues of fire that separated and came to rest on each of them. All of them were filled with the Holy Spirit and began to speak in other tongues as the Spirit enabled them.
> (Acts 2:1–4)

This is the Spirit which Jesus promised would come to the disciples after he had left them and gone to heaven:

> When the Counsellor comes, whom I will send to you from the Father, the Spirit of truth who goes out from the Father, he will testify about me.
> (John 15:26)

The Holy Spirit is first shown in the New Testament when Jesus is baptised by John the Baptist:

> When all the people were being baptised, Jesus was baptised too. And as he was praying, heaven

The baptism of Jesus.

was opened and the Holy Spirit descended on him in bodily form like a dove. And a voice came from heaven: 'You are my Son, whom I love; with you I am well pleased.'
(Luke 3:21–22)

This Holy Spirit has continued to guide the Christian Church since that time. One example of this guidance is when the Roman Catholic Church chooses a new Pope. The Cardinals (most senior members of the church) sit in a room with the door sealed and pray that the Holy Spirit will guide them to know who God has chosen as the next Pope.

Christians also believe that when they worship they may receive guidance from the Holy Spirit.

Christians may worship on their own (private worship) or together with other people (public or communal worship).

Private worship

Some Christians may choose a certain time of day when they worship. This worship takes many different forms. It might be Bible readings, prayer or meditation. Sometimes Christians pray privately. They may use this opportunity just to talk to God or they may use particular prayers.

Here are four of the best known prayers:

1 The 'Our Father' which Jesus taught to his disciples (Matthew 6:9–15):

Our Father in heaven,
hallowed be your name,
your kingdom come,
your will be done,
on earth as in heaven.
Give us today our daily bread.
Forgive us our sins
as we forgive those who sin
against us
Lead us not into temptation
but deliver us from evil.

Many Christians have said that prayers such as this should be changed so that they do not say that God is male. They think that it is very important to show that God can be thought of as female also.

2 The 'Jesus Prayer':

Lord Jesus, Son of God
be merciful to me, a sinner.

3 The 'Glory be':

Glory be to the Father and to the Son and to the Holy Spirit, as it was in the beginning, is now and ever shall be. Amen.

4 The prayer called the 'Hail Mary':

Hail Mary, full of grace,
the Lord is with thee.
Blessed art thou among women
and blessed is the fruit of thy womb, Jesus.
Holy Mary, Mother of God,
pray for us sinners, now, and at the hour of our death. Amen.

Some Christians spend time thinking about God by meditating. They sit quietly and try to clear their minds of ordinary thoughts so that they can 'hear' what God has to say to them. Many other religions also practise meditation as a form of worship. Some Christians meditate by saying the 'Hail Mary' while using rosary beads.

The Rosary
Whilst holding the rosary beads in their hand, worshippers:
● make the sign of the cross and say the 'Apostles' Creed'
● say the 'Our Father'
● say three 'Hail Marys'
● say the 'Glory be to the Father'
● announce the first mystery and then say the 'Our Father'

A set of rosary beads.

- say ten 'Hail Marys' while meditating on the first mystery
- say the 'Glory be to the Father'.

Then the person announces the second mystery and continues with this pattern of prayer until they reach the end of the fifth mystery.

After the rosary people say:

> **Hail, Holy Queen, Mother of Mercy, our life, our sweetness and our hope! To thee do we cry, poor banished children of Eve; to thee do we send up our sighs, mourning and weeping in this valley of tears. Turn then, most gracious advocate, thine eyes of mercy toward us, and after this our exile, show unto us the blessed fruit of thy womb, Jesus. O clement, O loving, O sweet Virgin Mary!**
>
> **Pray for us, O Holy Mother of God.**
>
> **That we may be made worthy of the promises of Christ.**
>
> **Let us pray. O God, whose only begotten Son, by His life, death, and resurrection, has purchased for us the rewards of eternal life, grant, we beseech Thee, that meditating upon these mysteries of the Most Holy Rosary of the Blessed Virgin Mary, we may imitate what they contain and obtain what they promise, through the same Christ Our Lord. Amen.**

After each decade (ten beads) people may also say the following prayer which is believed to have been requested by the Blessed Virgin Mary when she appeared at Fatima (1916–1917):

> **O my Jesus, forgive us our sins, save us from the fires of hell, lead all souls to Heaven, especially those who have most need of your mercy.**

> The Virgin Mary appeared six times to three shepherd children (now called the Three Seers) near the town of Fatima, Portugal between 13 May and 13 October, 1917.
>
> The Virgin said that she brought a message from God for everyone in the world. This took place during the First World War (1914–1918) and she promised that God would bring peace to the world if people followed her instructions for prayer and an end to fighting.
>
> She also requested that the Pope should publicly consecrate Russia to her Immaculate Heart.

The mysteries

Pope John Paul II (1920–2005) said that:
- the joyful mysteries should be said on Monday and Saturday
- the luminous mysteries on Thursday
- the sorrowful mysteries on Tuesday and Friday
- and the glorious mysteries on Wednesday and Sunday.

Joyful mysteries:
- The annunciation – when Gabriel appeared to Mary.
- The visitation – when Mary visited her cousin Elizabeth.
- The nativity – the birth of Jesus.
- The presentation – when Jesus was first taken to the Temple in Jerusalem.
- The finding of Jesus in the Temple.

Luminous mysteries:
- The baptism of the Lord.
- The wedding of Cana.
- The proclamation of the kingdom.
- The transfiguration – when Jesus appeared to his disciples with Moses and Elijah.
- The institution of the Eucharist.

Sorrowful mysteries:
- The agony in the garden.
- The scourging at the pillar – when Jesus was whipped.
- The crowning with thorns.
- The carrying of the cross.
- The crucifixion.

Glorious mysteries:
- The resurrection – when Jesus rose from the dead.
- The ascension – when Jesus ascended into heaven.
- The descent of the Holy Spirit.
- The assumption of the blessed Virgin Mary – when Mary was lifted up into heaven.
- The coronation of the blessed Virgin Mary.

Activity

23 of these mysteries are found in the New Testament:

(a) Find the references for as many of these mysteries as you can.

(b) Which two mysteries are not found in the New Testament?

Public worship

All worship is a form of praising God. It may take many different forms such as devoting your life to God, regularly worshipping God by prayer, attending church services or by the way in which you live:

> Therefore, I urge you, brothers, in view of God's mercy, to offer your bodies as living sacrifices, holy and pleasing to God – this is your spiritual act of worship.
>
> (Romans 12:1)

Some Christians may pray together at home.

One of the prayers which they may say is the Grace which is also often said after meals:

> May the grace of our Lord Jesus Christ, and the love of God, and the fellowship of the Holy Spirit, be with us all, now and evermore. Amen.

Many Christians belong to a local Christian community which may be based in a church or chapel. Most of these communities will worship on a Sunday though some may meet on other days as well.

Another form of Christian worship is called charismatic. Here, people try to 'open' themselves to the Holy Spirit. Often the result of this kind of worship is called **glossolalia** (speaking in tongues). People believe that the Holy Spirit has entered them and like the first disciples at Pentecost they begin to pray and praise God in languages which they themselves cannot speak or understand:

> Now there were staying in Jerusalem God-fearing Jews from every nation under heaven. When they heard this sound, a crowd came together in bewilderment, because each one heard them speaking in his own language. Utterly amazed, they asked: 'Are not all these men who are speaking Galileans? Then how is it that each of us hears them in his own native language? ...we hear them declaring the wonders of God in our own tongues!'
>
> (Acts 2:5–8, 11b)

One of the most famous modern incidents of glossolalia is the Toronto Blessing:

The Blessing started at the Toronto Airport Vineyard Church on 20 January, 1994.

John Arnott, the pastor, asked Randy Clark from St Louis to address a four-day series of revival meetings. After his first sermon people began to laugh hysterically, leap, dance, cry and roar. The phrase 'holy laughter' has been used to describe uncontrollable laughter from church congregations. This can include weeping, falling to the floor and animal noises such as barking like dogs or roaring like lions.

The Toronto Blessing spread all over the USA and Canada and has now travelled abroad.

Followers say this is the work of the Holy Spirit; others claim that the experiences are engineered.

Some Christians such as the Religious Society of Friends (Quakers) hold services where the worshippers sit in silence until the Holy Spirit prompts one of them to speak. A Quaker meeting house is a very simple building with no decoration or distinctive features apart from chairs surrounding a table which may hold the Bible.

Church services

Services often contain **hymns**. These are similar to prayers set to music. The hymns may be sung by the congregation or by a choir.

Bible reading is an important part of most church services. Many Christian denominations have a book called a lectionary, which shows which Bible passages, sometimes from both the Old and New Testaments, are to be read each day.

The **sermon** is also an important part of many services, when the priest or minister may talk about one of the Bible passages, about something to do with the Christian faith, or about a current event which the congregation needs to consider.

There may be different types of prayer used during communal worship. These may include:
● intercessory prayer
● penitential prayer
● petitionary prayer
● prayers of praise and thanksgiving.

Activity

Try to find, or write, examples of each of the four kinds of prayer listed above.

As well as prayer, many churches use special forms of services, called liturgy, in their worship. Most liturgies celebrate the Eucharist – the celebration of the Last Supper which Jesus ate with his disciples before his crucifixion. This is called by many different names such as the breaking of bread, **Holy Communion**, the **Lord's Supper**, the **Liturgy** or **Mass**. At this ceremony, after the bread and wine have been blessed, the priest or minister shares them with the congregation. This is called receiving communion. Some Christians may receive communion on Sundays or perhaps once or twice during the year. Others may make their communion every day.

The Eucharist may be a very simple event with a person reading Jesus' words from the Bible before sharing bread and wine with the other people present:

> For I received from the Lord what I also passed on to you: The Lord Jesus, on the night he was betrayed, took bread, and when he had given thanks, he broke it and said, 'This is my body, which is for you; do this in remembrance of me.' In the same way, after supper he took the cup, saying, 'This cup is the new covenant in my blood; do this, whenever you drink it, in remembrance of me.' For whenever you eat this bread and drink this cup, you proclaim the Lord's death until he comes.
> (1 Corinthians 11:23–26)

Alternatively, the Eucharist may be a very elaborate ceremony with music, singing, several priests wearing special clothes (vestments) and many prayers said before and after the central repeating of Jesus' words.

Many people believe that this ceremony is a symbolic repeating of what Jesus did whilst others, such as Roman Catholics, believe in a teaching called **transubstantiation** which means that, when the priest repeats Jesus' words, the bread and wine become the actual body and blood of Jesus.

Sharing bread and wine is an important part of Christian worship.

Other Christians, including denominations such as Methodists and Baptists, place the 'Ministry of the Word' at the centre of their worship. They hold services which focus on Bible readings and sermons (talks given by the minister).

Some Christians feel that the only way in which they can express their true spirituality is through devoting their whole life to God without any secular distractions. In order to do this they live in convents or monasteries as nuns or monks. They often have very little to do with the outside world and instead spend their time in prayer and worship and adopt a very simple lifestyle. In this life they take three vows:

1 Poverty – they have no personal possessions.

2 Chastity – they do not have any sexual relationships.

3 Obedience – they agree to follow the instructions of the leader of the community in which they live.

Although Christians believe that the Bible is the most sacred book because it contains the word of God and stories about Jesus and his teachings, they feel that it is so important that it has been translated into almost every language in the world so that everyone can have the opportunity to learn about Christianity.

Activity

Consider the difference between public and private worship. What do you think are the advantages and disadvantages of each type of worship?

Food and fasting

Christianity does not have strict rules or laws about food and fasting unlike some religions.

Jesus was a Jew and in the gospels there are accounts of him eating fish and drinking wine. Therefore it seems quite likely that he also ate meat.

Although some Christians may choose to be vegetarian, there is really no reason within Christianity for them to do this.

In the days of the early Christian Church, Peter had a vision which meant that Christians did not have to keep the strict food laws which the Jews followed:

> **About noon the next day, as they were on their journey and approaching the city, Peter went up on the roof to pray. He became hungry and wanted something to eat; and while it was being prepared, he fell into a trance. He saw the heaven opened and something like a large sheet coming down, being lowered to the ground by its four corners. In it were all kinds of four-footed creatures and reptiles and birds of the air. Then he heard a voice saying, 'Get up, Peter; kill and eat.' But Peter said, 'By no means, Lord; for I have never eaten anything that is profane or unclean.' The voice said to him again, a second time, 'What God has made clean, you must not call profane.' This happened three times, and the thing was suddenly taken up to heaven.**
>
> (Acts 10:9–16)

Although there are no rules about what Christians should or should not eat, some people do eat certain foods at certain times. For example, some people eat fish on Friday rather than meat. This is an old tradition which remembers that Jesus was crucified on a Friday.

There are also traditional foods which people eat such as mince pies at Christmas, hot cross buns on Good Friday and pancakes on Shrove Tuesday, but many of these are local customs rather than being really based on any Christian teaching.

Many Christian communities also celebrate Harvest Festivals in the autumn where God is thanked for continuing to provide food for humanity and the of creation.

The Church originally celebrated 1 August as Lammas Day – a festival marking the release of Peter from prison.

> **The night before Herod was to bring him to trial, Peter was sleeping between two soldiers, bound with two chains, and sentries stood guard at the entrance. Suddenly an angel of the Lord appeared and a light shone in the cell. He struck Peter on the side and woke him up. 'Quick, get up!' he said, and the chains fell off Peter's wrists.**
>
> (Acts 12:6–7)

Later, this feast day, known as *St Peter ad vincula*, became a celebration of the harvest, taking over former pagan customs.

In the United Kingdom, Harvest Festival in churches began in 1843, when the Rev. Robert Hawker held a special thanksgiving service at his church at Morwenstow, Cornwall. Many churches continue to celebrate a Harvest Festival in the autumn.

Fasting is usually when people go without food or drink for a period of time. The Jews have several fasts during their religious year and in particular Yom Kippur, the Day of Atonement, when they fast for 25 hours. Christianity no longer has any regular fasts. In the past, many Roman Catholics fasted for up to 12 hours before they received communion.

There are two penitential periods (times when people regret the wrongs that they have done) during the Christian year: Advent – the four weeks before Christmas and Lent – the 40 days before Easter Day. Originally, these were both periods of fasting.

Although probably no-one still fasts during Advent, many people still observe Lent. The 'fasting' during Lent lasts for 40 days so it starts on Ash Wednesday and continues until Easter Saturday. Fasting has always been forbidden on Sundays. As well as being a tradition and preparation for Easter, fasting also remembers the 40 days when Jesus was in the wilderness:

> **Jesus, full of the Holy Spirit, returned from the Jordan and was led by the Spirit in the wilderness, where for forty days he was tempted by the devil. He ate nothing at all during those days, and when they were over, he was famished.**
>
> (Luke 4:1–2)

In the past, many people gave up meat and rich foods for Lent. This is the reason that, in many countries, Lent is preceded by Carnival (carnem levare – giving up meat).

Now, most Christians try to give up luxuries and give money to charities or else they try to 'take up' something positive such as working for disadvantaged people.

Activity

To what extent do you think having rules about what people can or cannot eat might help a believer in their faith?

The architecture of Christian places of worship

Christian spirituality is also expressed in the art, architecture and music of the Church. Christianity has probably been the major influence on all European forms of art. Many of the greatest artists of the last thousand years have painted religious pictures based on Christianity. Every town has Christian buildings which are often a very important part of the architecture there. As well as this, all the great composers have written religious music, sometimes this has been hymns or choral music but many have also composed instrumental music which is inspired by Christian teachings and belief.

All these expressions of spirituality show Christians' belief in God. The art, architecture, music and liturgy of Christianity is all designed to praise God and to show how holy God is.

A figure of an eagle is often used as a stand for the lectern and represents the word of God being carried throughout the world.

Inside most churches you would expect to find a **font**. This is a bowl which holds water for baptisms. It is usually placed by the west door of the church and shows that this is the place where people enter the church and also enter the Christian faith.

Roman Catholic churches will have a holy water **stoup** just inside the door. Here, people dip their fingers into the water and then make the sign of the cross. They will also have confessionals, special boxes or screened off areas where people can speak to a priest and confess their sins.

Traditionally, the **altar** was raised up at the east end of the church. It is here that the Eucharist is celebrated. In the last century many churches moved the altar nearer the centre of the church so that it was closer to the congregation.

Near the congregation in many Anglican and Roman Catholic churches are the **pulpit** and the **lectern**. Usually the pulpit, from where the sermon is preached, is on the north side of the church and the lectern, for Bible readings, is on the south. The placing of the pulpit and the lectern is simply traditional.

In Protestant churches, which emphasise the Ministry of the Word, the combined pulpit and lectern may be in the centre of the east, or end wall with the table for the Eucharist in front of it.

Activity

Research, describe and explain the main features of worship in any one Christian church.

The use of music and art in Christian worship

Art and music have always been an essential part of Christian worship.

However, as is clear with the Quakers, who make no use of either art or music in their worship, there is a lot of variation from one denomination to another.

In many churches, particularly Anglican, Orthodox and Roman Catholic, art may

The places which Christians build for worship vary widely across the world, as well as from denomination to denomination.

An area may have a large cathedral which is elaborately decorated and can often be seen from a great distance. There are also many parish churches which may be a simple design or may be almost as richly decorated as their local cathedral, or mother church.

Many churches are built in the shape of a cross. Traditionally, the head of this cross pointed towards Jerusalem where Jesus was crucified and resurrected. Often, churches have towers, spires or steeples which point out the church from a distance and which also can be said to be pointing to heaven.

play a very important part. In most Anglican churches there may be stained glass windows and decoration within and outside the building. In Orthodox churches there are usually many icons (pictures) of the saints and Jesus. In most Roman Catholic churches there will be statutes of Jesus and the saints.

Some people say that they find these pictures and symbols helpful because they provide a focus for people's thinking and prayers. Others are opposed to any statues or pictures. They say that any picture or statue goes against the teachings of the **Ten Commandments**:

> **You shall not make for yourself an idol, whether in the form of anything that is in heaven above, or that is on the earth beneath, or that is in the water under the earth. You shall not bow down to them or worship them; for I the Lord your God am a jealous God...**
>
> (Exodus 20:4–5a)

Many churches also have hassocks, or kneelers, which are embroidered with Christian symbols.

Some churches, particularly Roman Catholic, will have Stations of the Cross around the walls. These 14 stations were developed by the Franciscans who were given custody of the holy places in Jerusalem. Each station recalls an event in the last day of Jesus' life. Seven of the events come from the gospels and the others are traditional.

These are the 14 Stations of the Cross and traditional Franciscan prayers are said at each one:

1 Jesus is condemned by Pilate.
2 Jesus receives the cross.
3 Jesus falls under the weight of the cross.
4 Jesus meets Mary.
5 Simon of Cyrene carries the cross for Jesus.
6 Saint Veronica wipes Jesus' face.
7 Jesus falls again.
8 Jesus speaks to the women of Jerusalem.
9 Jesus falls for a third time.

10 Jesus' clothes are removed.
11 The crucifixion.
12 Jesus dies.
13 Mary receives Jesus' body.
14 Jesus is buried.

Discussion

Music plays a very important part in Christian worship and many great musical works have been written for use in worship. Hymns and chants are often used in Christian worship. Although these are usually accompanied by an organ and choir, today many churches use more modern music with guitars and drums accompanying it.

Consider the different types of music you know and discuss what sort of music you might find helpful in worship.

Activity

Find out which of the Stations of the Cross are based on the gospels and which are traditional.

The ways in which symbols are used in Christianity

Symbols have always been an important part of Christian life and worship.

IXTOS

I	Iesous	Jesus
C	Christos	Christ
TH	Theou	of God
U	Uios	Son
S	Soter	Saviour

The fish is a very popular Christian symbol. It could be seen as reflecting the fact that many of the first disciples were fishermen. It is also an acronym. Each letter of Icthus represents a word which show the belief in Jesus Christ – Son of God – Saviour.

Another symbol expressing belief in Jesus as the Christ is known as the Chi-Rho. These are the first two letters of 'Christ' in Greek.

XR

The cross is perhaps the most common Christian symbol. There are many different designs of the cross.

The crucifix shows a cross together with the figure of Jesus nailed to it.

Another symbol is of Christus Rex – Christ the King who has overcome death.

There are many other symbols used in Christianity – for example, the Holy Spirit may be represented as fire, wind or a dove.

Candles are an important part of Christian worship. Their original purpose in worship was to give light but they are often seen as representing Jesus who was called 'Lux Mundi' – the light of the world.

Particularly in Roman Catholic and Orthodox churches, incense is used during services. This is made from wood or sweet-selling gums and is burnt in a censer, a container on long chains. The censer is swung and the smoke and smell of the incense is, again, said to represent people's prayers rising up to heaven and is used to bless and purify.

Activity

1 To what extent do you think symbols, statues, pictures or music might help a Christian in their worship?

2 If you could only choose one symbol to represent Christianity, which do you think would be the most appropriate and why?

Islam

This topic looks at:
- worship in the mosque and at home
- prayer and its role as a pillar of Islam
- the use of food and fasting by Muslims
- the architecture of the mosque
- the concepts of tawhid and shirk.

Muslim worship

In Islam, there are many ways in which spirituality and worship are demonstrated.

'Islam' means submission to the will of Allah and it is by living according to this will that Muslims can demonstrate their belief.

At the centre of Islamic life and belief are the Five Pillars:
- **Shahadah** – the declaration of faith which states:

> **There is no god except Allah, Muhammad ﷺ is the Messenger of Allah.**

- **Salah** – five compulsory daily prayers for communicating with, and worshipping, Allah. These are performed under specific conditions, in the manner taught by the Prophet Muhammad ﷺ and are said in Arabic.
- **Zakah** – this is literally 'the purification of wealth by the payment of an annual welfare due'. Muslims give 2.5% of their surplus income as zakah each year. Zakah began in al-Madinah to care for the widows and orphans. Wealth is a gift from Allah and should be shared. The remainder of a person's wealth is kept pure and people are kept free from greed and selfishness. As well as this, Muslims are urged to make additional voluntary payments called **sadaqah**.
- **Hajj** – the annual pilgrimage to Makkah, which each Muslim must carry out at least once in a lifetime if he or she has the health and wealth. A Muslim man who has completed Hajj is called Hajji, and a woman, Hajjah. The pilgrimage is made during Dhul Hijjah, the twelfth month.

- **Sawm** – fasting from just before dawn until sunset during the month of **Ramadan**, the ninth month. Muslims must abstain (stop themselves) from all food and drink (including water) as well as smoking and sexual relations.

The fulfilment of these Five Pillars is the duty of every Muslim as a demonstration of their obedience to Allah's wishes.

These five actions are all **ibadah** – acts of worship which are performed with the intention of obeying Allah.

A very important aspect of Islamic spirituality is jihad.

Greater jihad is 'personal individual struggle against evil in the way of Allah'. This is a daily feature in a Muslim's life as they must try to ensure that every aspect of their life is lived in accordance with Allah's will.

One of the major demonstrations of Islamic spirituality lies in Shari'ah. This is living according to Muslim law. In countries where the government is Muslim, the whole of the legal system is based on Shari'ah. Shari'ah itself is formed from the teachings and instructions found in the Qur'an and Sunnah.

All Muslim worship takes place in Arabic. This was the language of Muhammad ﷺ and the Qur'an was received and written in Arabic. All prayers are said in Arabic and Muslims have a duty to learn Arabic in order that they can understand worship and also read the Qur'an.

Unlike most other sacred writings, the Qur'an is not translated into other languages. It is permitted to make a version of it in non-Arabic languages but it is believed that these cannot be accurate and that to understand Islam and Allah's will it is necessary to learn to understand it in Arabic.

Muslim worship in the home consists of reading from the Qur'an and saying the five daily prayers.

Discussion

Do you think it is an advantage or a disadvantage for a religion to have strict rules to follow?

Activity

1 What do you consider to be the most important aspects of Muslim worship?

2 Explain what is meant by 'ibadah'.

Prayer

Muhammad ﷺ gave three important conditions for prayer:

1 Pray in a clean place.
2 Pray at five set times a day.
3 Pray facing **Makkah**, the holy city.

The Qur'an suggests that, if possible, people should pray with other believers:

> And be steadfast in prayer; practise regular charity; and bow down your heads with those who bow down (in worship).
>
> (Surah 2:43)

The daily prayers may be said alone or with others but Muhammad ﷺ said that communal prayer was 27 times better than praying alone.

Praying alone or together strengthens the worldwide community of Islam – the ummah.

The Qur'an also recommends praying regularly:

> Verily, I am Allah; there is no god but I: so serve thou Me (only), and establish regular prayer for celebrating My praise.
>
> (Surah 20:14)

The practices which Muhammad ﷺ set up in al-Madinah (see page 35) have formed the model for Muslim prayers since this time.

Salah (prayer) is fard (obligatory).

Muhammad ﷺ said:

> 'If one of you had a river right by his door and he bathed in it five times a day, do you think that there would be any dirt left on him?' They said, 'Not a trace'. He said, 'That is how it is with the five prayers; by means of them God washes away all sins.'
>
> (Hadith)

When Muhammad ﷺ visited heaven on the night journey to Jerusalem he asked how many times a day people should pray. It is said that originally Allah wanted people to pray 50 times a day but Moses persuaded him that five times was enough.

In the Qur'an it says:

> So (give) glory to Allah, when ye reach eventide and when ye rise in the morning;
>
> Yea, to Him be praise, in the heavens and on earth; and in the late afternoon and when the day begins to decline.
>
> (Surah 30:17–18)

The five set times for prayer are therefore:

> Fajr – from dawn until just before sunrise.
> Zuhr – after midday until afternoon.
> 'Asr – from late afternoon until just before sunset.
> Maghrib – after sunset until daylight ends.
> 'Isha' – night until midnight or dawn.

The Qur'an also insists that prayer must be done sincerely and should be accompanied by good deeds:

> Those who (want but) to be seen (of men), But refuse (to supply) (even) neighbourly needs.
>
> (Surah 107:6–7)

Preparing for salah – prayer

Although Muslims pray five times a day, each occasion is special. So, before they pray they ensure that they are physically clean with wudu which is a special kind of ritual washing. This physical washing represents being spiritually clean and ready to worship Allah.

In the name of Allah, the Compassionate, the Merciful.

- The hands are washed.
- The mouth is rinsed three times.
- Water is sniffed into the nostrils then blown out. This is done three times.
- The face is washed three times using both hands.
- The right arm and then the left are washed three times.
- The hair, neck and ears are wiped with wet hands.
- The right foot and then the left are washed to the ankle.

I bear witness that there is no god but Allah, and Muhammad ﷺ is the Messenger of Allah.

If Muslims are travelling, for example in the desert, they perform tayammum which is washing by touching sand and then wiping it over their hands, face and arms up to the elbows.

This clearly shows that although wudu is physical cleansing, the washing is symbolic of spiritual cleansing and purifying the soul.

Muslims do not have to perform wudu before every prayer time unless they have been asleep or to the toilet since the previous one. Also, if socks or stockings are worn, they do not need to wash their feet every time. Ghusl is a full bath which has to be taken after sexual intercourse before the Muslim can pray.

Before prayer Muslims cover their heads: a topi for men and a burka for women.

Worshippers then make niyyah which is a silent promise to offer prayer.

Facing the **Kab'ah** in Makkah, people then begin their prayers.

We shall see the turning of thy face (for guidance) to the heavens: now shall We turn thee to a qiblah that shall please thee. Turn then thy face in the direction

of the Sacred Mosque: wherever ye are, turn your faces in that direction. (Surah 2:144)

Prayer has an introduction and then two, three or four cycles of movements dependent on the time of day:

Fajr	2
Zuhr	4
Asr	4
Maghrib	3
'Isha'	4

The cycle or **rak'ah** involves reciting prayers while standing – qiyam, bowing – ruku and prostrating – sajda.

Du'a

Du'a is personal prayer and may be said after salah or at any time. Du'a means 'asking'.

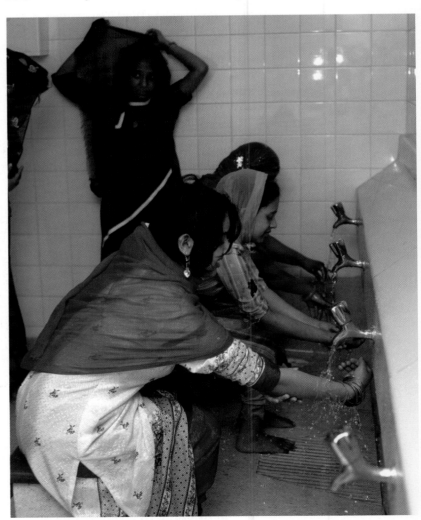

The Muslim stands, raises their hands to their ears, and says the takbir:

'Allahu Akbar'.

Allah is the greatest.

This shows they are separating themselves from distractions.

Then the opening surah of the Qur'an:

In the name of Allah, Most Gracious, Most Merciful,

Praise be to Allah, the Cherisher and Sustainer of the Worlds,

Most Gracious, Most Merciful;

Master of the Day of Judgement,

Thee do we worship,

And Thine aid we seek.

Show us the straight way.

The way of those on whom

Thou hast bestowed Thy Grace,

Those whose (portion)

Is not wrath,

And who go not astray.

The first rak'ah starts by again acknowledging the greatness of Allah. The right hand is placed over the left just below the chest:

O Allah, glory and praise are for You and blessed is Your name and exalted is Your Majesty. There is no God but You. I seek shelter from the rejected Shaytan.

The person bows and bends forward with their hands on their knees:

Allahu Akbar

then says three times:

Glory to my Lord the Almighty.

Standing upright:

Allah hears those who praise Him.

Our Lord, praise be to You.

Allahu Akbar

The Muslim lies on the ground with their forehead, nose, palms of the hands, knees and big toes touching the floor, showing total submission to Allah and says three times:

Glory to My Lord, the Most High.

The worshipper sits back on their heels placing the palms of their hands on their knees.

Then the prostration is repeated.

The worshipper stands up:

Allahu Akbar.

This is the end of one rak'ah.

The second rak'ah is the same.

The Muslim then sits with their left foot bent towards their right and resting their hands on their knees.

They say the Declaration and then a two rak'ah prayer in honour of the Prophet Muhammad ﷺ and his family.

'At Tashahhud' – the Declaration:

All prayer is for Allah, all worship and goodness.

Peace be upon you O Prophet, and the mercy of Allah

And His blessings.

Peace be upon us and on the righteous servants of Allah.

I bear witness that there is no god but Allah.

I bear witness that Muhammad ﷺ is His servant and messenger.

When the rak'ahs are complete, the Muslim turns their head to the right and then to the left blessing other Muslims:

Peace be on you and Allah's blessings.

I listen to the prayer of every
suppliant when he calleth on Me.
(Surah 2:186)

After Du'a Muslims wipe their hands across
their face to show that they have received
the blessing of Allah.

Food and fasting

Islam has strict rules about food.

Muslims are realistic about life. Eating
meat involves killing animals. It is the duty
of a Muslim man to know how to kill an
animal efficiently, quickly and mercifully. In
Britain, however, it is the law of the country
that animals must be slaughtered at an
abattoir by a specially licensed person.

Islamic law requires animals to be
slaughtered in a special way. The animal is
turned to face Makkah. The throat is cut by
a sharp knife across the jugular vein and
a prayer Tasmiyyah is said, 'by the name
of Allah'. No other form of slaughter is
allowed if the meat is to be halal (permitted
or lawful). All food which is not halal is
haram (forbidden). All the blood is drained
out. Muslims believe it is unclean to eat the
blood of an animal. Only a perfect animal
can be sacrificed to Allah. This slaughter is
called al-dabh.

It is against Islamic law to eat any products
from a pig, carrion or any animal which has
not been slaughtered by al-dabh.

The Qur'an also gives rules about what
Muslims should and should not eat which
are similar to those for Jews.

Forbidden to you (for food) are:
dead meat, blood, the flesh of
swine, and that on which hath
been invoked the name of other
than Allah. That which hath
been killed by strangling, or by
a violent blow, or by a headlong
fall, or by being gored to death;
that which hath been (partly)
eaten by a wild animal; unless ye
are able to slaughter it (in due
form); that which is sacrificed on

stone (altars); (forbidden) also is
the division (of meat) by raffling
with arrows: that is impiety. This
day have those who reject faith
given up all hope of your religion:
yet fear them not but fear Me.
This day have I perfected your
religion for you, completed My
favour upon you, and have chosen
for you Islam as your religion. But
if any is forced by hunger, with no
inclination to transgression, Allah
is indeed Oft-forgiving, Most
Merciful.   (Surah 5:3)

Impiety – lack of respect.

No inclination to transgression –
when they do not want to break
the law.

The Qur'an also deals with meat which has
been killed by Jews or Christians:

This day are (all) things good and
pure made lawful unto you. The
food of the People of the Book
is lawful unto you and yours is
lawful unto them.   (Surah 5:5)

People of the Book – Jews and
Christians.

However, this only applies to food which has
been killed according to the Jewish practice
of schechitah (the way in which Jewish meat
is slaughtered by a single sharp cut to the
animal's throat while a prayer is said) and
over which a blessing has been said.

Muslims may only hunt and kill animals
and birds for the purpose of food, they
are not allowed to hunt or shoot for sport.
Obviously it is not always possible to
slaughter an animal according to dabh but if
an animal or bird is still alive when they are
retrieved then they must be slain properly.

Animals which are used for hunting should
be trained not to kill for themselves. The
Prophet Muhammad ﷺ said:

If you despatch the dog and
he eats from the animal that is

caught, then do not eat from the animal for he has caught it only for himself. If you despatch a dog and he kills an animal and does not eat of it, then you can eat, for the dog has caught it only for its owner.

Muslims can eat all sea creatures, provided that they live completely in the sea, and are not required to kill them in any particular way. Creatures which live on land and in water like frogs are forbidden.

Some Muslims may choose to be vegetarian but there is no religious reason for this and meat plays an important part in Muslim worship such as the slaughter and distribution of meat to the community at the feast of Id-ul-Adha after the Hajj.

For the whole of the month of Ramadan, all adult Muslims are required to fast during the hours of daylight. Daylight is when a white thread and a black thread can be distinguished from each other.

Until the white thread of dawn appear to you distinct from its black thread. (Surah 2:187)

During the hours of fasting Muslims should not eat, drink, smoke or have any sexual activity. People are allowed to clean their teeth and accidental swallowing does not count.

If someone deliberately breaks their fast without a good reason they have to provide a meal for 60 people or, alternatively, fast for a further 60 days. Children under the age of puberty, women during menstruation, pregnancy or breastfeeding, the old, the sick, travellers and soldiers are exempt. However, apart from the elderly and children, all the others should make up the missing days as soon as possible.

Allah sees everything and knows what is in people's hearts so there is no point in trying to cheat.

At the end of each day Muslims say:

O God! For your sake we have fasted and now we break the fast with food you have given us.

Each day, Muhammad ﷺ broke his fast with some dates or a drink and most Muslims follow this tradition by eating something that is light. Later the whole family joins together for a big meal. However, Muslims are not supposed to eat too much at this meal because this would go against the whole idea of the fast.

The mosque

A Muslim place of worship is known as a mosque or masjid (place of prostration).

Muhammad ﷺ built the first mosque when he established the first Muslim community in 622 CE in al-Madinah. It is said that, because there was a debate over where Muhammad ﷺ should build his house (which later became the site of the first mosque), he let his camel stop where it wanted and built the house there.

Previously people had worshipped Allah at the Ka'bah in Makkah. Therefore, Muhammad ﷺ told his followers that they should face the Ka'bah when they prayed.

The masjid or mosque, is the central place of worship for Muslims. Muslim men gather there for **Salat-ul-Jumu'ah**, midday prayer on Fridays, and listen to the **khutbah** or speech given by the imam.

In the Qur'an rules are given about the mosque:

The mosques of Allah shall be visited and maintained by such as believe in Allah and the Last Day, establish regular prayers, and practise regular charity, and fear none (at all) except Allah. It is they who are expected to be on true guidance. (Surah 9:18)

In fact, the whole world can be thought of as a mosque because it is all God's creation. A mosque belongs to Allah and cannot be owned by any individual or organisation. In the same way a mosque cannot be sold, mortgaged or rented.

Many mosques are very beautiful buildings. The design may vary from place to place but there are certain features that all mosques must have.

The main open space in the mosque is the prayer hall. One wall, called the qiblah, must face the Ka'bah in Makkah and a **mihrab** or niche in the wall shows Muslims the direction in which they must face when they pray. In addition there is a platform or **minbar** on which the imam stands to give the khutbah. There will be a separate area for women to pray and this is behind a curtain or screen so that they will not distract the men.

Most mosques have at least one **minaret** from which the **adhan** or call to prayer is made. A dome represents the heavens and God's creation. Finally, there will be facilities with running water so that people can perform wudu.

Mosques are usually very simple buildings and yet they may be highly decorated. There are no pictures, statues or photographs showing living beings because this would be against Muslim teaching. However, the walls may be decorated with verses from the Qur'an, the name and attributes of Allah and the name of Muhammad ﷺ in Arabic calligraphy.

Although the mosque is the centre of the Muslim community, most daily worship takes place in the home where prayers may be said and where people can study the Qur'an. Because Muslims have to pray five times a day, many of these prayers will be said in their place of work or whilst travelling. The important aspect of prayer is that it is said, it does not matter where, provided that the place is clean and the Muslim can pray towards Makkah.

No music is used in Muslim worship. In fact many Muslims would say that no music is permitted within Islam.

The Qur'an says that:

> **But there are, among men, those who purchase idle tales, without knowledge (or meaning), to mislead (men) from the Path of Allah and throw ridicule (on the Path): for such there will be a humiliating penalty.** (Surah 31:6)

Music is seen as one of these 'idle diversions'. Also, the Prophet Muhammad ﷺ warned that:

> **there will be (at some future time) people from my Ummah (nation) who will seek to make lawful... the use of musical instruments.** (Sahih Al-Bukhari)

Tawhid and shirk

Tawhid and **shirk** are two very important ideas in Muslim belief and are closely related to each other.

Calligraphy decorating the walls of a mosque.

Tawhid is the belief in the Oneness of Allah – absolute monotheism. This idea was a significant part of the message of Muhammad ﷺ. It is found particularly in the later, Makkan surahs. Allah is not only the creator but also the sustainer of the universe and he rules and controls everything.

Muslims have to place Allah first in their lives. If, for example, Muslims were to live in order simply to make money, this would be shirk. Shirk is the sin of believing in anything other than Allah or of associating anything with Allah as equal to him and is the most serious sin possible.

It is for this reason that images, pictures or statues are forbidden in Islam. To make an image of a living person or creature is shirk because Allah is the sole creator.

Discussion

Consider whether pictures or religious symbols might help people in worship or whether they might distract them.

Summary

Spirituality and the sense of the numinous is a vital part of both of these religions but each does it in a different way which is particular to itself. Also the art, architecture, music and worship of each religion is different. In each instance, however, it is an attempt by believers to demonstrate their love for God and to express that love and their experience of God.

Questions

1 What do you understand by:
  (a) belief
  (b) spirituality
  (c) worship
  (d) prayer
  (e) numinous
  (f) awe and wonder
  (g) guidance?

2 Try to explain how people may feel that they are experiencing the numinous.

3 Explain how you think a believer in *either* Christianity *or* Islam might feel when they pray to God.

4 Look at what followers of *either* Christianity *or* Islam believe about their place of worship. Explain its importance and how the particular features and furnishings of the building show this.

5 How far would you agree that the most important aspect of religion is prayer and that as long as people pray to God it does not matter how they do it? Explain your answer.

6 Find out why, although there are monks and nuns in Christianity, there are none in Islam.

Practice GCSE questions

Christianity

1 (a) Describe how the use of food and fasting might show that Christians believe in God. [8 marks]

(b) Explain how praying every day might help Christians in their lives. [7 marks]

(c) 'Religious images help people to worship.' Do you agree? Give reasons to support your answer, and show that you have thought about different points of view. You must refer to Christianity in your answer. [5 marks]

2 (a) Describe a Christian place of public worship. [8 marks]

(b) Explain how the features of this building reflect Christian beliefs. [7 marks]

(c) 'People do not need symbols to worship God.' Do you agree? Give reasons to support your opinion and show that you have thought about different points of view. You must refer to Christianity in your answer. [5 marks]

Tips

In your answer you might write about the traditional use of fasting at Lent and possibly mention fasting at Advent and before Mass. You might also write about the way in which thanks is given for food by saying Grace before and/or after meals, and mention Harvest Festivals, as well as special foods being eaten to celebrate particular Christian festivals.

In your answer you might consider the benefits of prayer and the value of meditative practices in prayer as bringing peace and strength. You might also consider how people are strengthened by prayer and also that a regular structure of prayer can bring strength to a person's life.

You are free to answer this in any way you wish. You could consider the value of images as focusing worship, as well as considering that it could be too easy to be distracted into worshipping the image. You could refer to the Ten Commandments. You might also consider the arguments of different denominations as to what images, if any, are permitted.

In your answer you may choose any Christian place of worship from a cathedral to a meeting house. You need to make sure that your description is accurate and you could focus on specifics such as particular religious furnishings or look more generally at the design and, perhaps, the architecture.

Here, you should focus on some of the main features such as the cross, crucifix, statues, etc. It is important that you show you understand how these particular features reflect Christian belief.

In your answer you might argue that all religions use symbols but in different ways. You might decide that, nevertheless, worship should be personal between the worshipper and God and that, therefore, symbols are a potential hindrance.

Islam

1 (a) Describe how the use of food and fasting might show that Muslims believe in Allah.

[8 marks]

(b) Explain how praying every day might help Muslims in their lives.

[7 marks]

(c) 'Religious images help people to worship.' Do you agree? Give reasons to support your answer and show that you have thought about different points of view. You must refer to Islam in your answer.

[5 marks]

2 (a) Describe a Muslim place of public worship.

[8 marks]

(b) Explain how the features of this building reflect Muslim beliefs.

[7 marks]

(c) 'People do not need symbols to worship Allah.' Do you agree? Give reasons to support your answer, and show that you have thought about different points of view. You must refer to Islam in your answer.

[5 marks]

Tips

In your answer you may focus on fasting during Ramadan and need to give considerable detail about when food can and cannot be eaten and the regulations and exceptions surrounding this. You might comment on the general halal/haram laws about food. You might also consider the celebrations with special food which are made at the two Eid festivals.

In your answer you might consider the benefits of prayer and the value of meditative practices in prayer as bringing peace and strength. You might also consider how people are strengthened by prayer and also that a regular structure of prayer can bring strength to a person's life. You may comment on how prayer strengthens the ummah. Also, you might mention that regular prayer is one of the Five Pillars to be observed by all Muslims.

Here, you might consider the value of images as focusing worship. However, you also need to consider that, in Islam, images are forbidden and are shirk and that it could be too easy to be distracted into worshipping images which is one of the reasons why they are expressly forbidden.

In answering this question you may choose any type of mosque from a large specialist building to a small house mosque. You need to be accurate in your description. You should consider specifics such as the particular religious furnishings and also look more generally at design and, perhaps, architecture.

Here, you should focus on a few main features such as the minbar, mihrab, qiblah wall, dome, empty prayer space, etc. You should also give clear explanations of how these reflect belief, in particular, how the lack of pictures or statues reflect beliefs in tawhid and shirk.

In your answer you might argue that all religions use symbols but in different ways. You might decide that, nevertheless, worship should be personal between the worshipper and God and that, therefore, symbols are a potential hindrance.

Introduction

This unit looks at:

- religious ideas about the origins of the world and of humanity
- scientific ideas about the origins of the world and of humanity
- the relationship between people and the rest of the planet.

Religious ideas about the origins of the world and of humanity

Most religions have a belief that God created the world and, in their sacred writings, have a description of that act of creation.

Wherever these creation stories come from and whether or not any of them are actually true, we can be fairly sure, from what they say, that there was no human being there to see what happened and to report it. Also, although there are many similarities between some of the religious accounts of creation, there are many differences which might be seen to suggest that they cannot all be right.

Religions have sought to explain how God created the earth and all the forms of life on it, from plants and insects to human beings. People have also believed that the earth was the centre of the universe and that the sun and the planets revolved around it.

However, science has challenged these descriptions of creation.

Scientific ideas about the origins of the world and of humanity

The science of **cosmology** deals with the origins of the universe. It does not accept the idea that God created the Universe but, instead, has produced theories based on scientific evidence, such as the **Big Bang** theory. This would seem to challenge religious views. Scientists suggest that the earth is about 18 billion years old. The Big Bang was a massive explosion which made the entire universe. All the galaxies, stars and planets were formed. The world's latest high power telescopes have also helped to show evidence of the Big Bang.

The question must be whether, if the earth is just one planet amongst millions, there is anything really special about human life?

The other science which deals with creation is that of **evolution**. This theory had its origins in 1740 when the Swiss naturalist Charles Bonnet (1720–1793) published an article about aphids (insects that feed on plants). In his studies Bonnet said that all future generations of aphids were already contained within those which were already alive. He called this process 'preformationism' which is the earliest instance of the theory of evolution.

Evolutionary theory was made famous by the publication, in 1859 of *On the Origin of Species by Means of Natural Selection or the Preservation of Favoured Races in the Struggle for Life*, by Charles Darwin (1809–1882). Darwin had travelled on *The Beagle*, on a voyage that lasted five years and went around the globe.

Darwin's theory, based on his scientific research during the voyage, suggests that life on earth began with a very simple single cell and that life forms gradually evolved and developed from this. This theory also applies to humans and Darwin suggested that humans evolved and were not made on the last day of creation. Therefore the world was not made just for the benefit of humanity. Darwin believed that humans evolved from the great apes.

Many people refused to accept that humans could have evolved from apes.

Some religious people have challenged this view saying that it is untrue because it is at variance with the creation stories. At the time at which Darwin's book was published one very eminent geologist, called Edmund Gosse, claimed that not only was Darwin wrong in his theories but that the fossils which were found in rocks were simply placed there by God in order to test Christians' faith.

Often, religion and science have found themselves in conflict.

Science has sometimes been seen as having no room for God. However, there are many scientists who are also religious believers and think that it is only necessary to look more objectively at the accounts of creation in the sacred texts to see that God did create everything but in a way which science can now explain, at least in part.

Some people continue to believe literally in the biblical account of creation. These are often called 'creationists'.

A more recent response to this argument is called Intelligent Design. This argues that God created the universe because there are certain features of the universe and of living things which can be best explained by an intelligent cause, not a process such as **natural selection**. No scientist has any convincing evidence to support this theory.

Humans and the rest of the planet

Britain is known as a nation of animal lovers and there are many organisations concerned with the care of animals and the environment. These include:
- RSPB (Royal Society for the Protection of Birds)
- RSPCA (Royal Society for the Prevention of Cruelty to Animals)
- Greenpeace
- WWF (World Wide Fund for Nature)

The most recent figures for the domestic animal population of the United Kingdom were produced in 1975 when there were 5.83 million dogs and 4.45 million cats kept as household pets. Nearly a quarter of all homes had at least one pet.

Almost everyone would probably agree that animals should not be treated cruelly, people are shocked when they see pictures released by the RSPCA which show animals tied up, covered in sores, and starving to death. Many people are opposed to the use

Chickens being kept in battery houses.

of animals for sport, such as hunting (more than 13 million birds are shot for sport in the United Kingdom each year), and to animals being trained to do tricks, as in a circus, but very few people have objections to keeping dogs 'unnaturally' in their homes, or to the use of horses for work or for racing.

There has been widespread protest over the wearing of fur with 100 million animals killed for their coats each year. However, in some countries, such as those in the polar regions, the animals are being shot for food and people are wearing fur coats because it is the only sensible way for them to keep warm.

Probably the main use of animals in the world is as a source of food. The majority of the world's people are omnivores, they eat meat, fish, dairy products and fruit and vegetables. While some people are vegetarians and do not eat any meat, and some are vegans so they will not eat meat or dairy products, there are others who eat fish but not other animals. Some people feel that different types of animals should be treated differently.

People have the choice of what they eat. People also have influence over how animals are treated before they are slaughtered. Factory farming and the long-distance transportation of animals have been the subject of many protests in recent years.

All of the world's religions have given guidance or rules to their followers about what they should and should not eat.

It is also true that animals have been used very successfully in many types of medical research which are considered too dangerous to carry out on human beings.

The treatment of animals is often seen as being different from environmental issues. However, the lives of all animals, including humans, is very closely linked to the issues surrounding the environment that seem to appear in the media almost every day.

Environmental issues and the real application of the idea of stewardship may prove to be the most important issues facing humanity in the 21st century.

Science continues to 'interfere' with the natural order of the world with experiments in GM (genetically modified) foods. However, it is argued that these experiments will benefit humans by increasing the amount of food available.

Cloning experiments such as Dolly the sheep are also designed, ultimately, to help cure more humans.

Activity

1 In your opinion, should people be prepared to give up the 'luxuries of life' in order to ensure the planet for future generations?

2 Look at some of the publicity material produced by organisations such as the RSPCA and the Anti-vivisection League. How far do you think that people in the United Kingdom can really call themselves 'religious', or be described as a nation of animal lovers?

3 Look at some of the materials produced by groups such as Greenpeace and consider whether they are saying the right things to people about the environment. Could you produce something about an area which you are particularly concerned about which you think would be more effective?

Christianity

This topic looks at:
- Christian ideas about the origins of the world and of humanity
- Christian views about the differences between people and other animals
- Christian ideas about stewardship
- Christian responses to environmental issues.

Christian ideas about the origins of the world and of humanity

In the Bible there are two accounts of the creation of the world and of humanity. These are found at the beginning of Genesis, the first book in the Bible.

> **In the beginning God created the heavens and the earth. Now the earth was formless and empty, darkness was over the surface of the deep, and the Spirit of God was hovering over the waters. And God said, 'Let there be light,' and there was light.**
>
> (Genesis 1:1–3)

A painting of the creation of the world

Some people have interpreted this passage as saying that God created the world from nothing – *ex nihilo*. This is the teaching of the Roman Catholic Church. Some other Christians believe that the passage means that the raw material of the universe was already there before God began the process of creation. Which of these was the case may not seem very important but some people argue that if God was working with material which was already there, then he cannot be responsible if something goes wrong with the world.

In the first account of creation, which is in Genesis 1:1–2:3, God made creation in this order:

> Day one: Light and dark – day and night.
> Day two: Land and water.
> Day three: Plants.
> Day four: Sun, moon and stars.
> Day five: Fish and birds.
> Day six: Animals and humans.

A scientist might well say that there could be no light without the sun so this account does not make sense. However, its importance is that it explains how, according to the writers of the Bible, God planned the whole of creation with everything deliberately put in place.

The way the story is written suggests that each different life form was created by God from the beginning and each with a purpose.

> **And God said, 'Let the land produce living creatures according to their kinds: livestock, creatures that move along the ground, and wild animals, each according to its kind.' And it was so. God made the wild animals according to their kinds, the livestock according to their kinds, and all the creatures that move along the ground according to their kinds. And God saw that it was good.**
>
> (Genesis 1:24–25)

In this first account, God made humans last and placed them in charge of the earth:

> Then God said, 'Let us make man in our image, in our likeness, and let them rule over the fish of the sea and the birds of the air, over the livestock, over all the earth, and over all the creatures that move along the ground.' So God created man in his own image, in the image of God he created him; male and female he created them. God blessed them and said to them, 'Be fruitful and increase in number; fill the earth and subdue it. Rule over the fish of the sea and the birds of the air and over every living creature that moves on the ground.' Then God said, 'I give you every seed-bearing plant on the face of the whole earth and every tree that has fruit with seed in it. They will be yours for food. And to all the beasts of the earth and all the birds of the air and all the creatures that move on the ground – everything that has the breath of life in it – I give every green plant for food.' And it was so. God saw all that he had made, and it was very good. And there was evening, and there was morning – the sixth day.
>
> (Genesis 1:26–31)

This account says that creation took place in six days. However, the Hebrew word 'ayin' which is translated as 'day' just means a period of time. What is clear is that it says God made everything in a certain order.

Some people argue that as humans were told to 'fill the earth and subdue it' they have the right to dominate the earth and may not, necessarily, take the best interests of the planet and other life forms into account.

The second account of creation is different.

> When the Lord God made the earth and the heavens – and no shrub of the field had yet

appeared on the earth and no plant of the field had yet sprung up, for the Lord God had not sent rain on the earth and there was no man to work the ground, but streams came up from the earth and watered the whole surface of the ground – the Lord God formed the man from the dust of the ground and breathed into his nostrils the breath of life, and the man became a living being...

> The Lord God took the man and put him in the Garden of Eden to work it and take care of it...

> Now the Lord God had formed out of the ground all the beasts of the field and all the birds of the air. He brought them to the man to see what he would name them; and whatever the man called each living creature, that was its name. So the man gave names to all the livestock, the birds of the air and all the beasts of the field.
>
> (Genesis 2:4–7, 15, 19)

In this account, instead of the detail of the order in which things were created, the important point is that humans are shown to be the final part of creation and are placed in charge of the land and of all the living creatures. Although this does not have the same idea of ruling the earth and subduing it, the fact that the man is told to name the animals shows human power over all other forms of life.

Both accounts have created problems for some Christians. Some believers consider that the Bible is the exact word of God and that, therefore, everything in it must be accepted as true. This seems to mean that either the Bible or scientific theories are correct but not both and so the Bible must be right and science wrong.

In the 17th century, an English Bishop, James Ussher, tried to work out the exact time of the creation of the world and calculated that it was at 9am on 26 October 4004 BCE. Today, many people would probably laugh at this attempt to work out a scientific issue by using the Bible as though it was a totally accurate scientific account. However, it is not necessary to dismiss the biblical accounts of creation simply because we can now use modern scientific methods to discover what did happen during the creation of the world.

Some Christians have accepted that the creation stories are myths – they contain important truths but are not meant to be seen as factually correct. They could be seen as prayers thanking God for creation rather than being intended to give accurate details about what took place.

Many Christians would now say that the Bible and science answer two different questions:

Science answers the question of how the world was created while religion explains why.

The argument of the divine watchmaker (teleological) is also applied to creation (see Unit 1, page 2). The circumstances for the production of life in the universe are so exact that it seems to some people impossible that they could have simply come about by chance: God is necessary as a 'prime mover' for creation to have taken place.

Most people would now accept the Big Bang theory of the creation of the universe. This says that at the beginning of time there was an enormous explosion and that the universe we now see is the result of that. The effects of the explosion are still having an effect as the galaxies continue to move away from each other. This would mean that God must have been present before the Big Bang took place. In the 4th century, St Augustine suggested that this sort of argument was not a problem because as time was a part of the world, God must have invented time at the same point as the rest of creation.

Clearly it would be hard for anyone today to argue that Genesis gave an accurate scientific account of the creation, although it was not until 1996 that the Roman Catholic Church officially accepted that scientific theories of evolution were correct.

However, it is still illegal in certain parts of the USA which are predominantly Evangelical for scientific theories including evolution to be taught in schools.

St Augustine had already anticipated this difficulty in the 4th century when he said: 'In the beginning were created only germs or causes of the forms of life which were afterwards to be developed in gradual course.'

In fact, this is very similar to the theory of a gradual evolution. The biblical account is not therefore wrong, it is simply that it does not claim to be scientific. The account of creation in Genesis is designed to explain the relationship between God and nature, and like many of the accounts of creation in other religions, it explains the relationship without entering into a scientific debate. Nevertheless, some very fundamentalist Christians have found it impossible to accept that humans evolved and are actually related to apes, even though scientific research says that this is so.

Activity

Read Psalms 8 and 104 and compare these descriptions of creation with the ones in Genesis 1–3.

Christian views about the differences between people and other animals

Genesis also explains the relationship between God and humans, God created people but then allowed them to be free agents in their relationship with him and the world.

In Genesis the animals are made in the same way as the plants but humanity is made in 'imago dei' – the image of God. People appear to be a special creation, different from the animals. Also, Christians believe that when:

God... breathed into his nostrils the breath of life, and the man became a living being...

this was when humans received their soul. This makes humans different from all the rest of the animals which do not have souls. The lives of humans are sacred and they have special rights, duties and responsibilities which animals do not have.

Christian ideas about stewardship

Christianity teaches that when people were created they were intended to act as 'stewards' – someone who looks after others – in this case the earth:

> fill the earth and subdue it. Rule over the fish of the sea and the birds of the air and over every living creature that moves on the ground.

Humans have a responsibility to look after the earth which belongs to God:

> The earth is the Lord's, and all that is in it,
> The world, and those who live in it.
> (Psalm 24:1)

Christians try to respect all forms of life. It is a common mistake however to believe that Jesus said that 'all life is sacred' and for centuries there have been discussions about whether animals have souls. However, Jesus did say:

> Behold the fowls of the air: for they sow not, neither do they reap, nor gather into barns; yet your heavenly Father feedeth them.
> (Matthew 6:26)

And:

> Are not two sparrows sold for a penny? Yet not one of them will fall to the ground apart from the will of your Father.
> (Matthew 10:29)

Both of these teachings suggest that birds (and so, animals) are valuable to God and so should be valuable to humans.

There are many stories about Christian saints and animals.

One of the earliest is in a book called the Acts of Paul, probably written about 160–180 CE, which includes a story very similar to the Greek fable of Androcles and the lion, in which Paul escapes from the wild beasts in the arena at Ephesus by recognising a lion he had baptised earlier. The lion would not harm him.

St Francis of Assisi was born in 1181 and died in 1226. He is particularly remembered for a sermon which he preached to some birds in a field:

> My little sisters, the birds, you owe a lot to God, He created you, and you should always praise him wherever you are because he has given you freedom to fly anywhere, and has given you two or three sets of clothing. He also preserved you in Noah's ark and he has given you the sky to live in. You do not have to work and God feeds you and gives you streams and fountains to drink from, mountains and valleys where you can be safe and trees to nest in. Because you do not know how to spin or sew, God has clothed you and your children. Your creator loves you very much because he has given you so many things therefore you should never be ungrateful and should always praise God.

On another occasion he is said to have released a hare from a trap. The hare ran to him and he said, 'Come to me, brother hare,' and took it in his arms. When a fisherman gave him a large fish, he thanked him and then put it back into the water, telling it to praise God.

At the World Wide Fund for Nature in 1986, the Christian representative, Fr. Lanfranco Serrini, said that:

> Every human act of irresponsibility towards creatures is an abomination. According to its gravity, it is an offence against that divine wisdom which sustains and gives purpose to the interdependent harmony of the universe.

The Christian churches have also spoken out against the misuse and abuse of animals, though they have not said that necessary experiments for the preservation of human life should not be carried out.

The Church of England: 'Developments in science, medicine and technology' should be monitored 'in the light of Christian ethical principles.'

The Methodist Church: 'The universe as a whole is a product of God's creative and imaginative will. Men and women are to be stewards and curators not exploiters of its resources, material, animal and spiritual.'

The Religious Society of Friends (Quakers): '...believe that the air, sea, earth, forests, animals and ourselves are all intimately connected, and the way in which we treat all of those things reflects on ourselves and consequently on God.'

Christian responses to environmental issues

God's role as creator of the universe and everything in it is emphasised in the statement of belief called the Nicene Creed:

> We believe in one God,
> the Father, the almighty,
> maker of heaven and earth,
> of all that is,
> seen and unseen.

In the New Testament, Jesus also talks about God's creation when he is showing how important humans are:

> Consider how the lilies grow. They do not labour or spin. Yet I tell you, not even Solomon in all his splendour was dressed like one of these. If that is how God clothes the grass of the field, which is here today, and tomorrow is thrown into the fire,
> how much more will he clothe you, O you of little faith!
>
> (Luke 12:27–28)

St Francis of Assisi wrote a prayer known as the 'Canticle of the Sun':

> O Most High, Almighty, good Lord God, to you belong praise, glory, honour and all blessing! Praised be my Lord God for all his creatures, especially for our brother
> the sun who brings us the day and who brings us the light; far is he and shines with a very great splendour; O Lord,
> he signifies you to us.
> Praised be my Lord
> for our sister the moon,
> and for the stars, which he has set clear and lovely in heaven.
> Praised be my Lord for our brother the wind, and for the air and clouds, calms and all weather by which you uphold life in all creatures.

In recent years the Christian churches have become very concerned with environmental issues.

In 1988, Pope John Paul II issued an Encyclical (a formal statement issued by the Pope to the Bishops of the Roman Catholic Church) called *Sollicitudo Rei Socialis* (On Social Concerns) in which he said:

> The earth and all life on it is a gift from God given us to share and develop, not to dominate and exploit.

> Our actions have consequences for the rights of others and for the resources of the earth.

> The goods of the earth and the beauties of nature are to be enjoyed and celebrated as well as consumed.

> We have the responsibility to create a balanced policy between consumption and conservation.

> We must consider the welfare of future generations in our planning for and utilisation of the earth's resources.

The World Council of Churches issued a statement in which it said:

> The dignity of nature as creation needs to be bound up with our responsibility for the preservation of life.

In the Assisi Declarations Fr. Lanfranco Serrini said:

> **Christians repudiate all ill-considered exploitation of nature which threatens to destroy it and, in turn, to make man the victim of degradation.**

This statement showed that the churches condemned the way in which the natural world was being treated without any consideration of the consequences and felt that, in the end, nature would be destroyed and human beings would suffer for their actions.

These verses are from a poem by Kate Compston, a Christian minister:

> **Great spirit, still brooding over the world –**
> **We hear the cry of the earth, we see the sorrow of the land raped and plundered in our greed for its varied resources.**
> **We hear the cry of the waters, we see the sorrow of stream and ocean polluted by the poisons we release into them.**
> **We hear the cry of the animals, we see the sorrow of bird, fish, and beast needlessly suffering and dying to serve our profit or sport or vanity.**
> **Please teach us:**
> **a proper sensitivity toward your feeling creation**
> **a proper simplicity in the way we live in our environment**
> **a proper respect for the shalom of the universe.**
> **We turn from our arrogant ways to seek you again, Creator of all life.**
> **Redeem us – and redeem your world and heal its wounds and dry its tears.**
> **May our response to you bear fruit in a fresh sense of responsibility towards everything you have created.**

This passage is from the Iona Community Worship Book:

> **This we know, the earth does not belong to us,**
> **We belong to the earth.**
> **This we know, all things are connected,**
> **Like the blood that unites the family.**
> **This we know, we did not weave the web of life,**
> **We are merely a strand in it.**
> **This we know, whatever we do to the web,**
> **We do to ourselves.**
> **Let us give thanks for the gift of creation.**

Christianity does teach that people should only take and use what they need and that they should not be greedy or concerned with material wealth:

Then Jesus said to his disciples: 'Therefore I tell you, do not worry about your life, what you will eat; or about your body, what you will wear. Life is more than food, and the body more than clothes. Consider the ravens: They do not sow or reap, they have no storeroom or barn; yet God feeds them. And how much more valuable you are than birds! Who of you by worrying can add a single hour to his life? Since you cannot do this very little thing, why do you worry about the rest?

Consider how the lilies grow. They do not labour or spin. Yet I tell you, not even Solomon in all his splendour was dressed like one of these. If that is how God clothes the grass of the field, which is here today, and tomorrow is thrown into the fire, how much more will he clothe you, O you of little faith! And do not set your heart on what you will eat or drink; do not worry about it. For the pagan world runs after all such things, and your Father knows that you need them. But seek his kingdom, and these things will be given to you as well.' (Luke 12:22–31)

Fire destroying a forest.

Many Christians believe that it is the greed of the rich countries of the world which is causing so much damage to the environment. Some have joined organisations such as Greenpeace or the World Wide Fund for Nature to try to prevent the destruction of the environment; they believe that this is a way in which they can demonstrate their Christian stewardship. Some Christians have taken a very active part in protests against the use of animals in research and also work to try to prevent the environment being destroyed. The European Christian Environmental Network (ECEN) was set up in 1998 and works to enable the churches of Europe and Christian groups involved with the environment to:

- share information and common experiences
- reflect a wide variety of church traditions
- engage in a broad range of environmental work
- encourage each other in being a united witness to caring for God's creation.

Activity

Read Genesis 6:9–8:22. This is the traditional story of Noah.

Explain what people might learn about God and his care for the environment from this passage.

☾ ✦Islam

This topic looks at:
- Muslim ideas about the origins of the world and of humanity
- Muslim views about the differences between people and other animals
- Muslim responses to environmental issues.

Muslim ideas about the origins of the world

The Qur'an contains an account of creation which says that:

> **Your Guardian-Lord is Allah, Who created the heavens and the earth in six days, then He established Himself on the Throne (of authority): He draweth the night as a veil o'er the day, each seeking the other in rapid succession: He created the sun, the moon, and the stars, (all) governed by laws under His command. Is it not His to create and to govern? Blessed be Allah, the Cherisher and Sustainer of the worlds!**
>
> **Do no mischief on the earth, after it hath been set in order, but call on Him with fear and longing (in your hearts): for the Mercy of Allah is (always) near to those who do good.** (Surah 7:53, 56)

The Qur'an does not give an order of creation, but it says that Allah created everything. The word which is translated here as 'days' is ayyam which means 'long periods' or 'ages'. It would seem then that the Qur'an is simply saying that Allah created the universe over a long period of time.

The creation of humans is also explained:

> **I have created Jinns and men, that they may serve Me. No Sustenance do I require of them, nor do I require that they should feed Me. For Allah is He Who gives (all) Sustenance—Lord of Power—Steadfast (forever). For the Wrong-doers, their portion is like unto the portion of their fellows (of earlier generations): then let them not ask Me to hasten (that portion)! Woe, then, to the Unbelievers, on account of that Day of theirs which they have been promised!** (Surah 51:56–60)

The **Jinn** are spirits usually described as being made of fire. They are neither good nor evil. Allah also made **Mala'ikah** who are angels and messengers of Allah. They have no free will and no physical bodies, although they can take on human shape.

Islam has always been very closely linked to science, and modern theories of cosmology and evolution do not create any problem for Muslims. They believe that the Qur'an is the word of Allah and true, they also believe that Allah is in charge of the world and controls it, but this does not mean that science cannot explain what is said in the Qur'an. As humanity learns more, science helps people to understand more of what is in the Qur'an but which they could not understand before.

However, the Qur'an does contain some details that are surprising considering that it was written down long before many scientific discoveries were made:

Do not the Unbelievers see that the heavens and the earth were joined together (as one unit of Creation), before We clove them asunder? We made from water every living thing. Will they not then believe? And We have set on the earth mountains standing firm, lest it should shake with them, and We have made therein broad highways (between mountains) for them to pass through: that they may receive Guidance. And We have made the heavens as a canopy well guarded: yet do they turn away from the Signs which these things (point to)! It is He Who created the Night and the Day, and the sun and the moon: all (the celestial bodies) swim along, each in its rounded course.

(Surah 21:30–33)

This seems to be saying that life began in what scientists now call the 'primordial soup', as well as showing understanding of the fact that the sun and moon are in particular and separate orbits. Muslims explain this by saying that as such scientific discoveries had not been made at this time, it was God's wish to explain these things through the revelation of the Qur'an.

The Qur'an also explains the passage of water and its role in the growth of life:

Seest thou not that Allah sends down rain from the sky, and leads it through springs in the earth? Then He causes to grow, therewith, produce of various colours: then it withers; thou wilt see it grow yellow; then He makes it dry up and crumble away. Truly, in this, is a Message of remembrance to men of understanding. (Surah 39:21)

There is also knowledge that bodies can carry out physical changes on substances:

And verily in cattle (too) will ye find an instructive Sign. From what is within their bodies between excretions and blood,

We produce, for your drink, milk, pure and agreeable to those who drink it. And from the fruit of the date-palm and the vine, ye get out wholesome drink and food: behold, in this also is a Sign for those who are wise.

(Surah 16:66)

Neither arguments about cosmology or evolution create any real problem for Muslims, instead they demonstrate humanity's gradual understanding of what was already revealed.

Discussion

Consider why modern scientific developments do not always create the same difficulties for Muslims as they do for members of other religions.

Activity

1 Re-read Surah 21:30–33. Explain the ideas about creation which are in the passage.

2 Explain why modern theories of evolution might be acceptable to Muslims.

Muslim views about the differences between people and other animals

It is clear from the teachings of Islam that Allah is seen as the creator of the world and that humans are only here as 'vice-regents' or 'trustees'. Their task is not to destroy the world but to safeguard it for God and for future generations.

So set thou thy face steadily and truly to the Faith: (establish) Allah's handiwork according to the pattern on which He has made mankind: no change (let there be) in the work (wrought) by Allah: that is the standard Religion: but most among mankind understand not. (Surah 30:30)

Say: 'Shall I seek for (my) Cherisher other than Allah, when He is the Cherisher of all things (that exist)?' Every soul draws the meed of its acts on none but itself: no bearer of burdens can bear the burden of another. Your goal in the end is towards Allah: He will tell you the truth of the things wherein ye disputed. It is He Who hath made you (His) agents, inheritors of the earth: He hath raised you in ranks, some above others: that He may try you in the gifts He hath given you: for thy Lord is quick in punishment: yet He is indeed Oft-forgiving, Most Merciful. (Surah 6:164–165)

Both Judaism and Christianity have calendars that are based on the regular cycle of seasons through spring, summer, autumn and winter. Many of the festivals of these two religions are tied in to seasonal changes and began in the customs and celebrations of earlier religions. Islam, however, has a religious year which, at 354 days, is shorter than the Western calendar year of usually 365 days. The calendar is based on a 30-year cycle of 360 lunar months which vary between 29 and 30 days. By doing this Islam, unlike some other religions, avoided any link to earlier religious feasts and so the Muslim religious festivals fall at a different time from year to year.

Therefore, there is no 'harvest festival' in Islam but this does not mean that Muslims are not constantly giving thanks to Allah for his creation and for their food.

The Earth is green and beautiful, and Allah has appointed you his stewards over it.
The whole earth has been created a place of worship, pure and clean. Whoever plants a tree and diligently looks after it until it matures and bears fruit is rewarded.
If a Muslim plants a tree or sows a field and humans and beasts and birds eat from it, all of it is love on his part. (Hadith)

Islam believes that humanity has a responsibility to look after animals:

And take not life—which Allah has made sacred—except for just cause. (Surah 17:33)

The Prophet taught that animals must be treated well; they must not be branded or beaten. He told a story of a prostitute who, on a hot day, took water from a well to give to a dog. For this one act of kindness, he said, Allah forgave her all her sins.

The Qur'an states that all life, animal and human, belongs to Allah:

There is not an animal (that lives) on the earth, nor a being that flies on its wings, but (forms part of) communities like you. Nothing have we omitted from the Book, and they (all) shall be gathered to their Lord in the end. (Surah 6:38)

It is clear that humans have a duty towards all living beings.

Islam is not opposed to necessary animal experimentation when it safeguards humans but it does stress the importance of animals as part of Allah's creation:

...it was Our power that made the hills and the birds celebrate Our praises... (Surah 21:79)

This respect is shown in the life of Muhammad ﷺ. During his travels he saw an army of ants heading towards a fire so he ordered the fire to be put out so that the ants would not be harmed. Islam also teaches that when Muhammad ﷺ was fleeing from Makkah to al-Madinah and hid from his pursuers in a cave, a spider spun a web across the entrance and a dove nested on a ledge outside in order to protect him.

In the 13th century a Muslim lawyer called Izz ad-Din ibn Abd as-Salam drew up a bill of legal rights for animals based on Shari'ah (Muslim law).

This bill of rights protects animals but also shows that they are subservient to humans:

The unbeliever who prohibits the slaughtering of an animal [for no reason but] to achieve the interest of the animal is incorrect because in so doing he gives preference to a lower animal over a higher animal.

Muslim responses to environmental issues

Islam has always been known for its scientific knowledge and discoveries. Muslim medicine traditionally concentrated on the use of drugs and herbs rather than on surgery. Al-Razi (d. 925 CE) was the first scientist to distinguish between smallpox and measles and Ibn Sina (d.1037 CE) described how epidemics spread. Remembering also that many traditional Muslim countries are dry and arid with large areas of desert, it is not surprising therefore that Islam has shown itself particularly concerned with plant life and the environment.

The Qur'an is clear on the responsibility of humanity.

It is He Who hath made you (His) agents, inheritors of the earth.
(Surah 6:165)

At the World Wide Fund for Nature at Assisi in 1986, the Muslim representative, Dr Abdullah Omar Nasseef, stressed the human responsibility to look after the earth:

The central concept of Islam is tawheed or the Unity of God. Allah is Unity; and His Unity is also reflected in the unity of mankind, and the unity of man and nature. His trustees are responsible for maintaining the unity of His creation, the integrity of the Earth, its flora and fauna, its wildlife and natural environment. Unity cannot be had by discord, by setting one need against another or letting one end predominate over another; it is maintained by balance and

harmony. There Muslims say that Islam is the middle path and we will be answerable for how we have walked this path, how we have maintained balance and harmony in the whole of creation around us.

So unity, trusteeship and accountability, that is tawheed, khalifa and akhrah, the three central concepts of Islam, are also the pillars of the environmental ethics of Islam. They constitute the basic values taught by the Qur'an. It is these values which led Muhammad ﷺ, the Prophet of Islam, to say: 'Whoever plants a tree and diligently looks after it until it matures and bears fruit is rewarded.'

Islam sees the benefit and well-being of all humanity as being a human responsibility in looking after the world which God has created for us to live in and believes that every effort must be made to be 'green' and to slow down and halt destructive trends.

Muslim organisations such as the Islamic Foundation for Ecology & Environmental Sciences work closely with governments and other faith groups in caring for and protecting the environment.

Discussion

Consider Muslim attitudes towards animals and the reasons for their beliefs.

Activity

1 Explain the responsibilities which Muslims have as vice-regents.

2 What are the main environmental issues for Muslims?

3 Find out how Islam responds to the use of animals for medical research and for cosmetic or cigarette research.

Summary

Because they believe that God created the world for them to live in, the religions of the world also have a responsibility to safeguard that world for the future generations of all faiths. They must take an active part in ensuring that greed and ignorance do not destroy the future.

Creation harvest liturgy

Brothers and sisters in creation, we covenant this day with you and with all creation yet to be;
With every living Creature and all that contains and sustains you.
With all that is on earth and with the earth itself,
With all that lives in the water and with the waters themselves;
With all that flies in the skies and with the sky itself. We establish this covenant, that all our powers will be used to prevent your destruction.
We confess that it is our own kind who put you at risk of death. We ask you for your trust and as a symbol of our intention we mark our covenant with you by the rainbow.
This is the sign of the covenant between ourselves and every living thing that is found on the earth.

Questions

1 What do you understand by:
  (a) the environment
  (b) planet earth
  (c) nature
  (d) recycling
  (e) developing countries
  (f) vice-regent
  (g) vegetarianism and veganism
  (h) trustee or steward?

2 Explain why many religions feel that humanity has been given responsibility for the earth.

3 Find out what positive steps one of these religions is taking towards safeguarding the environment, and why it feels that it should be doing this.

4 Explain how far religious followers should be prepared to go in the positive action towards the environment.

5 Explain how religious people might make decisions about whether they should concentrate their energies on 'feeding the world' or 'safeguarding the environment'.

6 Explain whether you think that special rules about what people can and cannot eat are an advantage or a disadvantage for religious followers today.

7 Explain how far religious followers should be prepared to go in the positive action which they take towards protecting animal rights, and why they might do this.

8 How might religious people decide between giving money to animal charities and to organisations working for children, and how might they reach their decision?

9 Explain how religious followers might do more for animal welfare to fulfil their responsibilities as stewards of the earth.

Practice GCSE questions

Christianity

1 (a) Describe Christian teachings about the origins of humanity. **[8 marks]**

(b) Explain why Christians might believe that they should care for animals. **[7 marks]**

(c) 'Human beings are not capable of caring for the environment.'
Do you agree? Give reasons to support your opinion and show that you have thought about different points of view. You must refer to Christianity in your answer. **[5 marks]**

2 (a) Describe Christian ideas about the origins of the world. **[8 marks]**

(b) Explain how these ideas are different from scientific theories about the origins of the world. **[7 marks]**

(c) 'Science is right so religion is wrong.'
Do you agree? Give reasons to support your answer, and show that you have thought about different points of view. You must refer to Christianity in your answer. **[5 marks]**

Tips

When you answer this question remember that it is about the origins of humanity not the origins of the world. In your answer you might refer to the fact that humanity was the last part of creation, however, you need to go further than this. You might want to discuss either or both of the creation accounts in Genesis 1–2. You might also want to say that some Christians agree with scientific theories.

In your answer you might focus on the idea of stewardship and explain the responsibility which was therefore given to humans at the creation. You might want to consider and explain exactly what humans are instructed to do in the creation accounts. You might also want to look more generally at Christian ideas of responsibility towards animals and the world in the sense of caring for others.

You might decide, in answering this question, that humans are or are not responsible for caring for the environment. You might also want to argue that human beings are capable of being stewards but do not do so. From a religious perspective you might consider whether God would have placed humans as stewards if they were not capable of carrying out the task.

When you answer this question remember that it is about the origins of world not the origins of humanity. In your answer you will probably recount the stories of creation. You might deal with either or both of the two accounts in Genesis 1–2. You might also say that many Christians either do not accept the biblical accounts as actual fact in favour of scientific theories or that they look at the scientific theories as offering further explanation and detail for the biblical accounts.

In your answer you need to explain ideas about the Big Bang theory and draw comparisons with this. You might explain that some people find these ideas completely contradictory, whilst other people may wonder whether the scientific theories can be seen as offering explanations of the biblical accounts.

In your answer you are free to argue in a number of different ways and for either side or both in relation to their relative merits. You might decide that if a person is religious, then they are more likely to come out in favour of the religious theory each time, whilst other more 'enlightened' people would always accept the views of science.

Islam

1 (a) Describe Muslim teachings about the origins of humanity. [8 marks]

(b) Explain why Muslims might believe that they should care for animals. [7 marks]

(c) 'Human beings are not capable of caring for the environment.'
Do you agree? Give reasons to support your answer, and show that you have thought about different points of view.
You must refer to Islam in your answer. [5 marks]

2 (a) Describe Muslim ideas about the origins of the world. [8 marks]

(b) Explain how these ideas are different from scientific theories about the origins of the world. [7 marks]

(c) 'Science is right so religion is wrong.'
Do you agree? Give reasons to support your answer, and show that you have thought about different points of view.
You must refer to Islam in your answer. [5 marks]

Tips

When you answer this question remember that it is about the origins of humanity not the origins of the world. In your answer you need to focus clearly on the passages that you have studied from the Qur'an and exactly what they say about the creation of humanity and its importance.

In your answer you might focus on the idea of stewardship and explain the responsibility that was, therefore, given to humans at the creation as vice-regents on earth. You might want to consider and explain exactly what humans are instructed to do in the creation account. You might also want to look more generally at Muslim ideas of responsibility towards animals and the world in the sense of caring for others.

You might decide, in answering this question, that humans are or are not responsible for caring for the environment. You might also want to argue that human beings are capable of being stewards but do not do so. From a religious perspective, you might consider whether Allah would have placed humans as stewards or vice-regents if they were not capable of carrying out the task.

When you answer this question remember that it is about the origins of world not the origins of humanity. In your answer you will probably consider the Qur'anic account of creation. You might also say that many Muslims look at the scientific theories as offering further explanation and detail for the accounts in the Qur'an.

In your answer you need to explain ideas about the Big Bang theory and draw comparisons with this. You might explain that some people find these ideas completely contradictory, whilst other people may wonder whether the scientific theories can be seen as offering explanations of the Qur'anic accounts. You might explain that the Qur'an does not give much detail about how the world was created and that, therefore, most Muslims also accept scientific theories such as the Big Bang, which appear to support the teachings of the Qur'an.

In your answer you are free to argue in a number of different ways and for either side or both in relation to their relative merits. You might decide that if a person is religious, then they are more likely to come out in favour of the religious theory each time, whilst other more 'enlightened' people would always accept the views of science. You might also indicate that this is not really an issue in Islam.

Introduction

What happens when we die? What comes next?
These are some of the most important questions that people ever ask themselves. As far as we know animals do not worry about what is going to happen next. They live day to day and their concerns are feeding and breeding; much simpler than the sort of things that bother human beings.

Probably since the first person died humans have been worrying about what happens when they die, and about what will happen to them afterwards.

Many people believe that when they die that will be the end. They will not be conscious any more and so they will not know what is happening to them.

Others think that they continue to live on as ghosts and there are many stories about ghosts and poltergeists 'haunting' people and places.

Some people believe that after death they will be reborn and come back to life as a different person. There are many others who think that after death they will be rewarded, or punished, by God for the way in which they have lived their lives. This reward or punishment might be in some sort of heaven, or hell.

Gravestones remember the dead.

Beliefs about death

Death is the one certain thing about our lives. We cannot be sure whether we will be rich or successful. We cannot know if we will meet someone whom we will fall in love with but, even though we do not know when it will happen, we do know that eventually we will stop breathing and that we will die.

Death affects everyone during their lives. In an average year approximately 659,000 people die in the United Kingdom. For almost every one of these deaths, some people will be mourning and grieving because they have lost a relative or a friend.

Followers of some religions believe that, after they have died, they may be reborn many times. They may return to the earth in many different forms depending on how they have lived their lives. For example, if you were a particularly bad person, you might come back as an animal or even as an insect and you would have to die and be reborn many times before you had the opportunity of being a human being again. On the other hand, you might have lived such a good life that you are freed from this cycle of birth and rebirth and your soul is finally free to go to the afterlife.

This sort of belief in a continuing series of lives is usually called 'reincarnation' or 'rebirth'. However, both Christianity and Islam teach that people only live once, and therefore, they do not believe in reincarnation.

There are always accounts of people who claim to remember their previous lives and who, perhaps under hypnosis, can recall events of these earlier times. Although a lot of research has been carried out into whether these claims are true, no-one has so far been able to prove that such an event has taken place. Followers of Hinduism and Buddhism do not claim to be able to remember previous existences in this way.

Most followers of Christianity and Islam believe that they have only one life on earth. What they believe will happen to them when they die can be quite different.

Christianity

This topic looks at:
- Christian understanding of the distinction between 'body' and 'soul'
- heaven, hell and purgatory
- the relationship between moral behaviour and the afterlife
- funeral rites and beliefs about life after death.

Christian understanding of the distinction between 'body' and 'soul'

According to Christian teaching, as well as a physical, visible, body Christians also have an immortal soul. It is this soul which sets people apart from all other animals.

The Bible teaches that God created humanity in his own image:

> So God created man in his own image, in the image of God he created him; male and female he created them. (Genesis 1:27)

Some people have suggested that this does not mean that humans are like God in appearance but that all human beings have something of God in them and that this 'something' is their soul.

A similar account is found in the second creation story where:

> the Lord God formed the man from the dust of the ground and breathed into his nostrils the breath of life, and the man became a living being. (Genesis 2:7)

Again, it is this 'breath of life' which is the soul and is the difference between humans and other animals.

Eventually, Christians came to believe that the soul was separate from the body and lived on after the body had died.

In the New Testament, Paul explains that the body and the soul are often opposed to each other: the soul tries to follow God, while the body looks for pleasures. Paul wrote that when someone dies, their new 'spiritual body' lives on in heaven. However, it is not clear whether Paul meant the soul when he wrote about a spiritual body.

> The body that is sown is perishable, it is raised imperishable; it is sown in dishonour, it is raised in glory; it is sown in weakness, it is raised in power; it is sown a natural body, it is raised a spiritual body. If there is a natural body, there is also a spiritual body. (1 Corinthians 15:42–44)

According to Christianity, when Jesus died at his crucifixion and was resurrected three days later, he overcame the power of death and people were forgiven their sins. Jesus' death cleansed people from the 'original sin' of humanity which Adam and Eve had brought on themselves by disobeying God and eating from the Tree of Knowledge in the Garden of Eden. This meant the people's immortal souls were now able to survive death and reach heaven.

> Jesus said, 'I am the resurrection and the life. He who believes in me will live, even though he dies; and whoever lives and believes in me will never die.' (John 11:25–26)

The New Testament says that, after his crucifixion, Jesus went down into hell. There he freed the souls of the people from the times of the Old Testament who were waiting there:

> For Christ died for sins once for all, the righteous for the unrighteous, to bring you to God. He was put to death in the body but made alive by the Spirit, through whom also he went and preached to the spirits in prison. (1 Peter 3:18–19)

A wall painting showing the Day of Judgement.

Heaven, hell and purgatory

Christians believe that because of Jesus' death on the cross, they have been freed of the punishment of original sin and now have the opportunity to go to heaven. Christianity teaches that one day Jesus will come back to the earth, this is called the parousia, then God will judge everyone and those who have lived very bad lives will go to hell. Those who have followed Christian teachings and believe in Jesus will go to heaven. Some Christians believe that when someone dies their soul goes straight to heaven (or hell) while others think that everyone will be judged together on the Day of Judgement.

> Listen, I tell you a mystery: We will not all sleep, but we will all be changed – in a flash, in the twinkling of an eye, at the last trumpet. For the trumpet will sound, the dead will be raised imperishable, and we will be changed.
>
> (1 Corinthians 15:51–52)

Roman Catholics believe that there is an intermediate place known as Purgatory. Here, people who are Christians, but who still need to be cleansed of some of the sins that they have done on earth, are punished for a period of time before they are allowed to go to heaven.

Christians hope and believe that they will have the opportunity to go to heaven and be with Jesus for eternity.

Heaven

Christianity teaches that when people die their soul is raised from the dead and moves on to the afterlife. Christians hope that this will be in heaven and be eternal life with God. Heaven has traditionally been presented as a magical place with angels playing harps, but this is just a simple representation of an idea which is too difficult to express in normal human language.

A suggestion of what heaven might be like is found in the Book of Revelation:

> After this I looked, and there before me was a door standing open in heaven. And the voice I had first heard speaking to me like a trumpet said, 'Come up here, and I will show you what must take place after this.' At once I was in the Spirit, and there before me was a throne in heaven with someone sitting on it. And the one who sat there had the appearance of jasper and carnelian. A rainbow, resembling an emerald, encircled the throne. Surrounding the throne were twenty-four other thrones, and seated on them were twenty-four elders. They were dressed in white and had crowns of gold on their heads. From the throne came flashes of lightning, rumblings and peals of thunder. Before the throne, seven lamps were blazing. These are the seven spirits of God. Also before the throne there was what looked like a sea of glass, clear as crystal.
>
> In the centre, around the throne, were four living creatures, and they were covered with eyes, in front and in back. The first living creature was like a lion, the second was like an ox, the third had a face like a man, the fourth was like a flying eagle. Each of the four living creatures had six wings and was covered with eyes all around, even

under his wings. Day and night
they never stop saying:

'Holy, holy, holy
is the Lord God Almighty,
who was, and is, and is to come.'
(Revelation 4:1–8)

For some Christians, the end of time or the last days will also mean that people's bodies come back to life. It is for this reason that some Christians still feel that they should be buried rather than cremated.

Hell

In the past many Christians believed that people who did not believe in Jesus and follow his teachings would be sent to hell and would be punished there for eternity. This traditional view of hell describes it as a place of everlasting torture where people would burn in the fires of hell. People were threatened with hell-fire if they did not become Christians or if they rejected Christian teachings. Many Christians still believe in hell but may see it as a form of punishment where people are denied the sight of God (the beatific vision). Seeing God after death is often called the 'beatific vision' meaning the most beautiful thing that anyone could ever see.

This view has changed slightly and, although the Roman Catholic Church still believes that if people have heard about Jesus then they must follow him, it also says,

Those who, through no fault
of their own, do not know the
Gospel of Christ or his Church, but
who nevertheless seek God with
a sincere heart, and, moved by
grace, try in their actions to do his
will as they know it through the
dictates of their conscience – those
too may achieve eternal salvation.
(Ad gentes 7)

Some Christians may describe heaven as a beautiful garden paradise where everything is perfect and where they will live with God, and hell as an eternal bonfire where people will suffer horrible torments from the devil. Nowadays, however, most people would understand these ideas as states of happiness or unhappiness: in heaven you will be with God forever, while in hell you will never see God or know God's love again.

Purgatory

According to the Roman Catholic Church, very few people are ready to go straight to heaven. They may have lived good lives but are still not free from sin. Instead, they go to a state called purgatory. Their souls will stay here until they are completely free from sin and ready to go to heaven. People who reach purgatory do not risk being sent to hell. The period for which souls stay in purgatory is uncertain and anyway God does not operate in the same idea of time as we have in this life. Sometimes purgatory is said to be a period of thousands of years. Often people will pray for the souls of those who have died in the belief that this will shorten the time that they have to spend in purgatory. In the past people went on pilgrimages to certain places or paid money to the Church to shorten the time souls spent before going to heaven.

Many Christians may say that these beliefs are old fashioned and belong to a simpler age. They may suggest that heaven and hell are essentially states of mind rather than physical places. Some people have also suggested that heaven and hell are as much a part of our life now as they are of what happens when we die.

Moral behaviour and the afterlife

Christians believe that when they die God will judge them for the way in which they lived. One Christian belief is that people are judged on the concern they have shown for others less fortunate than themselves.

An example of Jesus' teaching about this is found in the parable of the Sheep and the Goats:

When the Son of Man comes in
his glory, and all the angels with
him, he will sit on his throne in
heavenly glory. All the nations will
be gathered before him, and he
will separate the people one from
another as a shepherd separates

the sheep from the goats. He will put the sheep on his right and the goats on his left.

Then the King will say to those on his right, 'Come, you who are blessed by my Father; take your inheritance, the kingdom prepared for you since the creation of the world. For I was hungry and you gave me something to eat, I was thirsty and you gave me something to drink, I was a stranger and you invited me in, I needed clothes and you clothed me, I was sick and you looked after me, I was in prison and you came to visit me.'

Then the righteous will answer him, 'Lord, when did we see you hungry and feed you, or thirsty and give you something to drink? When did we see you a stranger and invite you in, or needing clothes and clothe you? When did we see you sick or in prison and go to visit you?'

The King will reply, 'I tell you the truth, whatever you did for one of the least of these brothers of mine, you did for me.'

Then he will say to those on his left, 'Depart from me, you who are cursed, into the eternal fire prepared for the devil and his angels. For I was hungry and you gave me nothing to eat, I was thirsty and you gave me nothing to drink, I was a stranger and you did not invite me in, I needed clothes and you did not clothe me, I was sick and in prison and you did not look after me.'

They also will answer, 'Lord, when did we see you hungry or thirsty or a stranger or needing clothes or sick or in prison, and did not help you?'

He will reply, 'I tell you the truth, whatever you did not do for one of the least of these, you did not do for me.'

Then they will go away to eternal punishment, but the righteous to eternal life. (Matthew 25:31–46)

This parable shows that people who have cared for others will receive eternal life, whilst people who have simply ignored other people will be sent to hell.

Christians do believe they can be forgiven if they are truly sorry for their behaviour and believe in Jesus. This teaching can be found in the epistles of Paul:

Therefore, there is now no condemnation for those who are in Christ Jesus, because through Christ Jesus the law of the Spirit of life set me free from the law of sin and death. For what the law was powerless to do in that it was weakened by the sinful nature, God did by sending his own Son in the likeness of sinful man to be a sin offering. And so he condemned sin in sinful man, in order that the righteous requirements of the law might be fully met in us, who do not live according to the sinful nature but according to the Spirit.
(Romans 8:1–4)

These passages show Christian beliefs about the relationship between moral behaviour and life after death. God sets standards for people's behaviour. People may not be able to meet these standards but praying for forgiveness and showing faith in Jesus mean that they are not condemned to exile in hell. Roman Catholics in particular may go regularly to a priest and make their confession so that they can be forgiven their sins. This is called the Sacrament of Reconciliation and follows Jesus' teaching to his disciples:

Again Jesus said, 'Peace be with you! As the Father has sent me, I am sending you.' And with that he breathed on them and said, 'Receive the Holy Spirit. If you forgive anyone his sins, they are forgiven; if you do not forgive them, they are not forgiven.'
(John 20:21–23)

Activity

1 Find out about different Christian attitudes towards confession.

2 Write a summary of Christian beliefs about heaven, hell and purgatory.

Christian funeral rites and beliefs about life after death

When a person is known to be dying, a minister or priest may visit them to say prayers or to read from the Bible. Some people will wish to confess their sins to a priest before death, but others feel that this is a private matter between themselves and God. Roman Catholics receive a sacrament called the Anointing of the Sick from a priest who anoints them with holy oil as a preparation for death.

After death, Christians are either buried or cremated. A funeral service usually takes place in a church and may be followed by a burial in the graveyard of the church or in a public cemetery. Some Christians will have a requiem mass said at the funeral, this is a Eucharist where prayers are said for the dead person's soul.

People often decorate the church with white flowers for a funeral and flowers are put on the coffin and at the graveside. These represent the new life which the person is entering. Candles are also used to remind Christians that they are saved because of Jesus who is the 'Light of the World'. Candle smoke also symbolises the soul going up to heaven.

Funeral services usually begin with the statement:

> I am the resurrection and the life. He who believes in me will live, even though he dies; and whoever lives and believes in me will never die.   (John 11:25)

This was said by Jesus when he raised Lazarus from the dead and it is said at funerals to remind people of the Christian belief that people who have put their faith in Jesus will live again in heaven.

The Book of Revelation contains a description of what will happen on the Day of Judgement:

> Then I saw a new heaven and a new earth, for the first heaven and the first earth had passed away, and there was no longer any sea. I saw the Holy City, the new Jerusalem, coming down out of heaven from God, prepared as a bride beautifully dressed for her husband. And I heard a loud voice from the throne saying, 'Now the dwelling of God is with men, and he will live with them. They will be his people, and God himself will be with them and be their God. He will wipe every tear from their eyes. There will be no more death or mourning or crying or pain, for the old order of things has passed away.'
> (Revelation 21:1–7)

Flowers at a grave as a sign of remembrance.

Prayers are said around the grave and, as the coffin is lowered into the ground, the priest or minister will say: 'We commit this body to the ground, earth to earth, ashes to ashes, dust to dust.' Later, a gravestone will be erected at the site of the grave. This has details of the person's life and possibly a quotation from the Bible. Relatives of the deceased person may take flowers to place on the grave.

Some Christians may choose to be cremated rather than buried. They may simply not want to be buried or they may feel that cremation is a better way of disposing of a body. The service may be held in a church and then the coffin is taken to the crematorium. Sometimes the service takes place in a chapel alongside the crematorium. After the service, the coffin is usually covered by curtains as the mourners leave. The coffin is then incinerated (burnt). The ashes from the cremation are then given to the family of the dead person. Some people have the ashes buried, whilst others may choose to scatter them perhaps at a favourite place of the dead person.

Many Christians do not approve of cremations because of the teachings of the Apostles' Creed which says:

I believe in...
The resurrection of the body
And the life everlasting.

This is very similar to the beliefs of the ancient Greeks who thought that, in the afterlife, people continued to live in exactly the same physical condition as they died in. This idea of a physical body in heaven seems different from Paul's idea of a spiritual body.

This belief is also similar to the poem which is read every year at Remembrance Day services to recall those who died fighting for their country:

They shall grow not old, as we
that are left grow old:
Age shall not weary them, nor the
years condemn.
At the going down of the sun and
in the morning
We will remember them.

(Laurence Binyon)

This stresses the Christian belief that death is not something that people should be frightened of, but that they should look forward to a life in heaven when there will be no more suffering and where they will live happily with God forever.

Activity

1 Explain your own beliefs about what happens when people die and compare these with Christian teachings. Which do you think make the most sense?

2 Explain the differences between heaven, hell and purgatory. Can you suggest why some people do not believe in purgatory?

3 Consider what happens at a Christian funeral service. What parts of the service do you think might help those who are mourning? How do you think funeral services might be changed to make them less gloomy and more helpful to relatives and friends?

4 Explain why some people might prefer a burial to a cremation.

☪ Islam

This topic looks at:
- Muslim understanding of the distinction between 'body' and 'soul'
- heaven and hell
- the relationship between moral behaviour and the afterlife
- funeral rites and beliefs about life after death.

Muslim understanding of the distinction between 'body' and 'soul'

Muslims believe that after death there will be a Day of Judgement. People who have not followed Allah's wishes will go to hell where they will be punished. Good people will go to a perfect world of rest and pleasure with Allah for **akhirah** (life after death).

Muslims do not believe that people have an immortal soul which needs to be saved. They consider that this life is a test in which they have the opportunity to live as well as they can in submission to the will of Allah. Muslims believe that when someone dies they will stay in their grave until the Day of Judgement which will be on a date already chosen by Allah. On this day, the soul and body of each Muslim will be reunited and everyone will be raised from their graves. True followers of Allah will be 'reborn' in paradise. For Muslims, without a belief in life after death, life on earth would be meaningless.

Muslims believe that after death there will be a Day of Judgement – **Yawmuddin**. Surah 39 describes how, on the Day of Judgement, there will be the sound of a trumpet and people will fall down as if unconscious. The trumpet will then sound again and the dead will rise to join the living.

> The Trumpet will (just) be sounded, when all that are in the heavens and on earth will swoon, except such as it will please Allah (to exempt). Then will a second one be sounded, when, behold, they will be standing and looking on!

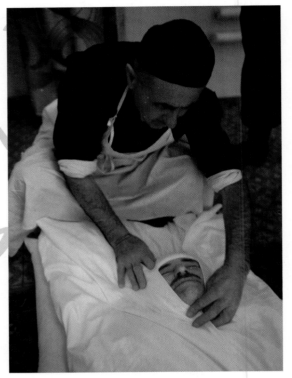
A Muslim being prepared for burial.

> And the Earth will shine with the Glory of its Lord: the Record (of Deeds) will be placed (open); the prophets and the witnesses will be brought forward and a just decision pronounced between them; and they will not be wronged (in the least).

A Muslim funeral.

And to every soul will be paid in full (the fruit) of its Deeds; and (Allah) knoweth best all that they do.

The Unbelievers will be led to Hell in crowd: until, when they arrive, there, its gates will be opened. And its keepers will say, 'Did not apostles come to you from among yourselves, rehearsing to you the Signs of your Lord, and warning you of the Meeting of This Day of yours?' The answer will be: 'True: but the Decree of Punishment has been proved true against the Unbelievers!'

(To them) will be said: 'Enter ye the gates of Hell, to dwell therein: and evil is (this) Abode of the Arrogant!'

And those who feared their Lord will be led to the Garden in crowds: until behold, they arrive there; its gates will be opened; and its keepers will say: 'Peace be upon you! Well have ye done! Enter ye here, to dwell therein.'

They will say: 'Praise be to Allah, Who has truly fulfilled His Promise to us, and has given us (this) land in heritage: We can dwell in the Garden as we will: how excellent a reward for those who work (righteousness)!'

And thou wilt see the angels surrounding the Throne (Divine) on all sides, singing Glory and Praise to their Lord. The Decision between them (at Judgement) will be in (perfect) justice, and the cry (on all sides) will be, 'Praise be to Allah, the Lord of the Worlds!'   (Surah 39:68–75)

This surah from the Qur'an teaches that those people who follow the words of Allah will live happily in a wonderful garden while people who reject these teachings will be punished.

In the long run evil in the extreme will be the End of those who do evil; for that they rejected the Signs of Allah, and held them up to ridicule.

It is Allah Who begins (the process of) creation; then repeats it; then shall ye be brought back to Him.

On the Day that the Hour will be established, the guilty will be struck dumb with despair.

No intercessor will they have among their 'Partners' and they will (themselves) reject their 'Partners'.

On the Day that the Hour will be established—that Day shall (all men) be sorted out. Then those who have believed and worked righteous deeds, shall be made happy in a Mead of Delight. And those who have rejected Faith and falsely denied Our Signs and the meeting of the Hereafter— such shall be brought forth to punishment.   (Surah 30:10–16)

Righteous – just.

Like Christians and Jews, Muslims believe that people only have one chance at life and you are judged on how you live it. When the judgement of Allah (God) finally comes he will already know everything and it will be fast and final:

To Allah belongeth the Mystery of the heavens and the earth. And the Decision of the Hour (of Judgement) is as the twinkling of an eye, or even quicker: for Allah hath power over all things.

It is He Who brought you forth from the wombs of your mothers when ye knew nothing; and He gave you hearing and sight and intelligence and affections: that ye may give thanks (to Allah).

Do they not look at the birds, held poised in the midst of (the air and) the sky? Nothing holds them up but (the power of) Allah. Verily in this are Signs for those who believe.   (Surah 16:77–79)

Islam does not believe that it is possible to describe the afterlife as it belongs to a totally different dimension, but they do believe that it lasts forever.

Heaven and hell

This surah from the Qur'an teaches that those people who follow the words of Allah will live happily in a wonderful garden, **al-Janna** (paradise):

> On the Day that the Hour will be established—that Day shall (all men) be sorted out. Then those who have believed and worked righteous deeds, shall be made happy in a Mead of Delight. And those who have rejected Faith and falsely denied Our Signs and the meeting of the Hereafter— such shall be brought forth to punishment.   (Surah 30:14–16)

When Muhammad ﷺ was carried up to heaven at the Mi'raj or night flight he passed through seven levels of heaven until he finally reached paradise. Some Muslims believe that how well they have lived on earth will decide how close they are to the prophets and Allah when they die.

People who have not followed Allah's wishes will go to the fires of hell – **Jahannam** – where they will be punished, and good people will go to a perfect world of rest and pleasure to be with Allah for akhirah (life after death). However, Allah is always merciful and even a bad person may eventually reach paradise after they have been punished. The exception will be anyone who is found guilty of shirk (see Unit 2, page 36) which cannot be forgiven.

Moral behaviour and the afterlife

Surah 17 says that true believers must follow a straight path if they are to escape punishment on Yawmuddin:

> Every man's fate We have fastened on his own neck: On the Day of Judgement we shall bring out for him a scroll, which he will see spread open.
>
> (It will be said to him:) 'Read thine (own) record: Sufficient is thy soul this day to make out an account against thee.'   (Surah 17:13–14)

Every person is responsible for their own actions because humans have been created with free will. People can follow or reject the teachings of Islam but they will face the consequences of their decision on the Day of Judgement.

Islam teaches the doctrine of fitrah. This says that every child is born with a predisposition or inclination to be a Muslim but may not be a Muslim because they are brought up in a different religion.

The Qur'an warns that when the Last Judgement occurs it will be too late for people to repent. The truth will be so obvious that there will be no opportunity to choose to believe with your own free will in Allah.

Islam recognises three types of sin: the first is shirk, associating someone or something with Allah; the second, zalim, consists of crimes such as murder, theft, suicide and illegal sexual relations; the third type covers lying, cursing and envy.

Muslims believe that they will be judged according to how well they followed the teachings of the Qur'an and the example of Muhammad ﷺ. To be judged favourably they need to have lived their lives in submission to the will of Allah and to have followed the teachings of the Five Pillars (see Unit 2, page 30).

When Allah makes his judgement, he will take into account not only people's deeds but also their intentions (niyyah):

> If a person intends to do something wrong but does not do it, this is a good deed.
>
> If a person intends to do something wrong and does it, this is a bad deed.
>
> If a person intends to do a good deed but cannot manage to carry it out, this is a good deed.
>
> If a person intends a good deed and carries it out, this is equal to ten good deeds.   (Hadith)

Discussion

Consider why a Muslim might feel that life after death is an essential part of their belief.

Activity

1 Explain what is meant by fitrah.

2 In your own words, explain what Muhammad ﷺ taught about intentions (niyyah).

Muslim funeral rites and beliefs about life after death

On their death bed Muslims will try to repeat the final words of the Prophet Muhammad ﷺ: 'Allah, help me through the hardship and agony of death.' When another Muslim hears of the death they will say, 'To Allah we belong and to Allah we return,' showing that they hope the person will be claimed by Allah to live in heaven.

Funerals take place within three days of death (if possible within 24 hours). The body is washed and covered in a simple white cloth. If the laws of the country permit, no coffin is used. Muslims are buried facing Makkah. In the United Kingdom this sort of burial is not allowed as bodies must be placed in closed coffins.

Muslims believe in a complete physical resurrection of the body and so do not approve of cremation. This verse points out that Allah will have no difficulty in putting these dead bodies back together, even including their fingerprints:

> Does man think that We cannot assemble his bones?
>
> Nay, We are able to put together in perfect order the very tips of his fingers. (Surah 75:3–4)

At the graveside Surah 1, **al-Fatihah**, is recited. This is a very important statement of belief in Allah and his mercy and is always said when praying:

> In the name of Allah, Most Gracious, Most Merciful.

> Praise be to Allah, the Cherisher and Sustainer of the worlds;
> Most Gracious, Most Merciful;
> Master of the Day of Judgement.
> Thee do we worship, and Thine aid we seek.
> Show us the straight way,
> The way of those on whom Thou hast bestowed Thy Grace, those whose (portion) is not wrath, and who go not astray. (Surah 1)

As the coffin is lowered into the ground, the mourners say the following words which show their belief that Allah will take the dead to paradise on the Day of Judgement:

> From the (earth) did We create you, and into it shall We return you, and from it shall We bring you out once again. (Surah 20:55)

It is traditional for the graves to be raised a little above the level of the ground to stop people walking or sitting on them, but elaborate monuments are forbidden.

It is normal for people to grieve but Islam teaches that this death should be accepted with trust and faith. The Prophet cried when his son died and it is natural for both men and women to cry at a death. However, Muslims must remember that the death is the wish of Allah. The time spent in mourning varies among different communities and can last from three days to three months and widows are permitted to mourn for longer. The community ensures that mourners are not left on their own and will visit the family, bringing food.

Discussion

Consider why Muslims do not allow elaborate monuments or tombstones.

Activity

1 Explain what Islam teaches about mourning.

2 Explain the importance of Muslim funeral rites.

Summary

Although Christians and Muslims believe in life after death, they have different beliefs about what exactly will happen to them when they die. One of the main concerns of religious people is how they will be judged and treated for the sort of life that they have led on earth. Some people believe that if they confess their sins before they die, or if they make some sort of repentance for the things that they have done wrong, then they will receive better treatment from God when they die.

People have different beliefs about heaven and hell: what they are and where they are. In the past many people thought that heaven and hell were simply physical places: heaven above the earth and hell below it. Nowadays, with scientific discoveries and a greater understanding of the earth and the universe, people have come to rather different conclusions.

Some people say that heaven and hell are types of existence and that it is only people's souls that are there, not their bodies. Others say that heaven and hell are where we live now and that we create them for ourselves. People who believe in this sort of 'afterlife' do not always take the teachings of religions literally.

What is certain about all of these beliefs is that people cannot really know what will happen after death until they have died. People may be certain in their faith and believe strongly that something will happen to them but, at the moment, there is no scientific proof about any other existence after death. It is a matter of faith and belief not of scientifically provable fact.

Questions

1 What do you understand by:
   (a) death
   (b) heaven
   (c) hell
   (d) purgatory
   (e) resurrection?

2 Explain how you think a believer in either Islam or Christianity might feel when someone they know dies. How does this differ from what a non-believer might feel when someone dies?

3 Look at what each religion believes about what happens when someone dies. Explain which religion you think gives most hope to: (a) someone who is dying; (b) a relative or friend of someone who is dying.

4 Explain how the way in which a funeral takes place may be designed to help the relatives and friends of the person who has died.

5 Explain what you think may happen to you when you die.

6 Consider how important living a 'good' life is in relation to what might happen to people when they die. What do you think a 'good' life is?

7 Do you think that people should be judged on the way in which they have lived their own lives or on the way in which their family, or the people in their country, or the people who follow their religion behave?

Practice GCSE questions

Christianity

1 (a) Describe Christian beliefs about life after death. [8 marks]

(b) Explain how these beliefs might affect the way in which Christians live. [7 marks]

(c) 'Funeral ceremonies are for the living, not the dead.'
Do you agree? Give reasons to support your answer, and show that you have thought about different points of view. You must refer to Christianity in your answer. [5 marks]

2 (a) Describe Christian beliefs about heaven and hell. [8 marks]

(b) Explain how these beliefs might affect the way a person lives. [7 marks]

(c) 'It cannot be true that there is life after death because there is no evidence for it.'
Do you agree? Give reasons to support your answer, and show that you have thought about different points of view. You must refer to Christianity in your answer. [5 marks]

Tips

In your answer you will probably choose to focus on beliefs about heaven, hell and purgatory. You could describe these and say what they mean in Christianity. You might also choose to show denominational differences. You could also continue to consider the issue of judgement and how the way a person lives their life may affect what happens to them when they die.

Here you might build on your answer to (a) and explain that, with the idea of a final judgement, these beliefs are a strong incentive to live according to the teachings of the Church. You may also explain that because of these beliefs Christians must try to live strictly according to biblical and Church teachings.

In answering this question you need to consider the purpose of a funeral ceremony. You might conclude that because the person is already dead then the ceremony is to show respect for them and to comfort those who are mourning. On the other hand, you might consider that the ceremony and the prayers said at it, as well as, perhaps, the prayers at a requiem mass, may help the person who has died on their way in to the next life.

In your answer you might choose to look at two different approaches. You might look at a traditional, or rather old-fashioned, idea of heaven with clouds, angels, harps and hell with fire, devils and pitchforks. However, you might also describe a more modern interpretation of these concepts, writing about whether the real difference is eternal life in the presence of God or without that presence.

Here you might suggest that people want to go to heaven when they die rather than hell and so will be careful about their behaviour, and ensure that they are living according to the teachings of the Bible. You might also suggest that people do not need to be thinking about these issues all through their life and that Christians should not worry about what happens to them when they die but simply trust in God.

In your answer you might want to argue that claims about people seeing ghosts and near-death experiences do provide evidence. You could also say that Jesus' resurrection was evidence. On the other hand, you may say that faith and belief are far more important than any claimed factual evidence.

Islam

1 (a) Describe Muslim beliefs about life after death. [8 marks]

(b) Explain how these beliefs might affect the way in which Muslims live. [7 marks]

(c) 'Funeral ceremonies are for the living, not the dead.'
Do you agree? Give reasons to support your answer, and show that you have thought about different points of view.
You must refer to Islam in your answer. [5 marks]

2 (a) Describe Muslim beliefs about heaven and hell. [8 marks]

(b) Explain how these beliefs might affect the way a person lives. [7 marks]

(c) 'It cannot be true that there is life after death because there is no evidence for it.'
Do you agree? Give reasons to support your answer, and show that you have thought about different points of view.
You must refer to Islam in your answer. [5 marks]

Tips

In answering this question you may focus on Muslim beliefs about heaven and hell and perhaps go on to deal with the issue of judgement. You might decide to give some details about the nature of paradise and its levels. You could also describe how a good or a bad life rests in the balance on the Day of Judgement and how this may affect a person's fate in the afterlife.

Building on your answer to (a) you might explain the idea of a final judgement, and consider whether these beliefs are a strong incentive to live according to the teachings of the Qur'an. You might also explain that given these beliefs there is a need to live strictly in accordance with Qur'anic teachings and to observe the Five Pillars.

In answering this question you need to consider the purpose of a funeral ceremony. You might conclude that because the person is already dead then the ceremony is to show respect for them and to comfort those who are mourning. On the other hand, you might consider whether, with the person's fate in the hands of Allah, there is any need for anything more.

In your answer you need to describe what Muslims believe about heaven and hell. You might suggest that these are basically simple beliefs which follow the writings in the Qur'an. You might describe the idea of a heavenly paradise (Jahanna) that will reward those who live according to the will of Allah.

In answering this question you may explain that people want to go to heaven when they die rather than hell and so will look at good behaviour. This will involve living according to the Five Pillars and the other teachings of the Qur'an in the hope of ensuring a place in paradise.

In your answer you might want to argue that claims about people seeing ghosts and near-death experiences do provide evidence. On the other hand, you may say that faith and belief are far more important than any claimed factual evidence and use examples from the Qur'an.

Introduction

'She/he's such a good person,' people sometimes say, or 'He/she's evil.' What do these expressions mean? How can people say that someone or something, is 'good' or 'evil' – what do the words themselves mean?

'Good' is a positive word which is used in lots of different situations. It can be something we like, something that is good for us: it is good to have a holiday or it is good to be given £1000.

'Evil', on the other hand, is not just something we do not like, it is much stronger than that. It is something which is damaging, not simply dangerous, because there is always a chance you may escape danger. Evil is more than that; it makes people suffer and does them harm.

When we use 'right' and 'wrong' we are making judgements about things – 'this is something of which I approve', 'this is something of which I do not approve'.

Something very similar happens when we use the words 'good' and 'evil'. We are making judgements based on what we do know, or what we think we know, and we are using some sort of code or set of rules by which we can judge things for ourselves.

Adolf Hitler was 'evil'.

So, if the way we decide in good and evil or right and wrong is something which we have learnt, where does this code come from?

From our families and the people around us, we learn a basic set of rules:
- Do not lie.
- Do not hurt people.
- Do not swear.
- Do not steal.
- Do what your parents tell you.

These are just some of the rules that most of us learn, but where do they come from originally? If these rules are easy and obvious, why do we want to break them?

Some people would argue that it is because there are people who are good and people who are evil:

This is too simple. All 'good' people make mistakes sometimes and do things in their life which are wrong and even 'evil' people may sometimes show love or affection for someone or something else. It could be said that Hitler loved his mistress Eva Braun.

The basic code of rules for life is, in some ways, very much like the Ten Commandments. Most religions teach that their rules come from God.

Mother Teresa was 'good'.

Religious people believe that God is the origin (beginning) of everything that is good. It is God who influences us to behave in the 'right' way.

So, what is it that makes people behave in the 'wrong' way? What is it that guides and influences people who we may describe as 'evil'?

Some religions have said that as God is a power of good and yet some people behave in an evil manner, there must also be a power of evil. This is the force or person which is sometimes referred to as Satan or the devil. God influences people to be good and the devil persuades them to be evil. The difference is that although God permits this power of evil to exist, nevertheless it is God who finally judges us on our life. If you live according to God's teachings, then he will reward you. If you live in the ways of the devil, God will punish you.

This seems very straightforward but many people would say that it is a weakness in humans themselves that causes them to choose not to follow these rules.

The fact that there is evil in the world has always caused problems for believers. If God is omnipotent, omniscient and omnibenevolent, how can evil continue to exist?

Believers says that there are two kinds of evil:
1 Moral evil – this is the actions of people which are cruel and uncaring.
2 Natural evil – events such as volcanoes, floods and hurricanes which harm or kill many people but do not appear to be caused by humans. Many of the people affected may live good and caring lives so why should God punish them if, indeed, God is responsible.

Is it that God is not all-powerful and cannot prevent these things happening or is God really responsible for them?

People who do not believe in religion at all would say that every human being has the choice: they can behave in a way which is positive and good for themselves and for others. Or they can choose a way which may seem good for themselves but is certainly bad for others.

However, there are still two questions which we have not answered:
● If God is good, then why does he let evil exist, whatever that evil is?
● If God created human beings and if he loves them, how can he let 'evil' things such as volcanoes, earthquakes and shipwrecks happen to them?

Christianity and Islam try to answer these questions. They explain what is good and what is bad and provide rules for their followers. As well as this, however, they also teach how we should treat people who break these rules – with forgiveness.

Discussion

How can we decide whether something or someone is good or evil?

Christianity

This topic looks at:

- beliefs about God and the devil or Satan
- responses to the problem of evil: the suffering of Christ
- coping with suffering through acceptance and prayer
- discovering the right way to behave through the Bible, the example of Christ and the conscience
- the reasons why Christians try to follow a moral code.

Beliefs about God and the devil

Christian teaching on good and evil is not a black or white issue.

Christianity teaches that when Adam and Eve sinned in the Garden of Eden by eating the fruit of the forbidden tree, not only did they choose to disobey God but also they were responsible for bringing sin on to human beings. This means that since that time all children have been born with 'original sin' (the sin of Adam and Eve), which can only be removed from them by baptism. Until recently the Roman Catholic Church taught that any baby which died without being baptised would spend eternity in limbo and could never enter heaven.

When a baby is being baptised in the Anglican Church the Priest says:

> We thank you, Father, for the water of baptism.
> In it we are buried with Christ in his death.
> By it we share in his resurrection.
> Through it we are reborn by the Holy Spirit.
> Therefore, in joyful obedience to your Son,
> we baptise into his fellowship those who come to him in faith.
> Now sanctify this water that, by the power of your Holy Spirit, they may be cleansed from sin

and born again.
> Renewed in your image, may they walk by the light of faith
> and continue for ever in the risen life of Jesus Christ our Lord;
> to whom with you and the Holy Spirit
> be all honour and glory, now and for ever.

The congregation say:

> Fight valiantly as a disciple of Christ against sin, the world and the devil, and remain faithful to Christ to the end of your life.

In the past, Christianity has taught that Lucifer, one of the archangels, was guilty of pride in his relationship with God. Because of this he was thrown out of heaven. He fell to hell where he became Satan, the devil. One of the origins of this story can be found in Luke's gospel where Jesus is talking to 70 disciples:

> I saw Satan fall like lightning from heaven.   (Luke 10:18)

There are also references to Satan in the Book of Revelation:

> And there was war in heaven. Michael and his angels fought against the dragon, and the dragon and his angels fought back. But he was not strong enough, and they lost their place in heaven. The great dragon was hurled down – that ancient serpent called the devil, or Satan, who leads the whole world astray. He was hurled to the earth, and his angels with him. Then the dragon was enraged at the woman and went off to make war against the rest of her offspring – those who obey God's commandments and hold to the testimony of Jesus.
> (Revelation 12:7–9, 17)

A mediaeval gargoyle.

When Jesus spent 40 days in the wilderness after his baptism he was tempted by the devil:

Jesus, full of the Holy Spirit, returned from the Jordan and was led by the Spirit in the desert, where for forty days he was tempted by the devil. He ate nothing during those days, and at the end of them he was hungry. The devil said to him, 'If you are the Son of God, tell this stone to become bread.'

Jesus answered, 'It is written: "Man does not live on bread alone."
The devil led him up to a high place and showed him in an instant all the kingdoms of the world. And he said to him, 'I will give you all their authority and splendour, for it has been given to me, and I can give it to anyone I want to. So if you worship me, it will all be yours.'

Jesus answered, 'It is written: "Worship the Lord your God and serve him only."

The devil led him to Jerusalem and had him stand on the highest point of the temple. 'If you are the Son of God,' he said, 'throw yourself down from here. For it is written:

"He will command his angels concerning you to guard you carefully; they will lift you up in their hands, so that you will not strike your foot against a stone."

Jesus answered, 'It says: "Do not put the Lord your God to the test."'
When the devil had finished all this tempting, he left him until an opportune time.   (Luke 4:1–13)

Christians believe that God is much stronger than the devil so the power for good is much stronger than the power for evil. However, because God has given people free will so that they can choose for themselves, they can choose whether they follow him or not and they are able to decide to do wrong as well as right.

Some people believe that the devil can enter people and affect their behaviour. Because of this, people and sometimes buildings are exorcised – prayers are said to remove the devil. However, most Christians today, although they may still believe in a power of evil, do not think that people are 'possessed by demons'. Usually there are medical reasons for what we might call 'madness'. Devils have also sometimes been blamed for natural disasters such as earthquakes and erupting volcanoes; again people now know that these are caused by nature. Of course, it is difficult to explain why God would let natural disasters like this happen.

Some Christians would argue that there is no such thing as the devil and that it is just that some people have evil ideas and wishes even though they know that these are wrong. In the Middle Ages fear of the devil was often used to persuade people to attend church and obey the bishops and the law.

There are questions which Christians might ask about evil and suffering and why God allows them:

- If evil came into the world because of Adam and Eve who disobeyed God, why did God allow them to disobey and why did they choose to do so if they were perfect?
- Some people say that evil and suffering are a test. Irenaeus (130–202) suggested that people need to suffer and to choose between right or wrong otherwise they would be just like robots. However, this idea has problems as sometimes the people who are suffering, such as very young babies, do not have the opportunity to learn anything from the experience.
- Augustine (354–430) said that evil was a lack of good. What we call evil is when people fail to live up to the standards that we expect of human beings. So evil is not a thing but a lack of good.

Activity

Explain what Christians believe when they say that humans were created 'in the image of God'.

Responses to suffering

Christians might say that evil and suffering are mysteries which cannot be explained. However, God cares for people and does not want them to suffer. When God chose to come to earth as Jesus, the Son of God, he taught people how to live according to God's will and then died on the cross so that people's sins could be forgiven. In this way, some Christians argue, God shared in human suffering.

As a response to this many Christians pray to God when they are suffering, believing that God will listen to them and help them, either by relieving the suffering or by helping them live through it.

Prayers are not always answered, of course, but believers trust in God to do the best for them.

The book of Job in the Bible tells the story of a holy man who is tested by Satan. Some Christians believe that sometimes God chooses to send suffering on people as a test of their faith. Because of this suffering,

Christians may feel that they want to help other people who are also suffering.

In the past, many people believed that illness was a punishment for sin. Although most Christians would not believe this today, the possible origins of the idea can be found in stories such as this one:

> **They came to the other side of the sea, to the country of the Gerasenes. And when he had stepped out of the boat, immediately a man out of the tombs with an unclean spirit met him. He lived among the tombs; and no one could restrain him any more, even with a chain; for he had often been restrained with shackles and chains, but the chains he wrenched apart, and the shackles he broke in pieces; and no one had the strength to subdue him. Night and day among the tombs and on the mountains he was always howling and bruising himself with stones. When he saw Jesus from a distance, he ran and bowed down before him; and he shouted at the top of his voice, 'What have you to do with me, Jesus, Son of the Most High God? I adjure you by God, do not torment me.' For he had said to him, 'Come out of the man, you unclean spirit!' Then Jesus asked him, 'What is your name?' He replied, 'My name is Legion; for we are many.' He begged him earnestly not to send them out of the country. Now there on the hillside a great herd of swine was feeding; and the unclean spirits begged him, 'Send us into the swine; let us enter them.' So he gave them permission. And the unclean spirits came out and entered the swine; and the herd, numbering about two thousand, rushed down the steep bank into the sea, and were drowned in the sea.**
>
> (Mark 5:1–13)

In fact, this is a story of an exorcism but some people would say that the man had evil spirits in him because of his sins.

Discovering the right way to behave through the Bible

The Bible is often used by Christians as a way to find out how they should live according to God's wishes. People study the Bible and, in particular, passages such as the Ten Commandments and the Sermon on the Mount (Matthew 5–7) as they contain what are seen as essential truths about what is right and wrong.

Many people try to put the biblical teachings into practice but it is often difficult to find teachings which relate directly to problems in the 21st century, thousands of years after it was written.

There are some teachings such as the Ten Commandments and others such as:

> **So in everything, do to others what you would have them do to you** (Matthew 7:12a)

that mean the same now as they did when they were written.

However, there are passages in the Bible which many people would see as reflecting out-dated views such as those about the role of women:

> **Likewise, teach the older women to be reverent in the way they live, not to be slanderers or addicted to much wine, but to teach what is good. Then they can train the younger women to love their husbands and children, to be self-controlled and pure, to be busy at home, to be kind, and to be subject to their husbands, so that no one will malign the word of God.** (Titus 2:3–5)

> **As in all the congregations of the saints, women should remain silent in the churches. They are not allowed to speak, but must be in submission, as the Law says. If they want to inquire about something, they should ask their own husbands at home; for it is disgraceful for a woman to speak in the church.** (1 Corinthians 14:34–5)

> **I want men everywhere to lift up holy hands in prayer, without anger or disputing.**

> **I also want women to dress modestly, with decency and propriety, not with braided hair or gold or pearls or expensive clothes, but with good deeds, appropriate for women who profess to worship God.**

> **A woman should learn in quietness and full submission. I do not permit a woman to teach or to have authority over a man; she must be silent. For Adam was formed first, then Eve. And Adam was not the one deceived; it was the woman who was deceived and became a sinner. But women will be saved through childbearing – if they continue in faith, love and holiness with propriety.** (1 Timothy 2:8–15)

> **Now I want you to realise that the head of every man is Christ, and the head of the woman is man, and the head of Christ is God. Every man who prays or prophesies with his head covered dishonours his head. And every woman who prays or prophesies with her head uncovered dishonours her head – it is just as though her head were shaved. If a woman does not cover her head, she should have her hair cut off; and if it is a disgrace for a woman to have her hair cut or shaved off, she should cover her head. A man ought not to cover his head, since he is the image and glory of God; but the woman is the glory of man. For man did not come from woman, but woman from man; neither was man created for woman, but woman for man.** (1 Corinthians 11:3–9)

Discovering the right way to behave through the example of Jesus

Before Jesus came to earth, people believed that they were punished for humanity's sins by being sent to hell and so the belief about the death and resurrection of Jesus is absolutely central to the whole of Christianity.

According to the New Testament, Jesus was put to death on the cross by the Roman authorities in Jerusalem because he was accused of blasphemy by the Jews. He was given the opportunity to deny the charges which were brought against him but he refused.

He was very badly treated by the Romans. He was whipped and a 'crown' of sharp thorns was pushed on to his head. After this he was made to carry his cross from the prison to the place where criminals were executed. Here he was nailed to the cross by his wrists and feet and left to die. During the three hours which he lived, nailed to the cross, he asked God, his father, to forgive the people who punished him:

> **Father, forgive them, for they do not know what they are doing.**
> (Luke 23:34)

Three days after his death he was seen again by the disciples: this is called the resurrection. He lived with them on earth for another 40 days until he finally returned to heaven.

Because Jesus did not fight against his execution but died innocently, the sins of humanity were forgiven: he atoned (made up) for them. Because Jesus defeated death and came back to life, from that time forward people who followed Jesus and accepted his teachings and that he is the Son of God, can be confident that when they die they will be with him in heaven.

> **Consequently, just as the result of one trespass (sin) was condemnation for all men, so also the result of one act of righteousness was justification that brings life for all men. For just as through the disobedience of the one man the many were made sinners, so also through the obedience of the one man the many will be made righteous.**
> (Romans 5:18–19)

This passage from a letter written by Paul explains how the sin of Adam and Eve was forgiven by Jesus' actions.

During the three days before the resurrection the Bible says that Jesus went to hell to free the good people who were there:

> **For Christ died for sins once for all, the righteous for the unrighteous, to bring you to God. He was put to death in the body but made alive by the Spirit, through whom also he went and preached to the spirits in prison who disobeyed long ago when God waited patiently in the days of Noah while the ark was being**

Jesus carries his cross to Calvary.

built. In it only a few people, eight in all, were saved through water.
(1 Peter 3:18–20)

On the night before he was put to death, Jesus had celebrated the Last Supper with his disciples. At this meal he shared bread and wine with them.

While they were eating, Jesus took bread, gave thanks and broke it, and gave it to his disciples, saying, 'Take and eat; this is my body.' Then he took the cup, gave thanks and offered it to them, saying, 'Drink from it, all of you. This is my blood of the covenant, which is poured out for many for the forgiveness of sins.'
(Matthew 26:26–28)

Christians remember this meal each time they celebrate the Eucharist. By saying these words and sharing bread and wine they believe that they are bringing Jesus back into their lives and also reminding themselves of his atonement for their sins.

The example of Jesus' life may be taken as a model by Christians. Because he was the Son of God, they believe that he always acted and spoke as God wishes. Some people may follow his example in relation to people who society considers to be outcasts or adopt his teachings about the use of wealth.

In this incident Jesus healed an outcast – a man with leprosy:

While Jesus was in one of the towns, a man came along who was covered with leprosy. When he saw Jesus, he fell with his face to the ground and begged him, 'Lord, if you are willing, you can make me clean.'

Jesus reached out his hand and touched the man. 'I am willing,' he said. 'Be clean!' And immediately the leprosy left him.

Then Jesus ordered him, 'Don't tell anyone, but go, show yourself to the priest and offer the sacrifices that Moses commanded for your cleansing, as a testimony to them.'

Yet the news about him spread all the more, so that crowds of people came to hear him and to be healed of their sicknesses.
(Luke 5:12–15)

Here is an example of Jesus' teaching about wealth:

Someone in the crowd said to him, 'Teacher, tell my brother to divide the inheritance with me.'

Jesus replied, 'Man, who appointed me a judge or an arbiter between you?' Then he said to them, 'Watch out! Be on your guard against all kinds of greed; a man's life does not consist in the abundance of his possessions.'

And he told them this parable: 'The ground of a certain rich man produced a good crop. He thought to himself, "What shall I do? I have no place to store my crops."

Then he said, "This is what I'll do. I will tear down my barns and build bigger ones, and there I will store all my grain and my goods. And I'll say to myself, 'You have plenty of good things laid up for many years. Take life easy; eat, drink and be merry.'"

But God said to him, "You fool! This very night your life will be demanded from you. Then who will get what you have prepared for yourself?"'

This is how it will be with anyone who stores up things for himself but is not rich toward God.
(Luke 12:13–21)

Discussion

The example of Jesus healing a leper shows his attitudes towards outcasts. Who do you think would be considered outcasts today?

Activity

Try to explain in your own words what Christians mean when they say that Jesus atoned for the sins of the world.

Conscience

Some people believe that they know what is right or wrong because they are following their conscience. People may feel guilty or ashamed when they do something wrong even though they are the only person who knows about it. Some people feel that they cannot do certain things because their conscience will not let them.

It is not clear what this thing called a 'conscience' is. Some Christians believe that it is a way in which God communicates with them and that if they pray for help, God will guide their conscience.

Other people may say that the conscience is the result of upbringing and that we learn about what is right and wrong from our parents and other people around us.

The reasons why Christians try to follow a moral code

Christians believe that they were created 'in the image of God' (Genesis 1:27).

They also believe that God is perfectly good. Therefore, humans were designed to following God's example and also to be perfectly good.

There are moral guidelines in the Bible about how people should behave according to God's wishes. Throughout the Old Testament, as well as in the Ten Commandments, there are many passages which contain teachings on how God wishes his people to behave towards him and towards each other. There are also examples of how God punished people when they disobeyed him.

In the New Testament, much of Jesus' teaching is found in parables: a short story which teaches a religious or moral lesson.

Two of the most famous of these are the Parable of the Good Samaritan (Luke 10:25–37) where Jesus is answering the question: 'And who is my neighbour', and the Parable of the Prodigal Son (Luke 15), which teaches about repentance (being sorry for what you have done) and forgiveness.

Many of Jesus' most important teachings are found in the Sermon on the Mount (Matthew 5–7) and Christians might look here for teachings about issues such as divorce, adultery and anger.

Some people may believe that they must behave morally in order to reach heaven when they die. They may fear that if they do not lead a good life they will be punished for eternity in hell. In the past the churches used this fear to encourage people to go to church more regularly. However, most Christians today would probably not accept such a simple view of heaven and hell.

Activity

Choose one of the examples given in this section on why Christians try to follow a moral code and explain how a Christian might use the teachings in their daily life.

This topic looks at:
- beliefs about the goodness of Allah and the nature of Shaytan/'Iblis
- responses to the problem of evil: submission to the will of Allah
- coping with suffering through submission to the will of Allah and prayer
- discovering the right way to behave through the Qur'an, the example of Muhammad ﷺ and the conscience
- the reasons why Muslims try to follow a moral code.

Beliefs about the goodness of Allah and the nature of Shaytan/'Iblis

It is a fundamental belief of Islam that Allah is good and merciful:

> In the name of Allah, Most Gracious, Most Merciful.
> Praise be to Allah, the Cherisher and Sustainer of the worlds;
> Most Gracious, Most Merciful;
> Master of the Day of Judgment.
>
> (Surah 1:1–4)

Muslims believe therefore that Allah will look after them and guide them so that they can follow his teachings and live in submission to his will. The reason that there is evil and suffering in the world is explained by the existence of **Shaytan** or **'Iblis** (the devil).

Muslims believe that all human beings are born without sin (fitrah). Therefore Muslims have free will and can choose whether to follow the will of Allah (Islam) or they can choose to do wrong.

Allah forgives people who acknowledge that they are wrong and pray for forgiveness. Islam teaches that goodness is always better than evil:

> Nor can goodness and Evil be equal. Repel (Evil) with what is better: Then will he between whom

> and thee was hatred become as it were thy friend and intimate!
>
> (Surah 41:34)

Islam teaches that Allah made Mala'ikah (angels) from nur (divine light); he created Adam, the first human, from clay; he also created spirits called Jinn and these came from fire. After Allah had made Adam, he ordered the angels and Jinn to bow down to his new creation. The angels obeyed but 'Iblis (the devil) a Jinn, refused.

> Behold! Thy Lord said to the angels: 'I am about to create man, from sounding clay from mud moulded into shape;
>
> When I have fashioned him (in due proportion) and breathed into him of My spirit, fall ye down in obeisance unto him.'
>
> So the angels prostrated themselves, all of them together:
>
> Not so Iblis: he refused to be among those who prostrated themselves.
>
> (Allah) said: 'O Iblis! What is your reason for not being among those who prostrated themselves?'
>
> Iblis) said: 'I am not one to prostrate myself to man, whom Thou didst create from sounding clay, from mud moulded into shape.'
>
> (Allah) said: 'Then get thee out from here; for thou art rejected, accursed.
>
> And the curse shall be on thee till the Day of Judgement.'
>
> (Iblis) said: 'O my Lord! Give me then respite till the Day the (dead) are raised.'
>
> (Allah) said: 'Respite is granted thee Till the Day of the Time appointed.'

(Iblis) said: 'O my Lord! Because Thou hast put me in the wrong, I will make (wrong) fair-seeming to them on the earth, and I will put them all in the wrong—

Except Thy servants among them, sincere and purified (by Thy Grace).' (Surah 15:32–35)

'Iblis said that he would tempt humans for ever to choose wrong rather than right.

'Iblis is sometimes called Shaytan (the devil). In his last sermon, Muhammad ﷺ warned his followers:

Beware of Shaytan, he is desperate to divert you from the worship of Allah, so beware of him in matters of your religion.

Islam says that during their lives people will be tempted. Life is a series of tests to which people have to find their own solutions:

Be sure we shall test you with something of fear and hunger, some loss in goods or lives or the fruits (of your toil), but give glad tidings to those who patiently persevere,

Who say, when afflicted with calamity: 'To Allah We belong, and to Him is our return'—

They are those on whom (Descend) blessings from Allah, and Mercy, and they are the ones that receive guidance. (Surah 2:155–157)

However, Shaytan is not equal to Allah and although he is used to test a Muslim's faith, he cannot harm people unless Allah permits it:

Secret counsels are only (inspired) by the Evil One, in order that he may cause grief to the Believers; but he cannot harm them in the least, except as Allah permits; and on Allah let the Believers put their trust. (Surah 58:10)

It is Allah who decides whether someone will be punished or forgiven. Muslims do not make public confessions of their sins.

Islam recognises three types of sin: the first is shirk, associating someone or something with Allah; the second, zalim, consists of crimes such as murder, theft, suicide and illegal sexual relations; the third type covers lying, cursing and envy.

According to the Qur'an, Adam and Hawwa' (Eve) were tempted by Shaytan and ate the fruit of the forbidden tree in Al-Jannah (paradise). Allah forgave Adam and Hawwa' their sins when they prayed to him:

They said: 'Our Lord! We have wronged our own souls: If thou forgive us not and bestow not upon us Thy Mercy, we shall certainly be lost.'

(Allah) said: 'Get ye down with enmity between yourselves. On earth will be your dwelling-place and your means of livelihood—for a time.'

He said: 'Therein shall ye live, and therein shall ye die; but from it shall ye be taken out (at last).' (Surah 7:23–25)

Allah said:

We said: 'Get ye down all from here; and if, as is sure, there comes to you Guidance from Me, whosoever follows My guidance, on them shall be no fear, nor shall they grieve.

But those who reject Faith and belie Our Signs, they shall be companions of the Fire; they shall abide therein.' (Surah 2:38–39)

This is very different from the version of this story found in the Jewish scriptures where Adam and Eve are banished for their sin and from the Christian interpretation of this story, where the sin of eating from the tree brought the idea of Original Sin into the world.

According to the Qur'an Adam and Hawwa' did not bring sin into the world. Therefore people are born without sin and in submission to Allah. This means that everyone has their own responsibility to choose between right and wrong.

It is important for Muslims to remember that there is life after death and the next life will be better than this one. Suffering and the existence of evil in the world is a test, but people who survive this life well will have increased rewards in the afterlife. Anyone who lives according to the teaching of the Qur'an will not suffer forever even if their life is hard. It is also the responsibility of Muslims to reduce suffering for others as much as possible. Muslims cannot know why Allah permits evil and suffering but they understand that it is all part of a larger plan that is beyond human comprehension.

> What is the life of this world but amusement and play? but verily the Home in the Hereafter—that is life indeed, if they but knew.
> (Surah 29:64)

Discussion

Consider the differences between the stories of Adam and Eve and Adam and Hawwa'. Explain the importance of these for Muslim belief.

Activity

1 Explain Muslim teachings about Shaytan/'Iblis and how he came to be the devil.

2 Explain how a Muslim would justify suffering.

Living according to the will of Allah – submission to the will of Allah

Muslims believe that all human beings are born without sin (fitrah). Therefore Muslims have free will and can choose whether to follow the will of Allah (Islam) or they can choose to do wrong. As Muslims also believe in predestination it can be difficult to understand this teaching about free will. Muslims are entirely free to make their own decisions, whether these are for good or bad, but Allah already knows what these decisions will be. There

would be no purpose in Allah stopping people from making the wrong decisions, only when they have the choice can they exercise their desire to do what is right, which is submission to the will of Allah.

It is Allah who decides whether someone will be punished or forgiven. Muslims do not make public confessions of their sins.

Islam means 'submission' and living according to the Five Pillars, the teachings of the Qur'an and the example of Muhammad ﷺ, is to live according to Allah's will.

The Five Pillars are fundamental to Muslim life and a Muslim may sin against Allah by not living according to them:

● Shahadah – declaration of faith which states:

> There is no god except Allah, Muhammad ﷺ is the Messenger of Allah.

● Salah – five compulsory daily prayers for communicating with, and worshipping, Allah. These are performed under specific conditions, in the manner taught by the Prophet Muhammad ﷺ and are said in Arabic. The prayers are said at fixed times and can be performed alone or with other people. Saying these prayers not only fulfils the instructions of the Qur'an and the Prophet, but also means that everyday concerns do not take over a Muslim's life. At regular intervals work has to stop and the Muslim has the opportunity to focus his or her thoughts on Allah.
● Zakah – this is literally 'the purification of wealth by the payment of an annual welfare due'. The observance of zakah means that Muslims are protected from greed and over-concern about money. After they have given the 2.5% in zakah, the rest of their money is 'purified' for their own use.
● Hajj – pilgrimage to Makkah. The annual pilgrimage to Makkah in Saudi Arabia is an obligation on all Muslims who are able to afford it and who are fit enough to undertake it. It provides an

opportunity not only to do the will of Allah but also to visit the holy places of Islam, to follow the journey taken by the Prophet and to share the experience and the prayers with other Muslims from all over the world.

- Sawm – fasting during Ramadan. The fast of sawm is of particular importance to Muslims because, for a month, they have the opportunity to focus their thoughts on Allah because of the requirement to fast, and also to share the experience of fasting with their immediate family and also the **ummah** (the worldwide community of Muslims), all of whom are fasting at the same time.
- A Muslim who believes in the statement of faith and lives his or her life according to this statement and the other four pillars is living in submission to Allah.
- Islam is a religion which brings together the spiritual and everyday aspects of life and aims to control a person's relationship with God (through his or her conscience) as well as human relationships. Islam therefore affects all aspects of life, spiritual, private and public.

Discovering the right way to behave through the Qur'an, the example of Muhammad ﷺ and the conscience

The combination of the words of the Qur'an and the teachings and example of Muhammad ﷺ guide Muslims in making moral decisions. Muslims study the Qur'an and the collections of Hadith in order to reach moral decisions. In this way they are following the words of Allah, given to the Prophet, and also the example of the life of Muhammad ﷺ himself.

One story about Muhammad ﷺ says that, as a child, he was visited by two angels. The angels took his heart and washed it in snow before replacing it in his chest. This showed that he would not be bothered by worldly matters and was different from other children.

One day Muhammad ﷺ was travelling with his uncle who was a merchant, as they were passing through Syria his uncle met a monk called Bahira.

Bahira noticed that a cloud was travelling with the camel train just as though it was sheltering someone from the sun. Bahira sent for Muhammad ﷺ and asked him many questions.

Eventually, he asked Muhammad ﷺ to swear by the idol gods of Makkah, al-Lat and al-Uzza. Muhammad ﷺ refused. Bahira said:

'This child will be a great leader. Take him back to your country and look after him well.'

Later, when Muhammad ﷺ worked for his uncle as a camel driver he gained the respect of everyone he met. He was called al-Amin, the trustworthy one.

The Qur'an and Hadith together give Muslims a clear idea of how Allah wishes them to behave. These provide them with the examples they need to direct their conscience and to determine 'right' from 'wrong'. Muslims believe that Islam helps them by controlling their relationship with Allah through their conscience. Their conscience is then guided by prayer and their submission to Allah's will.

The reasons why Muslims try to follow a moral code

Living in submission to Allah is the way a Muslim would want to live because it shows respect to Allah and shows the Muslim is thankful for the love and care which Allah has always shown. It is also necessary if a Muslim is to reach paradise on the Day of Judgement.

For Muslims, their daily struggle to live according to the will of Allah is known as greater jihad. This is a personal struggle for each individual as they strive to follow the teachings of the Qur'an. For example, Muslims should pray five times a day. There may be many excuses which someone could make for missing one or more of these prayers. Jihad is the effort people make when their conscience tells them that they should pray even though they would rather carry on doing something else which is perhaps giving them pleasure, or they may decide that they want to finish a piece of work before stopping.

Discussion

If Allah created humanity and wants humans to love him, how would you explain the fact that so many people suffer?

Activity

1 Explain how each of the Five Pillars might affect the life of a Muslim and how each would help to strengthen their faith.

2 Explain how Muslims might use both the Qur'an and the example of Muhammad ﷺ when they are trying to cope with suffering.

Summary

From this unit we can see that both of these religions have quite similar views on the relationship between good and evil and the way in which God thinks people should behave. They all believe that God is good and is the power of goodness.

Each religion also has a belief in a power of evil which is sometimes described as a being.

Some people believe that this force for evil is found in a supernatural being which may be the devil in Christianity or 'Iblis in Islam. Others might think that evil is simply the absence of good or perhaps a natural tendency in people that they have to work to overcome.

Both Muslims and Christians believe that evil can be overcome by submitting to the will of God/Allah and by trying to live according to religious teachings. Christians use their conscience and the teachings of the Bible to try to find out God's will. Muslims also use their conscience together with the Qur'an and the example of Muhammad ﷺ.

Again, for both Muslims and Christians, suffering is seen as something which has to be endured but they will pray to God/Allah for help and guidance.

Questions

1 What do you understand by:
   (a) natural disaster
   (b) good and evil?

2 How would you explain the fact that religious people can die in natural disasters?

3 In your opinion, is it possible that the devil is a real being, or do you think that it is natural for people to choose to behave wrongly?

4 If God is really good, why do you think that he allows evil to exist? Should he make all people behave well?

5 Explain how someone's conscience might help them to make the right moral decisions.

Practice GCSE questions

Christianity

1 (a) Describe Christian beliefs about good and evil. [8 marks]

(b) Explain the ways in which a Christian might try to find the answer to a moral problem. [7 marks]

(c) 'When people suffer they are being punished for something they have done.' Do you agree? Give reasons to support your answer and show that you have thought about different points of view. You must refer to Christianity in your answer. [5 marks]

2 (a) Describe Christian beliefs about God and the devil. [8 marks]

(b) Explain how these beliefs might help people who are suffering. [7 marks]

(c) 'If God was really good then people would not suffer.' Do you agree? Give reasons to support your answer, and show that you have thought about different points of view. You must refer to Christianity in your answer. [5 marks]

Tips

In answering this question you need to consider what is meant by good and evil. You may do this in relation to human behaviour (moral evil) and disasters such as hurricanes and floods (natural evil). You might consider these in relation to biblical and Church teachings. You might also consider good and evil in terms of God and the devil.

Here, you could explain how Christians might turn to the Bible for guidance, they might talk to a priest or minister, or discuss the problem with other Christians, they might pray for guidance, and they might turn to their conscience. You could expand on any of these while considering how someone might reach a decision.

There are different ways in which you might approach this question. You might consider that the whole idea is unfair and unreligious. You might also suggest that some people believe that suffering has always been seen by some as punishment for misdeeds. You might consider that some people believe that even illness itself can be a punishment for wrong doing.

In your answer you might say that God is by definition 'good' and that this goodness covers all dealings with God. You might also say God is the total opposite of evil, represented by the devil. However, you might also consider that some people see the devil as a servant of God.

Here, you might explain that Christians see God as all-good and that therefore he must care for creation. This might help people believe that however much they are suffering, nevertheless this suffering will eventually end and they will be rewarded according to this goodness. You might also mention that sometimes the New Testament links the ideas of illness and sin.

In your answer you might want to consider the views of people such as Irenaeus and Augustine. You might also look at other ideas as to why God apparently allows evil and suffering to exist. You might say that some people see the existence of evil and suffering as proof that God does not exist.

Islam

1 (a) Describe Muslim beliefs about good and evil. [8 marks]

(b) Explain the ways in which a Muslim might try to find the answer to a moral problem. [7 marks]

(c) 'When people suffer they are being punished for something they have done.' Do you agree? Give reasons to support your answer, and show that you have thought about different points of view. You must refer to Islam in your answer. [5 marks]

2 (a) Describe Muslim beliefs about Allah and Shaytan. [8 marks]

(b) Explain how these beliefs might help people who are suffering. [7 marks]

(c) 'If Allah was really good then people would not suffer.' Do you agree? Give reasons to support your answer, and show that you have thought about different points of view. You must refer to Islam in your answer. [5 marks]

Tips

In answering this question you need to consider what is meant by good and evil. You may do this in relation to human behaviour (moral evil) and disasters such as hurricanes and floods (natural evil). You might consider these in relation to Qur'anic teachings. You might also consider good and evil in terms of Allah and Shaytan.

Here, you could explain how Muslims might turn to the Qur'an for guidance, they might try to follow the example of the Prophet, they might talk to an imam, or they might discuss the problem with other Muslims, they might pray for guidance, and they might turn to their conscience. You could expand on any of these while considering how someone might reach a decision.

There are different ways in which you might approach this question. You might consider that the whole idea is unfair and unreligious. You might also suggest that some people believe that suffering has always been seen by some as punishment for misdeeds. You might consider that some non-Muslims believe that even illness itself can be a punishment for wrong doing.

In your answer you might say that Allah is by definition 'good' and that this goodness covers all dealings with Allah. You might also say Allah is the total opposite of evil, represented by the Shaytan.

Here, you might explain that Muslims see Allah as all-good and that therefore he must care for creation. This might help people believe that however much they are suffering, nevertheless this suffering will eventually end and they will be rewarded according to this goodness.

In your answer you might want to consider different views about the nature and purpose of suffering and consider that, for Muslims, this life is seen as a test. You might also look at other ideas as to why Allah apparently allows evil and suffering to exist. You might say that some people see the existence of evil and suffering as proof that Allah does not exist.

Introduction

This unit is concerned with:
- understanding the roles of men and women within a family
- issues related to marriage and divorce
- marriage ceremonies and the ways in which they reflect belief and provide guidance
- issues related to sexual relationships and contraception.

Are love and sex the same thing?

- Love: warm affection or attachment to a person.
- Sex: meaning sexual intercourse, often used in the phrase 'to have sex (with)'.

Most people would probably say that they know what human love is, even if they have only experienced love for a parent, or a brother or sister.

Probably everyone would also say that they knew what sexual activity is – they may not have experienced this with anyone, but they still know what is involved.

Some people might say that love and sex are really the same thing or perhaps they may behave as though they are the same thing. This is very obvious when people say that they 'made love'. In fact, the people concerned may not love one another at all, they are actually having sexual intercourse with each other.

This is an issue of very real and serious concern within religious teaching.

One of the questions which we are trying to answer, or at least discuss, is whether there are really two different words for the same thing or if there is a very real and important difference between them.

The religions we are studying do see a difference. On the other hand, the activities of many people of all ages, all over the world, often seem to suggest the opposite.

The other question is why religions treat the two as separate.

The marriage service of the Church of England as it appears in the Book of Common Prayer says that one of the purposes of marriage is as:

> a remedy against sin, and to avoid fornication (sex outside of marriage); that such persons as have not the gift of continency (self-restraint) might marry

This means that the Church believes that it is a sin for people to have sexual relations with each other unless they are married and it also suggests that marriage is only required when people cannot manage to live celibate lives.

This seems to imply that sex is wrong and that marriage somehow makes it rather less of a sin. However, as sexual intercourse is the way in which people have children and as, like other animals, we were clearly designed to produce new life, we need to ask why some religions have this view.

Marriage and divorce

Marriage is the way in which most religions believe that men and women should live together.

'Till death us do part' is a familiar phrase to most people, whether they are Christians or not.

It is part of the marriage service and is, perhaps, the strongest vow that two people can make to one another when they are married.

Despite this, however, the number of divorces in the United Kingdom continues to increase and there is also a steady decrease in the number of people getting married.
- In 1961 the total number of divorces was 27,000; in 1993 it was 180,000. By 1969 the number of divorces had doubled to 55,556 and doubled again by 1972 to 124,991. In 2005 the number was 155,052.

● From 1961 to 1991 the number of marriages fell from 350,000 to about 340,000. In 2005 the number was 284,000.

Marriage and the family lie at the centre of the teachings of most religions and both Christianity and Islam stress its importance. It seems, however, that more and more people are finding it too difficult to be married to one person for the whole of their lives.

An increasing number of people also choose to have their relationship made legal in a civil ceremony (at a Registry Office) rather than having a religious ceremony.

So perhaps we have to consider why people are finding alternatives to marriage.

One of the reasons may well be the way in which the law has changed:

In the United Kingdom, before 1857 people could only remarry by an Act of Parliament. Absolute divorce in a court was not allowed until 1857 and until 1936 was only allowed in cases of adultery. After 1936, cruelty and desertion were also allowed as reasons for granting a divorce. Finally, in the 1970s, the law allowed people to be divorced when it could be shown that a marriage had 'irretrievably broken down' (there was no way to make it better).

Another issue which is often linked with both divorce and cohabitation is the status of any children who are born.

Children who are born outside of a legal marriage, whether the parents are living together or not, are technically called illegitimate.

The law has now changed, and since 1988 the married status of the parents of a child is considered totally irrelevant. This has, to a large extent, changed social views about illegitimacy, although many people still believe that it is 'wrong' for children to be born 'outside of marriage'.

An aspect of marriage that occurs in many religious marriages is the giving of a dowry, this is a gift (often of money) from one partner to the other. In addition, some people make a contract which says, not only how they will treat each other in the marriage but also what will happen if they should divorce.

2006 saw the introduction of same-sex ceremonies called Civil Partnerships. For the first time this allowed homosexual or 'same-sex' couples to make a legally recognised public statement of their commitment to each other and to receive the same benefits only heterosexual couples had previously been able to enjoy.

So, the questions we have to ask are:
● Why do so many religious people think that marriage is so important?
● Why do people often disapprove of divorce?

There are also two other particular types of relationship which are practised in some parts of the world: polygamy is where a man is married to several wives at the same time; and polyandry where a woman has more than one husband.

Discussion

1 Why do you think the number of people getting divorced is rising so quickly?

Activity

1 Consider whether there really is a difference between love and sex and what that might be.

2 Do you think people really have changed their attitude towards marriage and cohabitation?

A same-sex partnership.

Christianity

This topic looks at:
- the roles of men and women within a Christian family
- Christian marriage ceremonies and the ways in which these reflect and emphasise Christian teaching about marriage
- Christian beliefs about the ethics of divorce
- Christian beliefs about sexual relationships and contraception.

The roles of men and women within a Christian family

The roles of men and women are often an area of dispute within religions, even in the 21st century. Although the majority of people would probably say that men and women are equal, some would still argue that God intended men and women to have different roles and that they were created for different purposes.

Often, the creation stories in Genesis are used to argue that women are secondary to men.

However, it is important to remember that there are two accounts of creation and that they are different.

In the creation story found in Genesis 1, men and women were created at the same time:

> **Then God said, 'Let us make man in our image, in our likeness, and let them rule over the fish of the sea and the birds of the air, over the livestock, over all the earth, and over all the creatures that move along the ground.'**
>
> **So God created man in his own image, in the image of God he created him; male and female he created them.**
>
> (Genesis 1:26–27)

The second account is different:

> **The Lord God said, 'It is not good for the man to be alone. I will make a helper suitable for him.'... But for Adam no suitable helper was found. So the Lord God caused the man to fall into a deep sleep; and while he was sleeping, he took one of the man's ribs and closed up the place with flesh. Then the Lord God made a woman from the rib he had taken out of the man, and he brought her to the man.**
>
> (Genesis 2:18, 20–23)

People have often used this account to suggest that the woman was created to be a companion and helpmate to the man.

People putting this view forward do not explain that the person who was created first in this second account was neither male nor female. It was as though this first person was split to create the man and the woman.

Although it was Adam who was told not to eat from the tree:

> **And the Lord God commanded the man, 'You are free to eat from any tree in the garden; but you must not eat from the tree of the knowledge of good and evil, for when you eat of it you will surely die.'**
>
> (Genesis 1:16–17)

It was Eve who took the fruit, at the suggestion of the serpent, and gave it to Adam. Again, this has been seen as showing that women are weaker than men and more likely to sin.

In fact, through the course of the Old Testament women such as Deborah (Judges 4:4–5) and the Queen of Sheba (1 Kings 10:1–3) are portrayed in many important roles and as strong people who are powerful and as rulers, not just as people who look after men.

In the New Testament, Jesus has friends who are women such as Mary and Martha

(John 11) and does not appear to see women as being inferior.

> Now a certain man was ill, Lazarus of Bethany, the village of Mary and her sister Martha. Mary was the one who anointed the Lord with perfume and wiped his feet with her hair; her brother Lazarus was ill.   (John 11:1–2)

However there are other texts in the New Testament which present a more traditional view:

> Wives, in the same way, be submissive to your husbands so that, if any of them do not believe the word, they may be won over without words by the behaviour of their wives, when they see the purity and reverence of your lives. Your beauty should not come from outward adornment, such as braided hair and the wearing of gold jewellry and fine clothes.
>   (1 Peter 3:1 7)

Some people believe that these teachings are still correct today and that 'women' should stay at home and care for her children and her husband.

However, the majority of Christians would probably say that men and women are created equal and should be treated equally.

> There is neither Jew nor Greek, slave nor free, male nor female, for you are all one in Christ Jesus. If you belong to Christ, then you are Abraham's seed, and heirs according to the promise.
>   (Galatians 3:28–29)

Christian marriage ceremonies, and the ways in which these reflect and emphasise Christian teaching about marriage

According to many Christians, marriage and the family lie at the centre of their religious teaching.

A modern nuclear family.

In the marriage service of the Church of England, the bride and groom make a number of vows to each other:

> I, [the person's name], take you, [the other person's name], to be my wife [or husband] to have and to hold from this day forward; for better, for worse, for richer, for poorer, in sickness and in health, to love and to cherish, till death us do part, according to God's holy law; and this is my solemn vow.

These vows are the promises that people make to one another about the way in which they will each treat the other person once they are married. Until fairly recently the bride promised to obey her husband but now usually they both make the same set of vows.

The priest or minister who is conducting the service explains why marriage is so important:

St John tells us how Jesus shared in such an occasion at Cana, and gave there a sign of new beginnings as he turned water into wine (see John 2:1–10).

Marriage is a gift from God because he intended men and women to live together.

Men and women should help and support one another and be faithful.

Marriage is for bringing up children.

Marriages have to take place in front of witnesses who see that the ceremony does take place and also that both people are getting married out of their own free will.

The importance of the service is stressed in the ceremony:

The preface

In the presence of God, Father, Son and Holy Spirit, we have come together to witness the marriage of N and N, to pray for God's blessing on them, to share their joy and to celebrate their love.

Marriage is a gift of God in creation through which husband and wife may know the grace of God. It is given that as man and woman grow together in love and trust, they shall be united with one another in heart, body and mind, as Christ is united with his bride, the Church.

Marriage is a way of life made holy by God,

Marriage is a sign of unity and loyalty which all should uphold and honour. It enriches society and strengthens community. No one should enter into it lightly or selfishly but reverently and responsibly in the sight of almighty God.

The vows

The vows you are about to take are to be made in the presence of

God, who is judge of all and knows all the secrets of our hearts; therefore if either of you knows a reason why you may not lawfully marry, you must declare it now.

The minister says:

N, will you take N to be your wife/husband? Will you love her/him, comfort her/him, honour and protect her/him, and, forsaking all others, be faithful to her/him as long as you both shall live?

The declarations

I, N, take you, N, to be my wife/husband, to have and to hold from this day forward; for better, for worse, for richer, for poorer, in sickness and in health, to love and to cherish, till death us do part; according to God's holy law. In the presence of God I make this vow.

The giving of rings

N, I give you this ring as a sign of our marriage. With my body I honour you, all that I am I give to you, and all that I have I share with you, within the love of God, Father, Son and Holy Spirit.

(Common Worship)

The Anglican Communion stresses that the marriage is made in the sight of God and that the promises are made 'with' God but it does not regard marriage as a sacrament. A sacrament is often defined as 'an outward visible sign of an inward, invisible grace'.

This free will is stressed in the Roman Catholic marriage ceremony where the couple to be married are asked:

And so, in the presence of the Church, I ask you to state your intentions:

Are you ready freely and without reservation to give yourselves to each other in marriage?

Are you ready to love and honour each other as man and wife for the rest of your lives?

> Are you ready to accept children lovingly from God, and bring them up according to the law of Christ and his Church?

The importance of marriage is stressed by Jesus in the gospels:

> But from the beginning of creation, 'God made them male and female. For this reason a man shall leave his father and mother and be joined to his wife, and the two shall become one flesh. So they are no longer two, but one flesh. Therefore what God has joined together, let no one separate.'
>
> (Mark 10:6–9)

One of the most important aspects of a Christian marriage is that, for most Christians, it is regarded as a sacrament.

The Roman Catholic Church recognises seven sacraments: baptism; confirmation; marriage; ordination; reconciliation; anointing of the sick; and the Eucharist. It is because marriage is a sacrament and is a promise made to and in front of God, that divorce is seen as such an important issue. In the Roman Catholic Church the marriage will be followed by a nuptial mass (a celebration of the Eucharist).

Activity

1 Describe the main features of a Christian wedding.

2 Explain why Christians still believe that marriage is so important. Try to give several reasons.

3 Why do you think that many people choose to have a Christian marriage ceremony rather than a civil marriage?

Christian beliefs about the ethics of divorce

Jesus taught that divorce was wrong. In the Sermon on the Mount he was explaining that even the laws about divorce in the Old Testament were not as strict as the ones God wanted:

> It was also said, 'Whoever divorces his wife, let him give her a certificate of divorce.' But I say to you that anyone who divorces his wife, except on the ground of unchastity, causes her to commit adultery; and whoever marries a divorced woman commits adultery.
>
> (Matthew 5:31–32)

This text is also used to argue that if people are divorced, then they should not be remarried.

Divorce is certainly not welcomed in Christianity but it is permitted in most churches. In the Roman Catholic Church, remarriage in a church after divorce is not allowed but sometimes people are given an annulment. An annulment is an official document granted by the Pope which states that the marriage was flawed and did not actually take place, for example, if one of the people married did not understand the commitment they were making in the ceremony. After an annulment has been granted the two people involved are then able to marry other people in a church ceremony if they wish. People who have had a civil divorce but not an annulment cannot be married again in a church. If they are living with another person or have had a civil marriage, they are not allowed to make their communion.

Since 1981 the Church of England has agreed to a person who is divorced marrying again. Most Protestant churches also follow this view, believing that all people are capable of making mistakes and that someone should not be forced to live alone for the rest of their life when there may be the opportunity of happiness for them in a new marriage.

The Orthodox Church permits up to three divorces followed by remarriage.

Most of the Christian churches try to help married people who are experiencing problems. They may run special groups where people can come together and talk about their problems in the hope that they can be resolved without them having to divorce.

Christian beliefs about sexual relationships and contraception

Although some Christians may tolerate the idea of people cohabiting, they do not generally welcome this.

The Roman Catholic Church is completely opposed to cohabitation:

> **The sexual act must take place exclusively within marriage. Outside marriage it always constitutes a grave sin and excludes one from sacramental communion. Some today claim a right to trial marriage where there is an intention of getting married later. However firm the purpose of those who engage in premature sexual relations may be, the fact is that such liaisons can scarcely ensure mutual sincerity and fidelity [faithfulness] in a relationship between a man and a woman.**
> (Catechism of the Catholic Church)

A number of the Protestant churches accept that cohabitation is seen as an option for many people today but, although they may welcome people who live in this sort of relationship into their communities, they still believe that living together outside of marriage is falling short of what God wanted.

All Christian groups stress that whatever the circumstances of a relationship, marriage or divorce, one of the primary concerns of the people involved must be the welfare of their children.

They may also stress the importance of respecting your body:

> **Do you not know that your body is a temple of the Holy Spirit... Therefore honour God with your body.** (1 Corinthians 6:19a, 20b)

The Christian Church takes the teaching of the Ten Commandments very strictly. The seventh commandment: You shall not commit adultery, is often interpreted to mean that people must not have a sexual relationship with anyone to whom they are not married, but simply that married people must not 'sleep' with someone else.

Jesus went further and said:

> **You have heard that it was said, 'Do not commit adultery.' But I tell you that anyone who looks at a woman lustfully has already committed adultery with her in his heart.** (Matthew 5:27–28)

It seems that Christians feel that sexual intercourse is always wrong unless it takes place within a marriage. They feel that God intended men and women to live together as married couples but not to cohabit.

In fact, Paul seemed to believe that people should really be celibate (someone who leads a single life, a confirmed bachelor or spinster; someone who has decided not to marry). He remained unmarried:

> **Now for the matters you wrote about: It is good for a man not to marry. But since there is so much immorality, each man should have his own wife, and each woman her own husband. ...Now to the unmarried and the widows I say: It is good for them to stay unmarried, as I am. But if they cannot control themselves, they should marry, for it is better to marry than to burn with passion.** (1 Corinthians 7:8–9)

It does seem from this that Christianity sees sex as a very strong and dangerous emotion from which people have to protect themselves.

Roman Catholic priests, monks and nuns are all required to take a vow of celibacy because it is believed that having a sexual partner would distract them from working for God. Some Christians feel that this is unhealthy and not normal: God created men and women and gave them the desire to have sexual relationships with each other so why should he want people to deny themselves. On the other hand, many Christians regard this as a sacrifice which they are making as a demonstration of their love for God.

Ideas of Christian love are also given in the New Testament:

> Dear friends, let us love one another, for love comes from God. Everyone who loves has been born of God and knows God. Whoever does not love does not know God, because God is love. This is how God showed his love among us: He sent his one and only Son into the world that we might live through him. This is love: not that we loved God, but that he loved us and sent his Son as an atoning sacrifice for our sins. Dear friends, since God so loved us, we also ought to love one another. No-one has ever seen God; but if we love one another, God lives in us and his love is made complete in us.
>
> (1 John 4:7–12)

We can see that Christians are urged to love one another in a platonic (non-sexual) way, as a way of showing God's love and living according to it.

Activity

Do you think that married priests would be more able to give advice to married couples who are experiencing difficulties in their marriage?

Same-sex relationships

As well as the discussion about love and sex, another issue which has always been a very important part of Christian teaching is homosexuality.

A homosexual is a person who is emotionally and sexually attracted to members of the same sex. The opposite is a heterosexual, who is attracted to members of the opposite sex. Female homosexuals are usually known as lesbians but both men and women often describe themselves as gay.

The Old Testament says that homosexuality is wrong and some people believe that this was the reason that God destroyed the cities of Sodom and Gomorrah in Genesis chapter 14.

Paul is very definite on the question of homosexuality and says:

> God gave them over to shameful lusts. Even their women exchanged natural relations for unnatural ones. In the same way the men also abandoned natural relations with women and were inflamed with lust for one another. Men committed indecent acts with other men, and received in themselves the due penalty for their perversion.
>
> (Romans 1:26–27)

For many years the Church has said that the feelings of homosexuality are acceptable but that people must live celibate lives because it would be a sin for them to take part in any sexual activity. In recent years this has been challenged by many people and there has been some attempt to soften the official church policy. However, although many of the clergy are willing to accept homosexuals and homosexual couples in their congregations only the Religious Society of Friends (Quakers) fully accepts homosexuals who are active sexually. Even the Methodist Church which has always been very open to discussion about this 'does not consider that homosexual genital practice... is acceptable'.

Here, then, we have a very clear example of where love and sex are certainly not regarded as the same thing.

The Roman Catholic Church also has a very strict attitude towards masturbation which it believes is always wrong.

Between one in 20 and one in ten people are homosexual so it seems that many Christians who are homosexual and, perhaps, live in same-sex relationships, are not permitted to be fully part of the Christian Church.

Contraception (birth control)

Christianity regards life as being sacred and as a gift from God.

However, many Christians today believe that they should interpret the teachings of the Bible for the age in which they live.

The Roman Catholic Church bases much of its teaching on Natural Law (what is in keeping with human nature). Because it is natural that conception may follow from intercourse, the Church does not approve of any form of contraception which would prevent this taking place. The only form of contraception which is permitted is the rhythm method (where sex only takes place at the time of the month when the woman is known to be least fertile) which makes use of the body's natural cycles.

It argues that humans have an obligation from God to 'Be fruitful and increase in number' and that this is in accordance with Natural Law.

The Methodist Church welcomes contraception as a means of spacing a family and providing fulfilment in marriage. The Anglican Church also decided that the responsibility for deciding upon the number and frequency of children was given by God to the parents' conscience 'in such ways as are acceptable to man and wife' (Lambeth Conference).

Activity

Suggest reasons why people would want to limit the number of children that they have. Would Christianity agree with any of these reasons?

Islam

This topic looks at:
- the roles of men and women within a Muslim family
- Muslim marriage ceremonies, and the ways in which these reflect and emphasise Muslim teaching about marriage
- Muslim beliefs about the ethics of divorce
- Muslim beliefs about sexual relationships and contraception.

The roles of men and women within a Muslim family

Marriage in Islam is more than the joining together of the bride and the groom. In Islam, it brings together two families. It is usual for the wife to live with the husband's family. Muslims often live in extended families and other relatives may also live close by and help with family life.

Marriage and family life are very important. In a traditional Muslim family the man works to support the family and the woman's duty is to bring up the children and look after the house. The father makes the main decisions whilst the mother is important within the home and must be shown respect by her husband and children. This is seen as the natural order of things and the way that Allah intended men and women to live.

Islam teaches that men and women are equal and that Allah will judge them equally according to the way in which they have lived.

To help men value women for who they are, rather than for their bodies, many women wear garments that leave only the hands and face exposed.

> **O Prophet! Tell thy wives and daughters, and the believing women, that they should cast their outer garments over their persons (when abroad): that is most convenient, that they should be known (as such) and not molested. And Allah is Oft-Forgiving, Most Merciful.**
>
> (Surah 33:59)

A woman must protect her husband's property; she must be faithful to him and she must dress modestly:

> **And say to the believing women that they should lower their gaze and guard their modesty; that they should not display their beauty and ornaments except what (must ordinarily) appear thereof; that they should draw their veils over their bosoms and not display their beauty except to their husbands, their fathers, their husband's fathers, their sons, their husband's sons, their brothers or their brothers' sons, or their sisters' sons, or their women, or the slaves whom their right hands possess, or male servants free of physical needs, or small children who have no sense of the shame of sex; and that they should not strike their feet in order to draw attention to their hidden ornaments. And O ye Believers! Turn ye all together towards Allah, that ye may attain Bliss.**
>
> (Surah 24:31)

The word hijab means 'veil' and is used both for the scarf and for the modest clothes which most Muslim women wear in order not to tempt men and to preserve their own dignity. Both Muslim men and Muslim women may be shocked by the clothing worn by girls and women in western secular society. Skimpy clothes and western fashions are often seen by Muslims not as the exercise of personal choice and freedom but as the exploitation of women by men and by the media. Of course, in the United Kingdom, some Muslim young women and girls sometimes wish to dress like their peer group and this could cause arguments in the home.

Muslim women and girls who wish to observe the rules of Islam often find there are less problems than in the past because schools and places of work in the west have become more accommodating in their dress codes.

When women are covered totally, they are said to be in purdah. This is a custom in some countries. The chador gives complete privacy.

The issue of women's clothes is more complicated than it looks on the surface. It is relevant to some other matters concerning women's rights in the modern world.

Young Muslim women in London.

Muslim women in traditional dress.

In some Muslim countries, women have not been educated and are treated almost as servants so the clothing is seen as a mark of servitude. In other Muslim countries, some educated women have chosen to revert to wearing traditional garb, using it as a symbol to disassociate themselves from what they see as a corrupting western influence. These women have done this by choice but they would not be willing to do so if wearing traditional clothes was made compulsory. When women are made to wear traditional clothes against their will and punished by individuals or by society for disobedience, then the issue has become one of human rights.

Muhammad ﷺ tried to make conditions better for the downtrodden, including women. From the time of Muhammad ﷺ Muslim women have had the right to own property. They can inherit wealth, although only half as much as a male relative. This is because men have dependants but women are not responsible for their male relatives.

According to Islam, the rights and responsibilities of a woman are equal to those of a man, but they are not identical and, therefore, they should be complementary to each other rather than competitive. However, it appears in the Qur'an that a final decision is to be taken by the husband.

> **Divorced women shall wait concerning themselves for three monthly periods. Nor is it lawful for them to hide what Allah Hath created in their wombs, if they have faith in Allah and the Last Day. And their husbands have the better right to take them back in that period, if they wish for reconciliation. And women shall have rights similar to the rights against them, according to what is equitable; but men have a degree (of advantage) over them. And Allah is Exalted in Power, Wise.**
>
> (Surah 2:228)

Women have the right to study, refuse a marriage, to divorce, to inherit, to keep their own names, to own property, to take part in politics, and to conduct business, whether they are married or unmarried.

Women are equal before Allah. They may attend mosque but they have separate washing facilities and usually perform salah in a separate area, often behind the men. This is to avoid distracting the men from their worship but also for the benefit of the women. It is considered to be a respectful and thoughtful arrangement, so that they can keep their dignity when prostrating before Allah. Women are expected to take part in Friday communal prayers at noon but they usually do this at home because it is understood by males and females alike that their role is to put the family's needs first. Women are allowed to work if they can do so without neglecting their family.

Men also are expected to show modesty and restraint. They, also, should be faithful and not indulge in sex outside marriage. The Qur'an says that:

> **Men are the protectors and maintainers of women, because Allah has given the one more (strength) than the other, and because they support them from their means.** (Surah 4:34)

Providing for a family is a great responsibility.

One significant point about Muslim family life is the respect given to the elderly in the extended family and the protection afforded to those on the fringe of family life, single relatives, who might otherwise be very lonely or neglected.

> **Thy Lord hath decreed that ye worship none but Him, and that ye be kind to parents. Whether one or both of them attain old age in thy life, say not to them a word of contempt, nor repel them, but address them in terms of honour. And, out of kindness, lower to them the wing of humility, and say: 'My Lord! Bestow on them thy Mercy even as they cherished me in childhood.'** (Surah 17:23–24)

Muslims very rarely put their parents in old folks' homes. The old are treated with

respect and their experience is regarded as a valuable asset for the whole family. Often the elderly find they have a new role to play in the family in that they are helpful with the young people and provide a willing listening ear when parents may be too busy to give enough time and attention.

Mutual care and concern in the family between all the members is seen as a reflection of Allah's compassion and a way of showing gratitude for his love.

Discussion

In many cultures it has been traditional to regard women as more impulsive and irrational than men. It is assumed that women are ruled by their emotions and that they are more interested in relationships than in matters such as politics and world affairs. How common is this attitude today and what do you think about the roles of men and women?

Muslim marriage ceremonies, and the ways in which these reflect and emphasise Muslim teaching about marriage

Marriages in the Muslim community are often arranged marriages but these can only take place with the consent of both parties. All Muslims are expected to marry and the age at which they do so depends on the civil law operating in the country in which the Muslims are living. Many Muslim marriages are arranged by families.

Courting or 'going out together' is not permitted and the couple who may be married are only allowed to meet each other when members of their families are present. Although marriages like this may be arranged by families, no-one can ever be forced to marry someone in Islam and if this did happen, then the marriage would be invalid.

Muslims may have up to four wives but each wife must be treated equally.

> **If ye fear that ye shall not be able to deal justly with the orphans, Marry women of your choice, Two or three or four; but if ye fear that ye shall not be able to deal justly (with them), then only one, or (a captive) that your right hands possess, that will be more suitable, to prevent you from doing injustice.** (Surah 4:3)

A man's other wives must agree before a Muslim may take another wife. Muhammad ﷺ had many wives. Many Muslims have only one wife because of the laws of the country in which they live. A Muslim man may marry a Jew or a Christian but a Muslim woman may only marry a Muslim man. Divorce is allowed in Islam though it is regarded as a last resort.

A Muslim marriage usually takes place in the home or the mosque. The couple gives their consent before a minimum of two witnesses. The ceremony is a very simple one. There is a declaration to the witnesses of the marriage that the bride and groom are marrying of their own free will.

Some Muslims include special vows in their marriage ceremony and these may include promising that they will try to make the marriage an act of submission to the will of Allah and a relationship of mercy, love, peace and faithfulness.

A Muslim wedding in Pakistan.

During the ceremony there are readings from the Qur'an.

> **O mankind! Reverence your Guardian-Lord, who created you from a single Person, created, of like nature, his mate, and from them twain scattered (like seeds) countless men and women– reverence Allah, through Whom ye demand your mutual (rights), and (reverence) the wombs (that bore you): for Allah ever watches over you.** (Surah 4:1)

The imam and the guests pray for the couple, wishing such things as wealth, long life and many children.

A marriage contract, the Aqd Nikah, is read as well as written. The bride and groom then sign three copies of this to show that they have agreed to the marriage. The contract also specifies the mahr (dowry) which the groom gives to the bride and which belongs to her for life. Sunni and Shi'ah Muslims have different arrangements for the mahr. Shi'ah Muslims pay the money immediately: some Sunni Muslims arrange to give part of it later.

> Sunni Muslims are the majority of the Muslim population of the world. They believe that, after Muhammad ﷺ, the first four Khalifas were Abu Bakr, 'Umar, 'Uthman and 'Ali.
>
> The minority, Shi'ah Muslims, believe that 'Ali was the real successor of Muhammad ﷺ.

Then there are prayers and readings and a ceremonial sermon usually led by the imam.

> **Almighty God created humanity, male and female, each in need of the other, and established the institution of marriage as a means of uniting souls in blessed bond of love...**

There are refreshments and celebrations after the contract is signed but these usually follow local customs. There may be a wedding feast called a walimah.

Sometimes the bride does not attend the ceremony. She may stay at home while the bridegroom attends the mosque with an agent and two witnesses who she has chosen to represent her part of the contract. Before they go to the mosque these people hear her agree three times at home that she is willing to be married and they speak on her behalf at the ceremony.

In the United Kingdom, there will be a civil wedding in front of a registrar as well as the religious ceremony.

The nature of marriage is laid down in the Qur'an:

> **And among His Signs is this, that He created for you mates from among yourselves, that ye may dwell in tranquillity with them, and He has put love and mercy between your (hearts): verily in that are Signs for those who reflect.** (Surah 30:20–21)

> **Permitted to you, on the night of the fasts, is the approach to your wives. They are your garments and ye are their garments. Allah knoweth what ye used to do secretly among yourselves; but He turned to you and forgave you; so now associate with them, and seek what Allah Hath ordained for you, and eat and drink, until the white thread of dawn appear to you distinct from its black thread; then complete your fast Till the night appears; but do not associate with your wives while ye are in retreat in the mosques. Those are Limits (set by) Allah: Approach not nigh thereto. Thus doth Allah make clear His Signs to men: that they may learn self-restraint.** (Surah 2:187)

This second quote comes from the rules for observing the fast of sawm during Ramadan but shows the importance of marriage and sexual relationships in Islam.

Marriage and the family are the basis of Islamic society:

> **No institution in Islam finds more favour with God than marriage.** (Hadith)

Men are urged to be careful about who they marry:

> **A woman is taken in marriage for three reasons; for her beauty, for family connections or the lure of wealth. Choose the one with faith and you will have success.** (Hadith)

Discussion

Do you think that there are jobs at home, or in the world of work, that are more suitable for men than for women? Give reasons to support your argument.

Activity

1 Describe the main features of a Muslim wedding.

2 Explain why Muslims still believe that marriage is so important. Try to give several reasons.

3 Explain what Muslims believe about polygamy (having more than one wife at the same time).

4 Explain what is meant in Islam by 'an arranged marriage'.

Muslim beliefs about the ethics of divorce

Although the principles of Muslim marriage are supported by Islam and are a common belief between the couple, Muslims realise that sometimes marriages break down. Marriage is a legal contract between two people and therefore it can be ended. This is done if continuation of the marriage brings misery to the couple and to their children and close relatives.

In the Hadith it says: 'Among all lawful things, divorce is most hated by Allah.' However, divorce is lawful, it is not forbidden by Islam.

The Qur'an says that:

> If a wife fears cruelty or desertion on her husband's part, there is no blame on them if they arrange an amicable settlement between themselves; and such settlement is best; even though men's souls are swayed by greed. But if ye do good and practise self-restraint, Allah is well-acquainted with all that ye do. (Surah 4:128)

A man cannot seek a divorce from his wife until it is certain that she is not pregnant, as it is possible that he might then change his mind. Once the divorce is announced there is a period of three months called 'iddah, this is a period in which reconciliation should be attempted. If there is no reconciliation, then the divorce takes place. A man and a woman can remarry twice, but after a third divorce remarriage to each other cannot take place unless the woman has been married to another man in the meanwhile.

> When ye divorce women, and they fulfil the term of their ('Iddat), do not prevent them from marrying their (former) husbands, if they mutually agree on equitable terms. This instruction is for all amongst you, who believe in Allah and the Last Day. That is (the course making for) most virtue and purity amongst you and Allah knows, and ye know not. (Surah 2:230–232)

The wife can free herself completely from the marriage by returning her mahr. During the period of 'iddah, she must stay in her husband's house and he must provide everything for her. He is not allowed to throw her out of the home. It is hoped that, in this way, there may eventually love each other again.

> O Prophet! When ye do divorce women, divorce them at their prescribed periods, and count (accurately), their prescribed periods: And fear Allah your Lord: and turn them not out of their houses, nor shall they (themselves) leave, except in case they are guilty

of some open lewdness, those are limits set by Allah: and any who transgresses the limits of Allah, does verily wrong his (own) soul: thou knowest not if perchance Allah will bring about thereafter some new situation. (Surah 65:1)

> Lewdness—indecent behaviour. Transgresses the limits—breaks the laws.

A woman is also able to obtain a divorce, either by an agreement with her husband (khul) or because of his treatment of her.

Children are regarded as illegitimate if their parents are not married and, according to Shari'ah, the father has no legal responsibility.

Activity

To what extent would you agree that it is a good idea to ensure that a woman is not pregnant before a divorce is granted?

Muslim beliefs about sexual relationships and contraception

For Muslims, sexual intercourse is an act of worship which fulfils emotional and physical needs, as well as being the means of having children. Children are the means by which humans can contribute towards Allah's creation. Sexual intercourse is seen as a gift from Allah and must only take place within a married relationship.

Marriage includes the responsibility of both husband and wife to meet each other's sexual needs.

Men are forbidden from being alone with women except for their wives in case they are tempted by them:

> Let no man be in privacy with a woman who he is not married to, or Satan will be the third. (Hadith)

It could be said that Islam has a very realistic attitude towards sex and realises that both men and women can be tempted to have sexual relationships outside of marriage.

Sexual activity of any kind outside of marriage is forbidden. Adultery by the husband or the wife is a serious crime:

> **Nor come nigh to adultery: for it is a shameful (deed) and an evil, opening the road (to other evils).**
> (Surah 17:32)

and the Qur'an clearly specifies the punishment.

> **The woman and the man guilty of adultery or fornication—flog each of them with a hundred stripes: let not compassion move you in their case, in a matter prescribed by Allah, if ye believe in Allah and the Last Day: and let a party of the Believers witness their punishment.** (Surah 24:2)

Homosexual and lesbian relationships are forbidden by Islam as unnatural. In practice it is often ignored, though some Islamic lawyers have argued that it should be punished with the death penalty because it is impure.

> **Of all the creatures in the world, will ye approach males,**
> **And leave those whom Allah has created for you to be your mates? Nay, ye are a people transgressing (all limits)!** (Surah 26:165–166)

> **If two men among you are guilty of lewdness, punish them both. If they repent and amend, Leave them alone; for Allah is Oft-returning, Most Merciful.**
> (Surah 4:16)

Activity

How far would you agree that the Muslim punishment for adultery is unfair or too severe?

Contraception (birth control)

Islam teaches that Allah created the world and everything in it. Life is therefore a special gift.

For Muslims, the birth of a child is not an 'accident' and does not happen by mistake, it is a gift of life from Allah.

> **To Allah belongs the dominion of the heavens and the earth. He creates what He wills (and plans). He bestows (children) male or female according to His Will (and Plan),**

> **Or He bestows both males and females, and He leaves barren whom He will: for He is full of Knowledge and Power.**
> (Surah 42:49–50)

Because of this view, contraception is not welcomed. However, in 1971, the Conference on Islam and Family Planning agreed that safe and legal contraception was permitted under certain circumstances:

- If there was a threat to the mother's health.
- If the use of contraception would help a woman who already had children.
- Where there was a chance of the child being born with mental or physical deformities.
- Where the family did not have the money to raise a child.

Generally, Muslims prefer the use of the rhythm method of contraception: intercourse only takes place at the time of the month when the woman is known to be least fertile. Other, artificial methods of contraception such as condoms or the Pill are used in preference to permanent sterilisation or vasectomy.

Discussion

Do you think that today, when people often live for more than 75 years, it is reasonable to expect that they should stay married for life? Try to support your answer with reasons.

Activity

1 Explain Muslim views about divorce.

2 Explain Muslim teaching about life being a gift from Allah.

3 Explain the reasons why you think contraception should be permitted.

4 Explain Muslim attitudes towards same-sex relationships.

Summary

In each of these religions it might seem that the rules about marriage and divorce are very strict. Perhaps this shows just how important marriage and the family are for believers in these faiths.

Christians and Muslims both believe that the family is central to their religion and to the way in which God means them to live. Because of this they all have ceremonies to bless the marriage and they all have rules about divorce which make it difficult for people to separate and remain within the religion. These rules are intended to make people think very carefully before they are married and also to try very hard to make marriage work.

It is also clear that both religions believe that people who wish to live together in a sexual relationship should be married and should not simply cohabit.

Although there are some differences, the views of these religions are very similar on the question of sex and love. Perhaps the principal reason for this is found in the fact that each religion stresses the importance of the family. This is the 'natural' way for people to live and also it is intended that families should bring new members into the religion and so more people can find God.

As we have seen, however, the teachings of these religions are often rather different from the way in which many people live their lives today, and the question we might be asking is whether it is the religion's or today's society which is right.

Questions

1 What do you understand by:
  (a) adultery
  (b) celibacy
  (c) cohabitation
  (d) polygamy and polyandry
  (e) homosexuality
  (f) contraception
  (g) marriage
  (h) divorce
  (i) illegitimate
  (j) civil marriage
  (k) dowry?

2 Do you think it is possible for a person to be a member of one of these religions and to cohabit?

3 How far would you agree with the teachings of these religions about homosexuality (male and female) and why?

4 Explain why religions have such a very strict attitude towards adultery.

5 Consider whether it is right for religious people to decide to deny their sexual desires and choose a life of celibacy, or whether this is 'unnatural'.

6 Explain why religious people may not want their son or daughter to marry someone who belongs to a different religion.

7 Explain how these religions treat men and women over the question of divorce.

8 Do you think that religions and society treat illegitimate children differently? Explain your opinion.

Practice GCSE questions

Christianity

1 (a) Describe a Christian marriage
service. [8 marks]

(b) Explain the importance of the vows made
at this service. [7 marks]

(c) 'People should live together first before
they decide to get married.'
Do you agree? Give reasons to support
your answer, and show that you have
thought about different points of view.
You must refer to Christianity in your
answer. [5 marks]

2 (a) Describe the roles of men and women in a
Christian family. [8 marks]

(b) Explain Christian attitudes towards
divorce. [7 marks]

(c) 'Every Christian should get married.'
Do you agree? Give reasons to support
your answer, and show that you have
thought about different points of
view. [5 marks]

Tips

In your answer you should describe the main features,
vows made before God and the congregation, exchange
of rings, blessings, etc. You might mention a nuptial mass.
You will gain some credit, but not very much, for extra
information about white dresses, bridesmaids, confetti and
receptions.

You should explain the significance of the vows being
made before God and marriage being seen as a sacrament.
You may consider the various aspects of the relationship
which are stressed in the vows and show how they may
help people in their future life together. You might also
show that the vows do not appear to permit divorce.

In answering this question from a Christian perspective
you might simply say 'no' and explain that Christianity does
not contemplate sexual relationships before marriage. For
another viewpoint you might consider the possible benefits
of a 'trial marriage' and also indicate that it reflects the
practice of much of today's society.

In your answer you may focus on the traditional roles of
men and women in a family and comment on changing
attitudes towards this. More clearly, Christian teaching
might be that Jesus appears to challenge this traditional
view sometimes, although on other occasions and in the
epistles the traditional role appears to be emphasised.

You need to explain that divorce is not allowed on the
basis of 'those whom God hath joined together…' Also
you need to comment on the fact that many churches do
permit divorce and remarriage whilst the Roman Catholic
Church does not and that annulment is not an equivalent to
divorce.

You might suggest that on the basis of 'go forth and
multiply' and 'better to marry than to burn' all Christians
should get married. On the other hand, you might also
point to the religious and to celibate priests to suggest that
this is not the case. You might also give an opinion about
extramarital sex.

Islam

1 (a) Describe a Muslim marriage service. [8 marks]

(b) Explain the importance of the promises made in the wedding contract. [7 marks]

(c) 'People should live together first before they decide to get married.'
Do you agree? Give reasons to support your answer, and show that you have thought about different points of view. You must refer to Islam in your answer. [5 marks]

2 (a) Describe the roles of men and women in a Muslim family. [8 marks]

(b) Explain Muslim attitudes towards divorce. [7 marks]

(c) 'Every Muslim should get married.'
Do you agree? Give reasons to support your answer, and show that you have thought about different points of view. [5 marks]

Tips

In your answer you should describe the main features, such as the signing of the marriage contract. You might also mention that the bride need not be present and that someone can speak on her behalf. You might also say that the marriage ceremony is more a secular event than a religious one and you might comment on the traditional clothes worn by the bride.

You should explain the importance of the promises made and show that the couple will live according to the teaching of the Qur'an and the Prophet as well as forming a civil contract. You may say that the husband will follow the Prophet's example in the respect he shows for his wife.

In answering this question from a Muslim perspective you might simply say 'no' and explain that Islam does not contemplate sexual relationships before marriage. For another viewpoint, you might consider the possible benefits of a 'trial marriage' and also indicate that it reflects the practice of much of today's society.

In your answer you may focus on the traditional roles of men and women in a family and comment on changing attitudes towards this. More clearly, Muslim teaching might be that husband and wife are equal but different and may focus on the mother's duty of instructing children in their faith at home.

You need to explain that Islam does not, of course, encourage divorce but is willing to accept it when it is clear that a couple is not suited and reconciliation is not possible. You might explain that both men and women can seek a divorce and the various conditions which are imposed on each.

You might suggest that it is a matter of personal choice but, on the other hand, the Prophet was married as are most imams and you might also comment that celibacy is not a popular concept in Islam.

Introduction

This unit is concerned with religious responses to ethical questions raised by medical issues. It looks at:

- attitudes towards abortion and fertility treatment
- attitudes towards euthanasia and suicide
- issues of the use of animals in medical research.

Is life really sacred?

In this unit we shall be considering the way in which religions look at human life and the way in which they react to certain situations.

Most religions believe that life is a gift from their God or Gods, even though they know that they were created by the actions of human beings. They often react quite strongly when it appears that humans are interfering with this God-given life.

The four issues which are being considered here are all related to **medical ethics**.

Sometimes people say that doctors are 'playing God' because they have to make decisions about people which can often result in life or death for the person concerned. However, many of the new advances in medicine have heightened the argument considerably and people are now talking about doctors and scientists 'playing God' in such a way and with such significance to all life on earth that many people are frightened about what might eventually happen.

Medical ethics is an area which often provokes very strong opinions and many of these may come from religion. Religions in general teach that life comes from God and is therefore sacred. People use the phrase **'sanctity of life'** to describe this.

The four issues here are:

- abortion
- fertility treatment
- euthanasia and suicide
- the use of animals in medical research.

Each of these issues is involved with the prevention, possible harming, or ending of life by human hands rather than by God's will.

A popular saying is: 'The Lord gives and the Lord takes away.' This is meant to imply that only God can influence life. However, increasingly, the beginning and ending of life is brought about by doctors and by ordinary human beings:

Abortion

An abortion is the 'deliberate premature expulsion of the foetus from the womb'. If the foetus is expelled naturally before it can live, it is called a miscarriage.

Abortions are usually performed for one of four reasons:

- To preserve the life, physical or mental well-being of the mother.
- To prevent a pregnancy that happened because a woman was raped.
- To prevent a child being born who would be mentally or physically damaged.
- To prevent a birth for social or economic reasons, e.g. the mother is very young.

In the United Kingdom abortions must be carried out during the first 24 weeks of pregnancy. Abortion is not permitted once the foetus is 'viable' which is when it could live outside of the womb. The operation cannot be carried out after 28 weeks.

People have different views about abortion. Some consider it to be murder as it is a human life. Others may consider that it is up to the woman to choose.

Fertility treatment

This is medical treatment given to people who want to

Mouse growing a human ear.

have children but are unable to do so for medical reasons. This can happen in different circumstances such as when the man cannot produce sperm capable of fertilising an ovum or because the woman cannot naturally produce eggs which are fertile.

There are different types of fertility treatment. Some involve the use of drugs to increase fertility. Perhaps the most common is IVF – **in vitro fertilisation**. Here, the sperm is placed with an egg in a test tube and fertilised there. The fertilised egg – the embryo – is then placed in the woman's womb. Quite often several eggs are fertilised at the same time because the procedure may need to be repeated until an embryo is established in the womb. Many people have concerns about what happens to these other embryos, which are usually frozen in case they are needed in the future. Most of these 'spare' embryos are eventually destroyed or may even be experimented upon. People argue that these embryos already have life and so have the right to live.

Other forms of fertility treatment may involve the use of sperm or eggs from people other than the couple who wants the baby and many people object to this third party being involved. This is called AID – artificial insemination by donor.

Euthanasia

This is sometimes called 'mercy killing'. **Euthanasia** is the act of painlessly putting someone to death. It comes from two Greek words: 'eu' and 'thanatos' meaning a 'good death'.

This may be done because the person is suffering from a painful and incurable disease or because they are very severely disabled. There are three types of **voluntary euthanasia:**
- People may decide to take their own life or refuse medical treatment that would keep them alive.
- A doctor may agree not to forcibly keep someone alive when they are in great pain and have expressed a wish not to be kept alive.
- A person may persuade someone else to help them die, but this counts as murder.

If the person is too ill to speak or give an opinion, a doctor together with relatives may decide to stop treatment and allow the person to die – this is **involuntary euthanasia.**

If a person is given drugs which help them to die, it is **active euthanasia**, whilst withholding drugs or medical treatment, or switching off life–support machines or a ventilator so that someone dies is **passive euthanasia.**

There are many debates amongst religious and non-religious people about whether anyone has the right to end their own life or to assist with the ending of another person's life.

Suicide

Suicide is when someone kills themselves. Suicide used to be regarded as a crime but now many people would see that the person concerned was probably suffering from extreme depression or a mental illness.

The use of animals in medical research

Animals have been used in medical research as well as to test all sorts of products that might come into contact with human beings.

Many people feel strongly that this should not be done because the animal has no choice in the matter. There are now very strict laws about the use of animals in research.

Doctors argue that without animal testing many of the developments in modern medicine, such as heart surgery would not have been possible. Vitamins, vaccines, modern anaesthetics and asthma treatments, were also first tested on animals.

Activity

1 To what extent do you agree that, in the 21st century, doctors are 'playing God'?

2 Do you think that there should be certain limits to medical research because there are some things that are not suitable for doctors to interfere with?

Christianity

This topic looks at:
- different Christian attitudes towards abortion
- Christian responses to issues raised by fertility treatment
- Christian attitudes towards euthanasia and suicide
- Christian beliefs about the use of animals in medical research.

Christianity regards life as being sacred and as a gift from God. This view is often called the 'sanctity of life' and there are several passages in the Bible which suggest this:

> **For you created my inmost being; you knit me together in my mother's womb.**   (Psalm 139:13)

> **Before I formed you in the womb I knew you, before you were born I set you apart; I appointed you as a prophet to the nations.**
> (Jeremiah 1:5)

> **Naked I came from my mother's womb, and naked I will depart. The Lord gave and the Lord has taken away; may the name of the Lord be praised.**   (Job 1:21)

However, many Christians today believe that they should interpret the teachings of the Bible for the age in which they live.

Different Christian attitudes towards abortion

Abortion is a complex issue in Christianity and has caused many problems and debates within the churches. None of the Christian churches feel that abortion should be encouraged or used in any but the most serious circumstances. In the early years of the Christian Church abortion was common in some cultures as was infanticide (killing unwanted babies).

Anti-abortionists argue from Natural Law and also from the Bible:

> **For you created my inmost being; you knit me together in my mother's womb.**   (Psalm 139:13)

> **Before I formed you in the womb I knew you, before you were born I set you apart**   (Jeremiah 1:5)

This text suggests that God knows the person before they are born and has a plan for them. Therefore, abortion can be seen as killing a human being, not just something that has the potential to be human.

The Roman Catholic Church is very strongly opposed to abortion in all cases. The only exception is in the instance of 'double effect' when a necessary operation to the mother may require a pregnancy to be terminated. This is not an abortion but the side-effect of an essential life-saving operation.

The Roman Catholic Church believes that the foetus is a living person from the moment of conception:

Ensoulment: Thomas Aquinas argued that the male foetus became a human being 40

Christians protesting outside an abortion clinic

days after conception and the female, 90 days after conception.

Quickening: this is the time when the baby starts to move in the womb. This is often supported by the experience of John the Baptist's mother, Elizabeth:

> **When Elizabeth heard Mary's greeting, the baby leaped in her womb, and Elizabeth was filled with the Holy Spirit.** (Luke 1:41)

Therefore, some Christians might say that an abortion is the same as murdering a human being. Christians from other denominations may not agree with this.

The Didache, one of the earliest Christian documents, said that: 'You shall not kill by abortion the fruit of the womb.'

In 1993 the General Synod of the Church of England said that far too many abortions were being carried out since the passing of the 1967 Abortion Act in the United Kingdom. It encouraged people to realise just how serious a moral decision they were making and that abortion should not be seen as an ultimate form of contraception. However, it still left the issue up to the consciences of the people concerned.

Some Christians try to employ the 'Golden Rule':

> **So in everything, do to others what you would have them do to you, for this sums up the Law and the Prophets.** (Matthew 7:12)

and the principle of Christian love, agape:

> **Dear friends, let us love one another, for love comes from God.**
>
> **Everyone who loves has been born of God and knows God.** (1 John 4:7)

Perhaps the most open view of abortion comes from the Religious Society of Friends (Quakers). Although abortion can be seen as going against their commitment to pacifism and non-violence, they would not value the life of an unborn child above that of the woman concerned.

Activity

Makes a list of the arguments that might be used by pro-life and pro-choice campaigners. Try to find as much supporting evidence for each point as you can.

Christian attitudes towards fertility treatment

Obviously, at the time the Bible was written there was no such thing as fertility treatment, therefore, there is no specific teaching on the subject.

There are several instances in the Bible where woman are unhappy because they were unable to have children:

Abraham's wife, Sarai, could not have children:

> **Now Sarai was barren; she had no children.** (Genesis 11:30)

However, eventually God gave her a child:

> **God also said to Abraham, 'As for Sarai your wife, you are no longer to call her Sarai; her name will be Sarah. I will bless her and will surely give you a son by her. I will bless her so that she will be the mother of nations; kings of peoples will come from her.'**
>
> **Abraham fell facedown; he laughed and said to himself, 'Will a son be born to a man a hundred years old? Will Sarah bear a child at the age of ninety?'** (Genesis 17:15–17)

This passage shows that, according to the Bible, it is entirely up to God whether a woman has a child or not.

Christians disagree about the use of fertility treatment. Some may again apply the Golden Rule and the principle of agape and argue that permitting fertility treatment is the most loving thing to do.

Others say that God has decided that a couple will not have children and that fertility treatment is therefore unnatural because it interferes with God's plan.

There are two main objections to fertility treatment. One is to do with the spare embryos which are created. If they are not implanted in the woman's womb they are frozen but eventually they are destroyed and this is seen as murder of a human being.

The other problem relates to the collection of the sperm from the man. This is done by masturbation which is regarded as a sin by many Christians. The reason for this is found in the story of Onan in the Old Testament. Jewish Law required that if a man died his brother should marry the widow. Onan refused to do this:

> **Judah got a wife for Er, his firstborn, and her name was Tamar. But Er, Judah's firstborn, was wicked in the Lord's sight; so the Lord put him to death.**
>
> **Then Judah said to Onan, 'Lie with your brother's wife and fulfill your duty to her as a brother-in-law to produce offspring for your brother.' But Onan knew that the offspring would not be his; so whenever he lay with his brother's wife, he spilled his semen on the ground to keep from producing offspring for his brother. What he did was wicked in the Lord's sight; so he put him to death also.**
>
> (Genesis 28:6–10)

In fact, Onan's sin was that he refused to marry his brother's widow. However, because the text says that he 'spilled his semen on the ground' many people have understood this as meaning that he was put to death for masturbation.

Activity

Read the following statements:

● Fertility treatment can be extremely expensive, it would be better for the couple to try adopting a child.

● If a couple desperately wants to have a child and cannot have one by normal means, it may cause them great distress.

> Consider the arguments for and against each of these statements. Which do you think is the most convincing?

Christian attitudes towards euthanasia and suicide

Euthanasia, whether voluntary or involuntary, is condemned by many Christians as murder and as breaking the sixth commandment:

> **You shall not murder.**
>
> (Exodus 20:13)

Many Christians also believe that God has known us from the very beginning and has laid down the path we are to follow:

> **For you created my inmost being;**
> **you knit me together in my**
> **mother's womb.**
> **I praise you because I am fearfully**
> **and wonderfully made;**
> **your works are wonderful,**
> **I know that full well.**
> **My frame was not hidden from you**
> **when I was made in the secret place.**
> **When I was woven together in the**
> **depths of the earth,**
> **your eyes saw my unformed body.**
> **All the days ordained for me**
> **were written in your book**
> **before one of them came to be.**
>
> (Psalm 139:13–16)

Some Christians claim that suffering may be good for the person's soul and that therefore any attempt to end their own life is wrong.

The Roman Catholic Church argues that any action which is intended to cause death is 'a grave violation of the law of God' (Evangelium Vitae). This covers the giving of an overdose of painkillers, as well as withholding treatment from a person if it is known that they will then die.

Large doses of painkillers that are required to ease suffering but which, by the law of 'double effect', may ultimately cause death are permitted. In the same way, any 'extraordinary treatment' such as keeping a person alive when they are in a Persistent Vegetative State is not required.

In a statement made in 1992, the Church of England recognised that although 'the deliberate taking of human life is prohibited except in self-defence or the legitimate defence of others', nevertheless there were very strong arguments that people should not be kept alive at all costs when they were suffering intolerable pain.

Similar distinctions are made by most of the other Christian churches. They fear that a change in the law to legalise euthanasia would be abused and elderly people might be put under pressure to accept euthanasia. They encourage support of the Hospice Movement which is committed to helping the elderly and terminally ill die with comfort and dignity.

The concern of a hospice is to provide palliative care, this means making the patient as comfortable as possible. The patients will eventually die but the aim is that they should have a peaceful end rather than any form of euthanasia.

Activity

1 Write a paragraph which distinguishes clearly between the doctrine of double effect and the teachings in this section from Evangelium Vitae.

2 Find out why Dame Cicely Saunders first established a hospice in England.

Suicide

For many hundreds of years suicide was seen as a sin and a crime. It was a sin against God because people were rejecting the gift of life that they had been given, and often it was also a crime in the country where it was attempted.

Many suicides were buried at crossroads. This was believed to confuse the ghost and prevent it from returning home. Crossroad burial was abolished in the United Kingdom in 1823. However, for some years afterwards suicides could only be buried in graveyards between 9pm and midnight and were not allowed a burial service.

The Roman Catholic Church does not permit 'sane' suicides to be buried in consecrated ground but, in fact, most people who commit suicide are judged to be insane either through stress and depression or through mental illness so this would rarely apply.

Most Christians would now regard suicide as the result of great unhappiness or illness rather than as a sin. Therefore, many Christians volunteer to work for organisations such as the Samaritans to try to prevent people from reaching the point where they do commit suicide.

The 'Samaritans' take their name from the Parable of the Good Samaritan in the New Testament. However, the founder of the Samaritans, Chad Varah, although he was a Christian minister, insisted that the Samaritans should not have any religious connections in their work.

Activity

Find out more about the work of the Samaritans.

Christian beliefs about the use of animals in medical research

Christianity teaches that humanity was the most important part of creation and that humans have been given the power and authority to rule over other animals.

> **God blessed them and said to them, 'Be fruitful and increase in number; fill the earth and subdue it. Rule over the fish of the sea and the birds of the air and over every living creature that moves on the ground.'** (Genesis 1:28)

Later, in the second account of creation:

> **the Lord God formed the man from the dust of the ground and breathed into his nostrils the breath of life, and the man became a living being.**
> (Genesis 2:7)

It is believed that this is when the first human received his soul. This 'breath of life' is not given to the other animals or plants and so is seen as setting humans apart.

Although many people eat meat and keep animals to work for them this is not seen as a reason to treat them inhumanely. Being cruel to animals is sometimes viewed as abusing the authority which God gave to humans.

Most Christians would probably agree that it is necessary to use animals for medical research that can help human beings. They are less likely to think animals should be used to test things such as cosmetics which are ultimately unnecessary.

The Church of England made the following statement:

> The Church recognises the need for animals to be used in certain research to improve medical understanding, veterinary or behavioural knowledge, and to test for the safety of chemicals, and understands that such testing is a requirement of law. It also, however, affirms that responsible stewardship of the natural world requires all animals to receive careful and sympathetic treatment, both during their lives and in the manner of their dying.
>
> (What the Churches say, CEM)

The Roman Catholic Church made the following statement at the Assisi Declaration on Nature:

> But it is especially through man and woman, made in the image and likeness of God and entrusted with a unique dominion [authority] over all visible creatures, that the Lord's goodness and providence [care, protection] are to be manifested [shown].

> Most certainly, then, because of the responsibilities which flow from his dual citizenship, man's dominion cannot be understood as licence to abuse, spoil, squander or destroy what God has made to manifest his glory. That dominion cannot be anything other than a stewardship in symbiosis with all creatures. On one hand, man's position verges on a viceregal partnership with God; on the other, his self-mastery in symbiosis with creation must manifest the Lord's exclusive and absolute dominion over everything, over man and over his stewardship. At the risk of destroying himself, man may not reduce to chaos or disorder, or, worse still, destroy God's bountiful treasures.
> Every human act of irresponsibility towards creatures is an abomination. According to its gravity, it is an offence against that divine wisdom which sustains and gives purpose to the interdependent harmony of the universe.   (Fr. Lanfranco Serrini)

Activity

1 The passage from the Asissi Declaration by Fr. Serrini is in a very formal style of writing but the ideas in it are quite straightforward. Taking one paragraph at a time and, using a dictionary if you need to, write you own version of what Fr. Serrini said.

2 Explain what, in your opinion, makes humans different from animals.

3 Consider whether medical drugs, which might be very dangerous, should be tested on animals before they are given to humans.

☪ Islam

This topic looks at:
- Muslim attitudes towards abortion
- Muslim responses to issues raised by fertility treatment
- Muslim attitudes towards euthanasia and suicide
- Muslim beliefs about the use of animals in medical research.

Islam teaches that Allah created the world and everything in it.

> To Allah belongs the dominion of the heavens and the earth. He creates what He wills (and plans). He bestows (children) male or female according to His Will (and Plan),
> Or He bestows both males and females, and He leaves barren whom He will: for He is full of Knowledge and Power.
>
> (Surah 42:49–50)

Life is therefore a special gift from Allah. It is clear that Allah decides whether any individual will be born and that everything happens according to his plans which are the correct ones. This, therefore, shows how sacred life is.

Muslim attitudes towards abortion

Although contraception is permitted in some circumstances, generally Islam will not allow abortion. Muslims consider the foetus as a human being and therefore abortion is thought of as a crime and so, if an abortion is carried out, blood money can be payable for the loss of life. Blood money is money which is paid by a murderer or someone responsible for a death to the family of the dead person. The paying of blood money means that the murderer will not then lose their own life for the crime. However, the deceased's family can decide whether they want blood money or the death penalty.

However, abortion is allowed if a doctor is convinced that continuation of the pregnancy will result in the mother's death. The later in the pregnancy that an abortion

takes place, the more human the foetus and so the greater the crime. Some Muslims believe that for the first four months of pregnancy the mother's rights are greater than those of the child, while after this time they have equal rights.

Although most Muslims believe that life begins at conception, it is clear that this does not mean that the foetus is then a person with full rights. Ensoulment does not take place until after 120 days from conception. The foetus becomes more of a person the older it is.

Imam Al-Ghazzali (1058–1111) distinguished between contraception and abortion by saying:

> Contraception is not like abortion. Abortion is a crime against an existing being. Existence has various stages. The first is the settling of the semen in the womb and its mixing with the secretions [egg] of the woman. It is then ready to receive life. Disturbing it is a crime. When it develops further and becomes a lump, abortion is a greater crime. When it acquires a soul and its creation is complete, the crime becomes even more grievous. The crime reaches its maximum seriousness after the foetus is separated from its mother alive.

Therefore, an abortion becomes most serious if the foetus is capable of life when it is taken from the mother's womb.

In Arabia, before the time of Muhammad ﷺ, unwanted baby girls were often buried alive and the Qur'an has very strict rules against this that are now also applied to the issue of abortion:

> Kill not your children for fear of want: We shall provide sustenance for them as well as for you. Verily the killing of them is a great sin.　　(Surah 17:31)

and the innocence of the child is stressed:

> When the female (infant) buried
> alive, is questioned—For what
> crime she was killed?
>
> (Surah 81:8–9)

If a pregnant woman is sentenced to death for a crime, she cannot be executed until after the baby is weaned – is no longer dependant on its mother for milk.

There are different beliefs among Muslim writers about when a foetus becomes a person.

> We believe that the soul is
> breathed in by the first 42
> days of pregnancy. What has
> led us to this opinion is the
> hard fact of embryology, that
> all stages – seed, clot of blood
> and morsel of flesh occur in the
> first 40 days of life.

> Before 120 days from conception,
> the foetus lacks a human soul.
> Only at the end of 120 days is
> the foetus ensouled. To consider
> in the same light abortions that
> are performed before the 120-
> day period and after, as the
> Anti-Abortion lobby does, is
> therefore both ridiculous and
> unIslamic. Muslim jurists prohibit,
> absolutely, any abortion taking
> place after ensoulment when the
> soul enters the body, but many of
> them permit it before 120 days
> under certain conditions, for
> example the poor health of the
> mother, or in the case of rape.

Activity

Explain what Muslims understand by 'ensoulment'.

Muslim attitudes to fertility treatment

The procreation of children is a very important part of a Muslim marriage. Therefore, it is very difficult for a couple when they find that they cannot have children of their own.

Islam often looks to the women in the Qur'an and in the life of Muhammad ﷺ as examples of how people have coped with infertility. For example, Sara, the wife of Ibrahim, was barren until she was 90. Then her future pregnancy is announced by angels:

> They said, 'Fear not,' and they
> gave him glad tidings of a son
> endowed with knowledge. But
> his wife came forward (laughing)
> aloud: she smote her forehead
> and said: 'A barren old woman!'
> They said, 'Even so has thy Lord
> spoken: and He is full of Wisdom
> and Knowledge.'
>
> (Surah 51:28–30)

Zakariya also prays to the Lord for a child and his elderly wife Ishba is cured of her barrenness and gives birth to a child, Yabya:

> And (remember) Zakariya, when
> he cried to his Lord: 'O my Lord!
> leave me not without offspring,
> though Thou art the best of
> inheritors.' So We listened to
> him: and We granted him Yabya:
> we cured his wife's (barrenness)
> for him. These (three) were ever
> quick in emulation (to copy) in
> good works; they used to call on
> Us with love and reverence, and
> humble themselves before Us.
>
> (Surah 21:89–90)

Women who cannot have children might argue that although Sara and Ishba were very old, they still had children eventually.

Muslims also look at the example of Muhammad ﷺ who had children with his first wife Khadijah, but none with any of his other wives: Sawda, Aisha, Hafsa, Umm Salamah, Zaynab bint Jahshm Juwayriyya, Rayhana, Umm Habiba, Safiyya, and Maymuna.

The possibility, in Islam, of a man having more than one wife is sometimes suggested as a way around a fertility problem but this is not a common practice in many Muslim countries and still does not deal with the suffering of the wife who wants children and cannot have them.

Although some Muslims believe that people should simply accept Allah's will if they cannot have children, others see infertility as a disease and argue that Muslims have a duty to seek treatment for any disease.

IVF is one possibility for Muslims. Although not all the fertilised eggs are placed in the uterus and some therefore eventually die, this is not seen as a problem. Muslims argue that these embryos are not human beings and therefore their death is not seen in the same way as an abortion. From Muslim tradition it might be argued that these 'spare' embryos could be used for stem cell research to cure other conditions. However, the embryos cannot be donated to another woman as any child born in this way would be viewed as illegitimate and break Muslim teaching about lineage (line of descendants).

> **It is He Who has created man from water: then has He established relationships of lineage and marriage: for thy Lord has power (over all things).** (Surah 25:54)

Discussion

Consider how Muslims might deal with the issue of infertility.

Activity

1 Explain Muslim attitudes about the time at which a foetus is considered to be a person.

2 Do you think that fertility treatment should be allowed for couples who are unable to have children? Give reasons for your answer.

Muslim attitudes to euthanasia and suicide

Muslims are opposed to euthanasia and also to suicide.

Because every soul is created by Allah, life is sacred. To kill yourself is therefore forbidden.

> **Nor kill (or destroy) yourselves: for verily Allah hath been to you most Merciful!** (Surah 4:29)

The sufferings people have to endure are a test of their iman (faith). Nothing which happens to a person, no matter how painful, is a good enough reason to end life, whether by suicide or euthanasia.

The Prophet Muhammad ﷺ said that anyone who killed themselves would go to hell:

> **Anyone who throws themselves down from a rock and commits suicide will be throwing themselves into Hell. A person who drinks poison and kills themselves will drink it for ever in Hell. A person who stabs themselves will stab themselves for ever in Hell.** (Hadith)

Muslims say that the time when someone will die can only be decided by Allah:

> **When their Term expires, they would not be able to delay (the punishment) for a single hour, just as they would not be able to anticipate it (for a single hour).** (Surah 16:61)

> **Nor can a soul die except by Allah's leave, the term being fixed as by writing.** (Surah 3:145)

If anyone does commit suicide, they have taken their life which did not belong to them and also it shows that the ummah has failed to take care of this individual.

Because of these teachings, euthanasia is forbidden in Islam. Euthanasia is therefore zalim, wrongdoing against Allah, other people, or yourself. Everyone has the responsibility to preserve and prolong life and although suffering is not seen as a good thing in its own right and everything possible should be done to relieve it, nevertheless it can help people to grow spiritually.

Muslims do not believe that people should be kept alive by artificial means:

> If, however, a number of medical experts determine that a patient is in a terminal condition, there is no hope for his/her recovery and all medication has become useless, then it could be permissible for them, through a collective decision, to stop the medication. If the patient is on life support, it may be permissible, with due consultation and care, to decide to switch off the life-support machine and let nature take its own time. Under no condition is it permissible to induce death. As long as a person is alive, it is his/her right to be fed. Medical experts and relatives should not withhold nutrition from a living person. They should do their best to provide him/her with necessary nutrition by whatever method is possible.
>
> (Muzammil Siddiqui of the Fiqh Council of North America)

> As for facilitating death by withdrawing artificial resuscitating apparatus from the patient who is clinically regarded as 'dead' or 'practically dead' because of the damage to the brainstem or brain, with which human beings live and feel; if the action of the physician is merely stopping the treatment instruments, it will be no more than giving up the treatment, in which case his action is legal and permissible, bearing in mind that these instruments can preserve the apparent life of the patient – represented by breathing and circulation – though the patient is actually dead, for he cannot conceive, feel or be sensitive to anything because of the damage of the source of all that, namely the brain. Keeping the patient

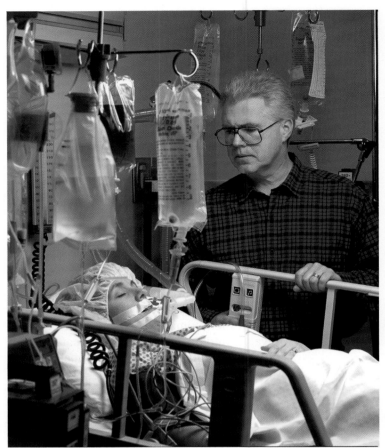

A terminally ill patient on a life-support machine.

> in that state would waste vital resources and would prevent other maybe curable patients from benefiting from the instruments being occupied for the practically dead patient.
>
> (European Council for Fatwa and Research)

Discussion

Consider whether there are any circumstances when religious people might say that someone was right to commit suicide.

Activity

How might a Muslim doctor or nurse answer someone who asked for an overdose of pain-relieving drugs, to make death come more quickly?

Muslim beliefs about the use of animals in medical research

The Qur'an states that all life, animal and human belongs to Allah:

> There is not an animal (that lives) on the earth, nor a being that flies on its wings, but (forms part of) communities like you. Nothing have we omitted from the Book, and they (all) shall be gathered to their Lord in the end. (Surah 6:38)

It is clear that humans have a duty towards all living beings.

Islam is not opposed to necessary animal experimentation when it safeguards humans but it does stress the importance of animals as part of Allah's creation:

> Seest thou not that it is Allah Whose praises all beings in the heavens and on earth do celebrate, and the birds (of the air) with wings outspread? Each one knows its own (mode of) prayer and praise. And Allah knows well all that they do. (Surah 24:42)

This respect is shown in the life of Muhammad ﷺ. During his travels he saw an army of ants heading towards a fire so he ordered the fire to be put out so that the ants would not be harmed.

Muhammad ﷺ called for compassion towards animals:

> If you kill, kill well, and if you slaughter, slaughter well. Let each of you sharpen his blade and let him spare suffering to the animal he slaughters.
>
> For (charity shown to) each creature which has a wet heart (i.e. is alive), there is a reward. (Hadith)

Muhammad ﷺ was also opposed to hunting for sport:

> Whoever shoots at a living creature for sport is cursed. (Hadith)

In the 13th century a Muslim lawyer called Izz ad-Din ibn Abd as-Salam drew up a bill of legal rights for animals based on Shari'ah (Muslim law).

At the World Wide Fund for Nature International in 1986, the Muslim representative, Dr Abdullah Omar Nasseef, stressed that humans had a responsibility to look after the earth and the animals:

> The essence of Islamic teaching is that the entire universe is God's creation. Allah makes the waters flow upon the earth, upholds the heavens, makes the rain fall and keeps the boundaries between day and night. The whole of the rich and wonderful universe belongs to God, its maker. It is God who created the plants and the animals in their pairs and gave them the means to multiply. Then God created mankind – a very special creation because mankind alone was created with reason and the power to think and even the means to turn against his Creator. Mankind has the potential to acquire a status higher than that of the angels or sink lower than the lowliest of the beasts.
>
> Our freedom is that of being sensible, aware, responsible trustees of God's gifts and bounty...
>
> Islam is a very practical world-view. It seeks, in all its principles and injunctions [commands], to give pragmatic [practical] shapes to its concepts and values. Indeed, the notions of *tawhid* and *khalifa* have been translated into practical injunctions in the *Shari'ah*. Such *Shari'ah* institutions as haram zones, inviolate [do not allow] areas within which development is prohibited to protect natural resources, and *hima*, reserves established solely for the conservation of wildlife and forests, form the core of the environmental legislation of Islam.

The Classical Muslim jurist, Izz ad-Din ibn Abd as-Salam, used these aspects of the *Shari'ah* when he formulated the bill of legal rights of animals in the thirteenth century. Similarly, numerous other jurists and scholars developed legislations [laws] to safeguard water resources, prevent over-grazing, conserve forests, limit the growth of cities, protect cultural property and so on. Islam's environmental ethics then are not limited to metaphysical [abstract] notions; it provides a practical guide as well.

Therefore, although Muslims see all life as important as it is created by Allah, human life has greater importance than other forms of animal life.

Discussion

Consider how far Muslim attitudes towards animals differ from those of animal activists.

Activity

1 Explain Muslim attitudes towards euthanasia and the use of life-support machines.

2 Do you think that humans have the right to use other animals for food and medical experiments? Give reasons for your answer.

Summary

Despite the differences between them, these religions have very similar views on most of these issues. We might conclude that 'Life really is sacred' and that followers of these faiths believe that they are given life by God and must do all they can to respect and preserve it.

All of these issues: abortion; fertility treatment; euthanasia; and the use of animals in medical research will affect most of us or people we know at some time in our lives, and none of them are matters that can be easily dismissed.

Questions

1 What do you understand by:
   (a) abortion
   (b) euthanasia
   (c) suicide
   (d) a hospice
   (e) Persistent Vegetative State?

2 Do you think that people should make up their own minds about euthanasia or should they be mainly guided by religious teachings?

3 What factors should be taken into account when someone is thinking about having an abortion?

4 Consider the arguments for and against hospice care and euthanasia.

5 'In the 21st century people are well educated enough to make up their own minds about these issues and do not need religions to tell them what to do.'
   Explain how far you would agree or disagree with this statement.

Practice GCSE questions

Christianity

1 (a) Describe Christian attitudes towards fertility treatment. **[8 marks]**

(b) Explain Christian attitudes to the use of animals in medical research. **[7 marks]**

(c) 'Every woman has the right to have a baby.'
Do you agree? Give reasons to support your answer, and show that you have thought about different points of view. You must refer to Christianity in your answer. **[5 marks]**

2 (a) Describe Christian attitudes towards abortion. **[8 marks]**

(b) Explain why some Christians might be against fertility treatment. **[7 marks]**

(c) 'It is up to God to decide if a woman is going to have a baby.'
Do you agree? Give reasons to support your answer, and show that you have thought about different points of view. You must refer to Christianity in your answer. **[5 marks]**

Tips

In your answer you might consider that some people are in favour of fertility treatment as it enables a woman to fulfil part of her mission in life, which is to have children and the commandment to 'go forth and multiply'. You might also consider the opposition to this: interfering with God's work, the use of 'spare' embryos and the way in which the semen is collected.

In answering this you need to do more that focus on 'it's not a nice thing to do' and 'suppose the animals did it to us'. You could consider issues of equality and also the benefits to humans of testing. You might explain whether animals should be treated equally as humans or whether they are a lesser part of creation.

Here, you might agree with the statement arguing that it is part of the duty and the right of every married woman to have children. On the other hand, you might consider the use of medical resources in helping an infertile couple and also whether a child is a right or a gift. You must also remember to include Christian teaching in the answer.

In your answer you will probably consider that God gave life and so only God can take it away, that abortion is murdering a new life, that life begins at conception, ensoulment, etc. You might give church teachings as well as biblical ones. You might also consider other viewpoints such as a 'woman's right to choose'.

Here, you may explain that some Christians welcome fertility treatment as a scientific development that helps couples who are desperate to have a baby but are unable to do so. You should also explain that some people consider it goes against the teaching of Natural Law and that a barren woman must accept her state.

In answering this you might consider that everything about life is God's will and that it should not be interfered with but accepted. On the other hand, you may consider the argument that God has allowed people to discover the techniques of fertility treatment and so it should be available to those who need it.

Islam

1 (a) Describe Muslim attitudes towards fertility treatment. [8 marks]

(b) Explain Muslim attitudes to the use of animals in medical research. [7 marks]

(c) 'Every woman has the right to have a baby.'
Do you agree? Give reasons to support your answer, and show that you have thought about different points of view. You must refer to Islam in your answer. [5 marks]

2 (a) Describe Muslim attitudes towards abortion. [8 marks]

(b) Explain why some Muslims might be against fertility treatment. [7 marks]

(c) 'It is up to Allah to decide if a woman is going to have a baby.'
Do you agree? Give reasons to support your answer, and show that you have thought about different points of view. You must refer to Islam in your answer. [5 marks]

Tips

In your answer you might consider that some people are in favour of fertility treatment as it enables a woman to fulfil part of her mission in life, which is to have children. You might also consider the opposition to this: interfering with Allah's work and the use of 'spare' embryos. You might also explain that some Muslims may be in favour of fertility treatment as developments in medical science are a gift from Allah.

In answering this you need to do more that focus on 'it's not a nice thing to do' and 'suppose the animals did it to us'. You could consider issues of equality and also the benefits to humans of testing. You might explain whether animals should be treated equally as humans or whether they are a lesser part of creation. You should make reference to the teachings of Muhammad ﷺ.

Here, you might agree with the statement arguing that it is part of the duty and the right of every married woman to have children. On the other hand, you might consider the use of medical resources in helping an infertile couple and also whether a child is a right or a gift. You must also remember to include Muslim teaching in the answer.

In your answer you will probably consider that Allah gave life and so only Allah can take it away, that abortion is murdering a new life, that life begins at conception, ensoulment, etc. You might also consider the Muslim view that the woman's life is more important than the foetus up until a certain point and, therefore, abortion may be permitted in certain cases where the mother's life is at risk.

Here, you may explain that some Muslims welcome fertility treatment as a scientific development that helps couples who are desperate to have a baby but are unable to do so and that it is the wish of Allah that humans should discover these treatments. You should also explain that some people believe that a barren woman must accept her state.

In answering this you might consider that everything about life is Allah's will and that it should not be interfered with but accepted. On the other hand, you may consider the argument that Allah has allowed people to discover the techniques of fertility treatment and so it should be available to those who need it.

Introduction

How often have you heard someone say 'But it's not fair'? How often have you said it yourself? 'It's not fair' is used to describe almost any situation regardless of its importance: it rains when you want to go out, you cannot afford to buy a new pair of trainers or someone will not buy them for you, a close friend or relative dies, a tornado kills a hundred people, a person is refused a job because they are black, a woman is paid less than a man for doing the same work, someone is not invited to join a group of friends because they belong to a different religion.

The Oxford English Dictionary says that 'fair' is used to describe something which is free from bias, fraud, or injustice; so it would seem that 'fair' really means reasonable.

Often when we say 'it's not fair' we mean that we do not like what has happened, it seems unreasonable, yet in many cases it is just that things are not quite as we want them.

However, the last three examples given above are rather more serious.

Eleanor Roosevelt holding a copy of the Universal Declaration of Human Rights.

Prejudice and discrimination

The first two articles of the United Nations Declaration of Human Rights state:

- Article 1. All human beings are born free and equal in dignity and rights. They are endowed 'with [given] reason and conscience and should act towards one another in a spirit of brotherhood.
- Article 2. Everyone is entitled to all the rights and freedoms set forth in this Declaration, without distinction of any kind, such as race, colour, sex, language, religion, political or other opinion, national or social origin, property, birth or other status.

It is not enough to say that something is not 'fair'. Thousands of people in the world still suffer from various forms of discrimination and prejudice. These may be based on such issues as race, colour, religion, language, sex, sexuality, disability and social class. The discrimination takes the form of some people who have power, exercising that power over people who do not. A simple formula for this is:

Discrimination = Prejudice + Power
- Prejudice is an idea or feeling that one person holds and which affects another person.
- Discrimination is when they act on this prejudice and treat the other person badly.

There are very few of us who have not suffered from discrimination at some time. It may not have been terribly important but it always hurts when someone else excludes us and makes us appear different in some way. Young children are often the cruellest people when it comes to discriminating but we might say that they are not old enough to know any better.

Adults cannot claim this kind of defence, and it should be the responsibility of all people who consider themselves to be civilised to make an attempt to ensure that they do not discriminate and that they fight discrimination wherever they find it.

We can say that only time and education will fight prejudice, but discrimination is something which people can do something about now.

The majority of people in the world would probably say that they belong to one religion or another, or indeed to a particular denomination (branch) of a religion. As each of these people will almost certainly believe that their particular religion is true or the 'right' one, many will probably also think that the other thousands of religions and denominations are all or mostly wrong. Some religions such as Hinduism and Judaism do not encourage converts, not because they think they are better than other people but because they believe that there is no need for people to convert. Other religions, including Islam and Christianity are proselytising or evangelising religions. This means that they believe that it is their task, as believers, to go out and convert other people to their religion. Although it is easy to see why people might think that they should do this, it is equally simple to see how this might sometimes cause offence and annoyance to people.

After a discussion on prejudice and discrimination it is also important to consider forgiveness and reconciliation.
- Forgiveness is the act of pardoning or forgiving someone for something they have done wrong.
- Reconciliation is the ending of a dispute or the restoring of a friendly relationship between people who have been in dispute.

These two concepts are fundamental to all religious teaching and form an essential part of both Islam and Christianity.

Activity

1 Make a list of the different types of prejudice

2 Consider whether there are some people who should be discriminated against.

Christianity

This topic looks at:
- Christian teachings about equality
- Christian attitudes towards racism
- the role of women in a Christian society
- Christian attitudes towards other religions
- Christian beliefs about forgiveness and reconciliation.

Biblical teaching about equality

Christianity teaches that all people are equal and that no-one is superior or better than anyone else in God's eyes. To a Christian, it should make no difference whether people are male or female, black or white, rich or poor for everyone should be treated equally and shown the same love. For a person to make someone suffer or feel inferior for any reason is to break one of the Commandments **given by Jesus:**

> **You shall love your neighbour as yourself.** (Matthew 22:39)

Jesus taught that it was essential for people to love others, and that then humanity would be saved from bitter struggles and wars.

> **I give you a new commandment, that you love one another. Just as I have loved you, you also should love one another.** (John 13:34)

This teaching is also found in the Acts of the Apostles:

> **Then Peter began to speak: 'I now realise how true it is that God does not show favouritism but accepts men from every nation who fear him and do what is right.'** (Acts 10:34–35)

Christianity is opposed to all forms of prejudice and discrimination.

> **We all long for Heaven where God is, but we have it in our power to be in Heaven with Him at this very moment. But being happy with Him now means:**
>
> **Loving as He loves,**
> **Helping as He helps,**
> **Giving as He gives,**
> **Serving as He serves,**
> **Rescuing as He rescues,**
> **Being with Him twenty-four hours,**
> **Touching him in his distressing disguise.** (Mother Teresa)

This prayer of Mother Teresa's was intended to explain that issues of prejudice and discrimination should be dealt with by always following God's example in their lives.

Christian attitudes towards racism

One day Jesus was asked by someone how they could ensure that they inherited eternal life:

> **'What is written in the Law?' he replied. 'How do you read it?'**
>
> **He answered: '"Love the Lord your God with all your heart and with all your soul and with all your strength and with all your mind"; and, "Love your neighbour as yourself."'**
>
> **'You have answered correctly,' Jesus replied. 'Do this and you will live.'**
>
> **But he wanted to justify himself, so he asked Jesus, 'And who is my neighbour?'**
>
> **In reply Jesus said: 'A man was going down from Jerusalem to Jericho, when he fell into the hands of robbers. They stripped him of his clothes, beat him and went away, leaving him half dead. A priest happened to be going down the same road, and when he saw the man, he passed by on the other side. So too, a Levite,**

when he came to the place and saw him, passed by on the other side. But a Samaritan, as he travelled, came where the man was; and when he saw him, he took pity on him. He went to him and bandaged his wounds, pouring on oil and wine. Then he put the man on his own donkey, took him to an inn and took care of him. The next day he took out two silver coins and gave them to the innkeeper. "Look after him," he said, "and when I return, I will reimburse you for any extra expense you may have."

'Which of these three do you think was a neighbour to the man who fell into the hands of robbers?'

The expert in the law replied, 'The one who had mercy on him.'

Jesus told him, 'Go and do likewise.'   (Luke 10:26–37)

This parable shows clearly that Christians should treat everyone equally.

It also reflects the teaching of the Old Testament:

When an alien lives with you in your land, do not ill-treat him. The alien living with you must be treated as one of your native-born. Love him as yourself, for you were aliens in Egypt. I am the Lord your God.
(Leviticus 19:33–34)

Paul's teaching about how Christians should treat other people appears to be very straightforward:

From one man he made every nation of men, that they should inhabit the whole earth; and he determined the times set for them and the exact places where they should live.   (Acts 17:26)

There is neither Jew nor Greek, slave nor free, male nor female,

for you are all one in Christ Jesus.   (Galatians 3:28)

The Christian Church itself has been guilty of racism and intolerance (unwilling to accept people who are different) and sometimes people have preached God's message at the expense of local communities and colonies. During the Crusades thousands of people were killed in the name of Christianity and one of the worst slaughters in history took place when attempts were made to force the peoples of South America to become Christians. In South Africa for many years the Dutch Reformed Church taught that black people were inferior to the whites; during times of colonisation (when European countries took over other countries) Christians have killed the native people or forced them to convert to Christianity, and many Christians were slave-owners in the American Deep South. In the 20th century, Christian countries have fought each other and non-Christian countries; the First and Second World Wars; wars in Vietnam, Korea, the Falklands/Malvinos, South Africa, Iraq, and Northern Ireland, were all fought by countries which claimed to be Christian.

In many countries black people, in particular, have had to protest and often fight against white people in order to be treated equally, even though those white people were themselves Christians.

This has been particularly true in South Africa and in the USA. In both countries there have been laws which prevented black and white people from being treated equally. Many Christians, both black and white protested for many years to get rid of these laws so that people could live as equals regardless of their colour.

One of the most famous Americans to protest against these laws was Martin Luther King Jr. (1929–1968). Martin Luther King Jr. was a black Baptist

Bishop Desmond Tutu.

Fr. Trevor Huddleston.

the true meaning of its creed: "We hold these truths to be self-evident, that all men are created equal."

I have a dream that one day on the red hills of Georgia, the sons of former slaves and the sons of former slave owners will be able to sit down together at the table of brotherhood...

I have a dream that my four little children will one day live in a nation where they will not be judged by the colour of their skin but by the content of their character.'

Martin Luther King Jr. was shot on 4 April 1968 while making a speech in Memphis, Tennessee by a white escaped convict called James Earl Ray. No reason has ever been given for his assassination.

Martin Luther King Jr.'s work led to major changes in the law, finally bringing equality to both black and white people.

Discussion

Look carefully at the quotation from Galatians 3:28. To what extent does it say that everyone is equal?

Activity

South Africa was, for many years, governed by a system called apartheid which discriminated against all non-white people. Find out about the work of either Fr. Trevor Huddleston or Bishop Desmond Tutu and how they put their Christian beliefs into practice.

minister whose father was also a Baptist minister. He had experienced segregation himself and spent most of his life protesting to get a change in the law. He was influenced by MK Gandhi and believed that the way to force change was through peaceful protest.

This is an extract from the famous speech he made on the steps of the Lincoln Memorial in Washington, DC, on 28 August 1963:

'I have a dream that one day this nation will rise up and live out

The role of women in Christian society

The Christian Church has sometimes been accused of sexism. The language of the Church has been in favour of men – God is almost always referred to as male.

125

Because some Christians take what the Bible says very literally, and as having absolute authority, passages such as 'God made Man in his own image' are often used against those who demand greater equality in the Church and in society as a whole.

Paul says that women are to be quiet in church and keep their heads covered:

> **Women should remain silent in the churches. They are not allowed to speak, but must be in submission, as the Law says. If they want to enquire about something, they should ask their own husbands at home; for it is disgraceful for a woman to speak in the church.**
>
> (1 Corinthians 14:34–35)

> **Now I want you to realise that the head of every man is Christ, and the head of the woman is man, and the head of Christ is God. Every man who prays or prophesies with his head covered dishonours his head. And every woman who prays or prophesies with her head uncovered dishonours her head –**
>
> (1 Corinthians 11:3–5a)

The Bible was written in times very different from now when this was a normal way of seeing the different roles of men and women.

Jesus showed great respect towards women:

> **Now while Jesus was at Bethany in the house of Simon the leper, a woman came to him with an alabaster jar of very costly ointment, and she poured it on his head as he sat at the table. But when the disciples saw it, they were angry and said, 'Why this waste? For this ointment could have been sold for a large sum, and the money given to the poor.' But Jesus, aware of this, said to them, 'Why do you trouble the woman? She has performed a good service for me. For you always have the poor with you, but you will not always have me. By pouring this ointment on my body she has prepared me for burial. Truly I tell you, wherever this good news is proclaimed in the whole world, what she has done will be told in remembrance of her.'**
>
> (Matthew 26:6–13)

However, people sometimes use the following passage to suggest that Jesus criticised his mother:

> **When the wine gave out, the mother of Jesus said to him, 'They have no wine.' And Jesus said to her, 'Woman, what concern is that to you and to me?'** (John 2:3–4a)

Some Christians still feel that there is a clear distinction between the roles of men and women and believe that women should stay at home, look after the house and bring up children while men go out to work to earn money and also make all the important decisions. Some people say that this is correct and necessary because men are physically stronger than women.

However, there are many other Christians who believe that men and women were created equal and should be treated equally.

In Unit 6 there are several examples of biblical teachings about women.

The two stories of creation in Genesis give different accounts of the creation of men and women:

> **So God created humankind in his image, in the image of God he created them; male and female he created them.** (Genesis 1:27)

In this account it is clear that men and women were created at the same time and they appear to be equal.

> **Then the Lord God formed man from the dust of the ground,**

and breathed into his nostrils the breath of life; and the man became a living being.

Then the Lord God said, 'It is not good that the man should be alone; I will make him a helper as his partner.'

So the Lord God caused a deep sleep to fall upon the man, and he slept; then he took one of his ribs and closed up its place with flesh. And the rib that the Lord God had taken from the man he made into a woman and brought her to the man. Then the man said,

'This at last is bone of my bones and flesh of my flesh; this one shall be called Woman, for out of Man this one was taken.'   (Genesis 2:7, 18, 21–23)

In the second account it appears that the man was made first and the woman second. However, this is a problem with the translation of the Hebrew text into English. When God has only made one human being the word translated 'man' actually means a person but has no

indication of sex. When the second human is made the first is identified as male and the second as female.

Jesus' teachings about women in the New Testament are not always clear but he does appear to have treated women as equals and, according to Mark's gospel, it was a woman to whom he first appeared after his resurrection:

Now after he rose early on the first day of the week, he appeared first to Mary Magdalene, from whom he had cast out seven demons. She went out and told those who had been with him, while they were mourning and weeping. But when they heard that he was alive and had been seen by her, they would not believe it.   (Mark 16:9–11)

The Church is slow to change and many of the old ideas and prejudices still exist. In the Anglican Church in the USA, women have been eligible for ordination for some years, as they have in Canada and New Zealand. However, the Church of England did not permit women to be ordained until 1994. Women priests have been welcomed by many people but others have left the Church of England and have joined the Roman Catholic Church. The Roman Catholic Church teaches that because Jesus was a man and that a priest represents Jesus in certain circumstances, priests should also be men. They also say that Jesus only chose men to be his disciples. However, in recent years some Christians have said that in the early Christian Church women had a more important role than they are allowed today.

After the ascension of Jesus, Mary, Jesus' mother, was with the disciples in the Upper Room:

Then they returned to Jerusalem from the hill called the Mount of Olives, a Sabbath day's walk from the city. When they arrived, they went upstairs to the room where they were staying. Those present were Peter, John, James and Andrew; Philip and Thomas,

An Anglican priest.

Bartholomew and Matthew; James son of Alphaeus and Simon the Zealot, and Judas son of James. They all joined together constantly in prayer, along with the women and Mary the mother of Jesus, and with his brothers.   (Acts 1:12–14)

This passage from Paul is often used to show that woman had greater importance in the early Church:

I commend to you our sister Phoebe, a servant of the church in Cenchrea. I ask you to receive her in the Lord in a way worthy of the saints and to give her any help she may need from you, for she has been a great help to many people, including me.

Greet Priscilla and Aquila, my fellow workers in Christ Jesus. They risked their lives for me. Not only I but all the churches of the Gentiles are grateful to them.

Greet also the church that meets at their house.   (Romans 16:1–5)

Discussion

For many years, women have struggled to have the same status as men and in the United Kingdom women did not have equal voting rights with men until 1928. Some people have said that Christianity also does not give women equal status with men.

To what extent do you agree that women should be able to be ordained as priests?

Christian attitudes towards other religions

Christians believe that people should have the right to practise their own religion but they also believe that only Christianity has the complete truth about God:

Jesus answered, 'I am the way and the truth and the life. No-one comes to the Father except through me.'   (John 14:6)

This passage appears to suggest that only followers of Jesus will be able to go to heaven when they die. Christians might argue that Jesus died to atone for the sins of the world and that his resurrection proves that he is the only way in which people can reach God.

In previous centuries many Christians went abroad as **missionaries**, they believed that, as Christians, it was their duty to travel the world and convert everyone to follow their religion. Although there are still missionaries today, most of them are more concerned with helping people in developing countries rather than trying to convert them – people might say that they show the example of Jesus in their lives and that this is enough.

However, Christianity is an **evangelical** religion and many Christians still feel that it is their duty to lead others to convert to Christianity.

The New Catechism of the Roman Catholic Church states that:

The Church still has the obligation and also the sacred right to evangelise all men.

Some Christians believe that this is a misunderstanding of Jesus' message and that people should follow their own religion and their own God. They argue that a person's religion may depend upon where they were born in the world and that the Christian God will not punish someone who is a devoted follower of a non-Christian religion. In recent years Christianity has shown much more respect to other religions and there are many services held where people from different religious traditions take part.

As well as working with members of different religions, many Christians also work towards **ecumenism** – trying to bring together the many different branches and denominations of the Christian Church. Often there are joint services between different denominations to show that, although there may be differences between them, they are all Christians with the same essential beliefs.

An example of this is Taizé. Taizé is a Christian community in a small village in France. It was founded in 1940, during the Second World War by Brother Roger Schutz. Taizé began by offering hospitality to refugees, particularly Jews escaping from Nazi Germany. Today there are more than 100 brothers mainly Protestants working there. Since the late 1960s Taizé has worked towards improving relationships between Protestants and Catholics.

Activity

Find out more about Taizé.

Christian beliefs about forgiveness and reconciliation

At the time of Jesus, capital punishment for crimes was an accepted part of life. Although Jesus did not say that the death penalty was wrong, he said many things which suggest that people should be forgiven.

An example of Jesus' forgiveness is found in John's gospel:

> **The teachers of the law and the Pharisees brought in a woman caught in adultery. They made her stand before the group and said to Jesus, 'Teacher, this woman was caught in the act of adultery. In the Law Moses commanded us to stone such women. Now what do you say?' ...he straightened up and said to them, 'If any one of you is without sin, let him be the first to throw a stone at her.' ...At this, those who heard began to go away one at a time, the older ones first, until only Jesus was left, with the woman still standing there. Jesus**

> **straightened up and asked her, 'Woman, where are they? Has no-one condemned you?' 'No-one, sir,' she said. 'Then neither do I condemn you,' Jesus declared. 'Go now and leave your life of sin.'** (John 8:3–5,7b,9–11)

This does not mean that Jesus was not capable of being angry. When he found shopkeepers and money lenders trading inside the Temple in Jerusalem he threw them out:

> **To those who sold doves he said, 'Get these out of here! How dare you turn my Father's house into a market!'** (John 2:16)

However, forgiveness and love for other people were at the centre of his teaching and so are at the centre of Christianity:

> **Teacher, which is the greatest commandment in the Law?' Jesus replied: "'Love the Lord your God with all your heart and with all your soul and with all your mind." This is the first and greatest commandment. And the second is like it: "Love your neighbour as yourself."'** (Matthew 22:36–39)

Jesus was teaching that not only should people follow God's laws but that one of the most important laws was that they should love and forgive one another.

> **Then Peter came to Jesus and asked, 'Lord, how many times shall I forgive my brother when he sins against me? Up to seven times?' Jesus answered, 'I tell you, not seven times, but seventy-seven times.'** (Matthew 18:21–22)

Seventy-seven times is a number used here to represent the idea that Christians should always forgive.

When Jesus taught his disciples how they should pray he said:

> **This, then, is how you should pray:**

> **'Our Father in heaven, hallowed be your name, your kingdom come, your will be done on earth as it is in heaven. Give us today**

our daily bread. Forgive us our debts, as we also have forgiven our debtors. And lead us not into temptation, but deliver us from the evil one.'

For if you forgive men when they sin against you, your heavenly Father will also forgive you. But if you do not forgive men their sins, your Father will not forgive your sins.   (Matthew 6:9–15)

Particular places such as Coventry Cathedral, which was rebuilt after being bombed in the Second World War, have become centres for reconciliation and forgiveness.

Christians can go to their priest or minister to seek help when they feel they need to be forgiven for something they have done wrong.

In the Roman Catholic Church this is called the Sacrament of Reconciliation. The person who is seeking forgiveness goes to the priest and asks to be forgiven. Priests have the power to forgive sins on behalf of God because Jesus gave this power to his disciples:

Again Jesus said, 'Peace be with you! As the Father has sent me, I am sending you.' And with that he breathed on them and said, 'Receive the Holy Spirit. If you forgive anyone his sins, they are forgiven; if you do not forgive them, they are not forgiven.'
(John 20:19–23)

After making their confession to the priest, the penitent (person who is seeking forgiveness) may be asked to say a certain number of prayers or do some work in the community or the church as penance, then the priest says:

God, the Father of mercies, through the death and resurrection of his Son has reconciled the world to himself and sent the Holy Spirit among us for the forgiveness of sins; through the ministry of the Church may God give you pardon and peace, and I absolve you from your sins in the name of the Father, and of the Son, and of the Holy Spirit. (the penitent answers) Amen.

The service of the Eucharist is also a time for forgiveness and reconciliation:

While they were eating, Jesus took bread, gave thanks and broke it, and gave it to his disciples, saying, 'Take and eat; this is my body.'

Then he took the cup, gave thanks and offered it to them, saying, 'Drink from it, all of you. This is my blood of the covenant, which is poured out for many for the forgiveness of sins.'
(Matthew 26:26–28)

Activity

1 Jesus taught people to forgive 'seventy-seven times'. How do you think people should forgive and how often?

2 Do you think that there are some crimes that cannot be forgiven? Explain your answer.

Islam

This topic looks at:
● Muslim teachings about equality
● Muslim attitudes towards racism
● the role of women in a Muslim society
● Muslim attitudes towards other religions
● Muslim beliefs about forgiveness and reconciliation.

Muslim teachings about equality from the Qur'an

The Qur'an teaches that all people are created by Allah and are therefore equal:

> And among His Signs is the creation of the heavens and the earth, and the variations in your languages and your colours; verily in that are Signs for those who know.
> (Surah 30:22)

> O mankind! We created you from a single (pair) of a male and a female; and made you into nations and tribes, that ye may know each other (not that ye may despise each other). Verily, the most honoured of you in the sight of Allah is (he who is) the most righteous of you. And Allah has full knowledge and is well-acquainted (with all things).
> (Surah 49:13)

It can be seen from this passage that Islam makes a positive statement about people of different languages and colours.

Muslim attitudes towards racism

Muslims are not a particular racial group: followers of Islam can be found all over the world and so there can never be any excuse for racism or prejudice. A person will see themselves as a Muslim first, regardless of their colour or nationality.

In his last sermon Muhammad ﷺ said:

> All mankind is descended from Adam and Eve, an Arab is not better than a non-Arab and a non-Arab is not better than an Arab; a white person is not better than a black person, nor is a black person better than a white person except by piety and good actions. Learn that every Muslim is the brother of every other Muslim and that Muslims form one brotherhood.

The first muezzin (the person who gives the call to prayer) chosen by Muhammad ﷺ was an Ethiopian former slave called Bilal. Racism has become an issue for many Muslims, not because they themselves are racist, but because of the way in which they are often treated by non-Muslims. It is often difficult to distinguish between racism and religious prejudice.

Muslims may fight racism but must obey those in authority unless they are required to go against the will of Allah.

> The Prophet invited us so we swore allegiance to him; and among the conditions which he laid down on us to follow was this: that he had a promise from us to hear and obey, whether we liked or disliked an order, and whether we were in adversity (trouble) or ease, even if our rights were not granted; and that we should not dispute the authority of those entrusted with it adding, 'Unless you see an act of open disbelief in which you have a clear argument from Allah.'
> (Hadith)

The role of women in Muslim society

Islam teaches that men and women are equal and that Allah will judge them equally according to the way in which they have lived.

To help men value women for who they are, rather than for their bodies, women wear garments that leave only the hands and face exposed.

And say to the believing women that they should lower their gaze and guard their modesty; that they should not display their beauty and ornaments except what (must ordinarily) appear thereof; that they should draw their veils over their bosoms and not display their beauty except to their husbands, their fathers, their husband's fathers, their sons, their husband's sons, their brothers or their brothers' sons, or their sisters' sons, or their women, or the slaves whom their right hands possess, or male servants free of physical needs, or small children who have no sense of the shame of sex; and that they should not strike their feet in order to draw attention to their hidden ornaments. And O ye Believers! Turn ye all together towards Allah, that ye may attain Bliss. (Surah 24:30–31)

Many non-Muslim westerners cannot understand Islamic teaching about women and feel that the need for women to be covered up in public and the way in which they are brought up is wrong. Some Muslim women, however, say that being covered is a statement of freedom because they feel that they are protected from being stared at and so are free to lead their lives without hindrance from men.

Men must also dress modestly and must always be covered from the navel to the knees.

According to Islam, the rights and responsibilities of a woman are equal to those of a man, but they are not identical and, therefore, they should be complementary to each other rather than competitive.

And women shall have rights similar to the rights against them, according to what is equitable; but men have a degree (of advantage) over them. And Allah is Exalted in Power, Wise. (Surah 2:228)

Shabina Begum took her school to court after the school refused to let her wear the jilbab. She lost her claim that she had been 'constructively excluded' as it was decided that the right to education and freedom of religion had not been violated.

In Islam this difference is seen as both natural and desirable. Men must support the family while women bear and rear children. Women have the right to study, refuse a marriage, to divorce, to inherit, to keep their own names, to own property, to take part in politics, and to conduct business, whether they are married or unmarried.

Some governments, saying that they are Islamic, impose harsh and repressive laws on women but these are not part of Islamic teaching.

Muhammad ﷺ stressed the respect which should be shown to women:

Paradise lies at the feet of your mother. (Sunan An-Nasa'i)

A man asked Prophet Muhammad ﷺ, 'O Messenger of Allah! Who deserves the best care from me?' The Prophet said, 'Your mother.' The man asked, 'Who then?' The Prophet said, 'Your mother.' The man asked yet again, 'Who then?' Prophet Muhammad ﷺ said, 'Your mother.' The man asked once

more, 'Who then?' The Prophet then said, 'Your father.'

(Sahih Al-Bukhari)

Activity

There have been many debates in recent years about Muslims and school uniforms such as the case of Shabina Begum pictured on page 132. Think about the issues carefully and consider whether religious believers should be able to wear particular clothes to school if they believe this is what their religion requires them to do.

Muslim attitudes towards other religions

Like Christianity, Islam sees itself as the only true religion and Muslims believe that they have a duty to lead other people into the faith:

Strongest among men in enmity to the Believers wilt thou find the Jews and the Pagans; and nearest among them in love to the Believers wilt thou find those who say, 'We are Christians': because amongst these are men devoted to learning and men who have renounced the world, and they are not arrogant.

(Surah 5:82)

If anyone desires a religion other than Islam (submission to Allah), never will it be accepted of him; and in the Hereafter he will be in the ranks of those who have lost (all spiritual good).   (Surah 3:85)

Muslims believe that all people are born with a natural instinct to be Muslims – this is called **'fitrah'**. People may belong to other religions but this is because of the way they were brought up. Therefore, when someone 'converts' to Islam, they are reverting or coming back to the religion into which they were born, not 'converting' as such.

A non-Muslim becomes a Muslim when he believes in his heart: 'There is no God but Allah and I bear witness that Muhammad ﷺ is His Messenger.'

Reverts are recommended to make this statement in front of at least two adult Muslim witnesses. They are also recommended to take a Muslim name, to follow a course on basic Islam and to associate with other Muslims.

It is not necessary for male reverts to be circumcised.

Muslims do not generally accept the validity of other religions and to do so would go against the teaching of the Qur'an and of Muhammad ﷺ. However, they still believe that all people are deserving of respect.

The position in relation to Jews and Christians is different, however, because they are all People of the Book – the Divine Word of Allah which was given to each group in turn until the true and final revelation came to Muhammad ﷺ.

Muslim beliefs about forgiveness and reconciliation

Allah forgives people who acknowledge that they are wrong and pray for forgiveness. Islam teaches that goodness is always better than evil:

Nor can Goodness and Evil be equal. Repel (Evil) with what is better: then will be between whom and thee was hatred become as it were thy friend and intimate!   (Surah 41:34)

Islamic law, Shari'ah, is based on the Qur'an and says how people are to be punished for crimes which they commit against others.

However, Shari'ah has very strict rules and procedures to safeguard the person who is being judged, to ensure that they have a fair trial and that the punishment is only that specified for the crime committed:
● People must be tried by a legal court.
● Murder of a robbery victim is punished by death.
● Bodily harm of a robbery victim is punished by cutting off a hand and a foot.
● Less serious crimes are punished by prison sentences.

Muslims believe that Allah is a merciful and forgiving ruler and judge and Muslims are required to follow this example:

> **Those who are kind and considerate to Allah's creatures, Allah bestows His kindness and affection on them.**
> (Abu Dawud, Tirmidhi)

So Muslims must follow the will of Allah and also follow his example in being forgiving to others.

Shari'ah, Islamic law, is based on the Qur'an and the belief that Allah is a forgiving judge.

Activity

1 Explain Muslim attitudes towards forgiveness and explain what is meant by Surahs 7:199 and 41:34.

2 Find out more about Shari'ah and how it works in a Muslim country.

Summary

So, how should we respond when something really isn't 'fair'? It seems that each of these religions believes that we should take some action to try and put things right. Whatever we do, it is likely to be a long time before we can really say that everyone is treated fairly and that there are no longer any wars being fought because people are living in peace. Nevertheless, this is a goal which each of these religions believes we should try to reach so that everyone can have a better, happier and fairer life.

Questions

1 What do you understand by:
  (a) prejudice
  (b) discrimination
  (c) fair, reasonable and equitable
  (d) racism
  (e) sexism
  (f) conversion?

2 Consider whether religious people should involve themselves in political questions such as issues of sexism and racism.

3 How far do you think members of different religions should try to overcome their differences and work together for the good of everyone? Is this a realistic aim?

4 Explain Muslim or Christian ideas about the role of women. What do you think a follower of one of these religions might say to someone who thought that this was unfair?

5 Find an example of a Muslim or Christian who has worked to combat racism and describe their work.

Practice GCSE questions

Christianity

1 (a) Describe Christian attitudes towards other religions. [8 marks]

(b) Explain Christian teachings about racism. [7 marks]

(c) 'People do not deserve to be treated equally.'
Do you agree? Give reasons to support your answer, and show that you have thought about different points of view. You must refer to Christianity in your answer. [5 marks]

2 (a) Describe Christian beliefs about equality. [8 marks]

(b) Explain Christian teaching about the role of women in society. [7 marks]

(c) 'Men and woman are not equal.'
Do you agree? Give reasons to support your answer, and show that you have thought about different points of view. You must refer to Christianity in your answer. [5 marks]

Tips

In your answer you should say that Christianity is a proselytising or evangelising religion and its teachings are that it is the only way to God and salvation. In addition you may want to consider the more modern liberal views held by some Christians.

In answering this question you may deal with general opinions about equality but also focus on biblical texts such as the passages of Leviticus and Galatians and church teachings. Remember that the Bible does not actually say that everyone is equal and the quotes from Paul are often misused in this context.

You are likely to disagree strongly with the statement and refer to Christian teaching in support, but you may also consider that there are some people whose actions and beliefs do not entitle them to equal treatment such as murderers, rapists and drug dealers. You might also consider that people who are disadvantaged in certain ways may need special treatment.

In your answer you could say that the New Testament does not actually teach that everyone is equal, except when talking about God's creation and the references in Paul which emphasise that all Christians are equal. You might also refer to texts in both the Old and New Testament which suggest that people should be treated equally. You might use church teaching to strengthen the argument.

In answering this question you might explain that Christianity has historically put women in a secondary role in society and the teaching about women priests might be used to illustrate this. Jesus' example of the treatment of his mother could stress one point, whilst the woman with the alabaster jar indicates another view.

Here, you are given a free rein to argue in both directions. Christian teaching might be used to show that men and women are equal. You might also argue that, whatever a religion might say, men and women are not, in fact, treated equally by society.

Islam

1 (a) Describe Muslim attitudes towards other religions. [8 marks]

(b) Explain Muslim teachings about racism. [7 marks]

(c) 'People do not deserve to be treated equally.'
Do you agree? Give reasons to support your answer, and show that you have thought about different points of view.
You must refer to Islam in your answer. [5 marks]

2 (a) Describe Muslim beliefs about equality. [8 marks]

(b) Explain Muslim teaching about the role of women in society. [7 marks]

(c) 'Men and woman are not equal.'
Do you agree? Give reasons to support your answer, and show that you have thought about different points of view.
You must refer to Islam in your answer. [5 marks]

Tips

In your answer you should say that Islam is a proselytizing or evangelising religion and its teachings are that it is the only way to Allah and salvation. In addition you may want to consider the more modern liberal views held by some people, though remember to refer specifically to Muslim teachings. You might also point out the respect that Islam shows towards the other Peoples of the Book.

In answering this question you may deal with general opinions about equality but also focus on texts from the Qur'an, which stress the centrality of equality in Muslim teachings. You may use references such as Allah making humanity in all its diversity to bring pleasure to people.

You are likely to disagree strongly with the statement and refer to Muslim teaching in support but you may also consider that there are some people whose actions and beliefs do not entitle them to equal treatment such as murderers, rapists and drug dealers. You might also consider that people who are disadvantaged in certain ways may need special treatment.

In your answer you could say that Islam teaches very clearly that everyone is equal and should be treated equally. The message is contained in the Qur'an when Allah creates humanity and says that different appearances and colours are to add variety and wonder, no-one should argue that some people are better than others.

In answering this question you might wish to consider media stereotypes about the treatment of women in society and cite extreme fundamentalist societies. On the other hand, you should explain that Islam itself teaches that woman have the right to run businesses, make and keep their own money and have the respect of men.

Here, you are given a free rein to argue in both directions. Muslim teaching might be used to show that men and women are equal though different. You might also argue that, whatever a religion might say, men and women are not, in fact, treated equally by society.

Introduction

This unit is concerned with religious responses to moral issues related to poverty and the use of money. It looks at:

- the causes of hunger, poverty and disease
- attitudes towards the poor and needy, giving to charity
- teachings about the use of money (e.g. gambling, lending)
- moral and immoral occupations.

The religions in this book both say that they believe in one God and they believe that this is a good God who would want everyone to be happy.

As God wants a good life for everyone, each religion teaches that its followers should work to make the world a better place for everyone.

In the world there is a very clear divide between the northern and southern hemispheres, with the north being generally much richer than the south. These southern poorer countries are now generally referred to as the developing world. In these developing countries most people have a very poor quality of life compared to those who live in the developed countries of the north.

In the developing world there may be no running water; no regular supplies of food; poor housing, if any; no medical care; and no education. This contrasts sharply with the lifestyle of most people north of the equator.

It is not easy to say why so many people are poor and suffer from hunger and disease. The media frequently reports the effects of bad weather and poor harvests as well as corrupt governments and civil and international wars. However, it cannot be denied that, in the past, many of the countries of the western world looted and exploited these developing countries, robbing them of their wealth and natural resources. The rich countries still control the world's wealth and resources and the continuous appeals in the 21st century for fair trade for farmers in these countries show that the exploitation continues.

It is difficult, then, for religious people to accept a world where many people are poor and suffering whilst others are more comfortable in their lives.

In the past, some religious people have invested money in countries and industries where people are exploited and treated in a way that is completely against the teachings of the religion.

Today, most people would think that this is wrong and would say that religions should work towards ending poverty and helping people to improve their living standards.

Central to this discussion is the Universal Declaration of Human Rights which was signed by the General Assembly of the United Nations on 10 December 1948. This laid out the basic rights to which the people of the world should be entitled. Most important for us, perhaps, is the First Article of the Declaration which says:

All human beings are born free and equal in dignity and rights. They are endowed with reason and conscience and should act towards one another in a spirit of brotherhood.

Bill Gates is the world's richest man and has approximately $56 billion. This makes him richer than many countries in the world.

Preamble to the Universal Declaration of Human Rights:

Whereas recognition of the inherent [inseparable] dignity and of the equal and inalienable [can not be changed] rights of all members of the human family is the foundation of freedom, justice and peace in the world,

Whereas disregard and contempt for human rights have resulted in barbarous [very cruel] acts which have outraged the conscience of mankind, and the advent of a world in which human beings shall enjoy freedom of speech and belief and freedom from fear and want has been proclaimed as the highest aspiration [desire] of the common people,

Whereas it is essential, if man is not to be compelled to have recourse, as a last resort, to rebellion against tyranny and oppression [abusive power from governments] that human rights should be protected by the rule of law,

Whereas it is essential to promote the development of friendly relations between nations,

Whereas the peoples of the United Nations have in the Charter reaffirmed their faith in fundamental human rights, in the dignity and worth of the human person and in the equal rights of men and women and have determined to promote social progress and better standards of life in larger freedom,

Whereas Member States have pledged themselves to achieve, in co-operation with the United Nations, the promotion of universal respect for and observance of human rights and fundamental freedoms,

Whereas a common understanding of these rights and freedoms is of the greatest importance for the full realisation of this pledge...

Sometimes people may find that the wish or desire to have something may put them into conflict with what their religion teaches. The teaching of the tenth commandment is central to this way of thinking:

You shall not covet your neighbour's house. You shall not covet your neighbour's wife, or his manservant or maidservant, his ox or donkey, or anything that belongs to your neighbour.
(Exodus 20:17)

Religious people must ask themselves whether they are behaving honestly and properly towards others, as their religion teaches, this includes when they are at work and will effect what kind of jobs they do.

Activity

There are many very rich people in the world, some of these are people such as popstars and footballers. They have more money than they will ever be able to spend.

(a) To what extent do you feel that it is 'fair' or 'just' that people should be so rich?

(b) Do you think they should be required by law to give some of their money to charity?

(c) Do you think they should not be allowed to earn so much?

Give reasons to support your answers.

Christianity

This topic looks at:
- Christian teaching about concern for the poor and the right uses of money
- giving to charity in Christianity
- Christian teaching about moral and immoral occupations.

Christian teaching about concern for the poor and the right uses of money

Christianity has many teachings which are to do with the treatment of other people. The duty of caring for the poor is central to Christian belief. Many Christians would see this following passage as one of the most important teachings of Jesus:

> One of the teachers of the law came and heard them debating. Noticing that Jesus had given them a good answer, he asked him, 'Of all the commandments, which is the most important?'
>
> 'The most important one,' answered Jesus, 'is this: "Hear, O Israel, the Lord our God, the Lord is one. Love the Lord your God with all your heart and with all your soul and with all your mind and with all your strength." The second is this: "Love your neighbour as yourself.'"There is no commandment greater than these.' (Mark 12:28–31)

This duty is also found in the Old Testament:

> If one of your countrymen becomes poor and is unable to support himself among you, help him as you would an alien or a temporary resident, so he can continue to live among you. Do not take interest of any kind from him, but fear your God, so that your countryman may continue to live among you. You must not lend him money at interest or sell him food at a profit. (Leviticus 25:35–37)

Jesus made clear his mission by quoting from the book of Isaiah and explained that he came to help the poor in whatever way he could:

> The Spirit of the Lord is on me, because he has anointed me to preach good news to the poor. He has sent me to proclaim freedom for the prisoners and recovery of sight for the blind, to release the oppressed, to proclaim the year of the Lord's favour. (Luke 4:18–19)

He explained this further to his disciples in the Sermon on the Plain from Luke's gospel:

> Looking at his disciples, he said: 'Blessed are you who are poor, for yours is the kingdom of God. Blessed are you who hunger now, for you will be satisfied.' (Luke 6:20–21)

Here, however, he is explaining that people will be happy in the kingdom of heaven rather than on earth.

Jesus explained to his followers that they should give away their riches in order to follow God. He said that:

> it is easier for a camel to go through the eye of a needle than for a rich man to enter the kingdom of God. (Luke 18:25)

Christianity is not opposed to people having wealth and enjoying their life but this can only be done after they have taken steps to help the poor. It is wrong for a Christian to be rich when other people are starving. At the time of Jesus many people believed that possessing wealth was a gift from God and Jesus warned them of the dangers of this:

> Then he said to them, 'Watch out! Be on your guard against all kinds of greed; a man's life does not consist in the abundance of his possessions.'

And he told them this parable: 'The ground of a certain rich man produced a good crop. He thought to himself, "What shall I do? I have no place to store my crops."

Then he said, "This is what I'll do. I will tear down my barns and build bigger ones, and there I will store all my grain and my goods. And I'll say to myself, 'You have plenty of good things laid up for many years. Take life easy; eat, drink and be merry.'"

But God said to him, "You fool! This very night your life will be demanded from you. Then who will get what you have prepared for yourself?"'

This is how it will be with anyone who stores up things for himself but is not rich toward God.

(Luke 12:15–21)

No-one can serve two masters. Either he will hate the one and love the other, or he will be devoted to the one and despise the other. You cannot serve both God and Money.

Therefore I tell you, do not worry about your life, what you will eat or drink; or about your body, what you will wear. Is not life more important than food, and the body more important than clothes? Look at the birds of the air; they do not sow or reap or store away in barns, and yet your heavenly Father feeds them. Are you not much more valuable than they? Who of you by worrying can add a single hour to his life?

And why do you worry about clothes? See how the lilies of the field grow. They do not labour or spin. Yet I tell you that not even Solomon in all his splendour was dressed like one of these. If that is how God clothes the grass of the field, which is here today and

tomorrow is thrown into the fire, will he not much more clothe you, O you of little faith? So do not worry, saying, 'What shall we eat?' or 'What shall we drink?' or 'What shall we wear?'

(Matthew 6:24–31)

Jesus taught his followers that they had a duty to look after other people and he gives the following teaching in the Parable of the Sheep and the Goats:

For I was hungry and you gave me something to eat, I was thirsty and you gave me something to drink, I was a stranger and you invited me in, I needed clothes and you clothed me, I was sick and you looked after me, I was in prison and you came to visit me.

(Matthew 25:35–36)

This gives an example of how Christians should behave towards others.

The first Christians followed his teachings according to the Acts of the Apostles:

All the believers were together and had everything in common. Selling their possessions and goods, they gave to anyone as he had need. (Acts 2:44–45)

Activity

Explain why Jesus said that it was easier for a poor person to get into heaven than a rich one.

Giving to charity in Christianity

As he looked up, Jesus saw the rich putting their gifts into the temple treasury. He also saw a poor widow put in two very small copper coins. 'I tell you the truth,' he said, 'this poor widow has put in more than all the others. All these people gave their gifts out of their wealth; but she out of her poverty put in all she had to live on.' (Luke 21:1–4)

As well as giving the example of poor people who still gave charity, Jesus also taught that charity should be carried out privately and not publicly:

> Be careful not to do your 'acts of righteousness' before men, to be seen by them. If you do, you will have no reward from your Father in heaven.
>
> So when you give to the needy, do not announce it with trumpets, as the hypocrites do in the synagogues and on the streets, to be honoured by men. I tell you the truth, they have received their reward in full. But when you give to the needy, do not let your left hand know what your right hand is doing, so that your giving may be in secret. Then your Father, who sees what is done in secret, will reward you.
>
> (Matthew 6:3–4)

Today, as the world seems to become more and more secular (non-religious), many people feel that making money is the main purpose of their lives. The enormous success of the National Lottery and of 'scratch cards' in the United Kingdom shows how much people want money.

There are several teachings about the use of money in the epistles of the New Testament:

> People who want to get rich fall into temptation and a trap and into many foolish and harmful desires that plunge men into ruin and destruction. For the love of money is a root of all kinds of evil. Some people, eager for money, have wandered from the faith and pierced themselves with many griefs. (1 Timothy 6:9–10)
>
> If anyone has material possessions and sees his brother in need but has no pity on him, how can the love of God be in him? (1 John 3:17)
>
> On the first day of every week, each one of you should set aside a sum of money in keeping with his income, saving it up, so that when I come no collections will have to be made. (1 Corinthians 16:2)

The Second Vatican Council of the Roman Catholic Church said that there was no separation between the religious and the secular world. It is all God's; therefore faith and justice are linked together.

The Catechism of the Catholic Church says that:

> True happiness is not found in riches or well-being, in human fame or power, or in any human achievement... God blesses those who come to the aid of the poor and rebukes those who turn away from them.

It continues by stressing that:

> Rich nations have a grave moral responsibility towards those which are unable to ensure the means of their development by themselves.

In the past, many people supported the poor through paying church tithes. Tithing is an ancient custom where people gave a tenth of their income to the church to be used for various purposes, including caring for the poor. Tithing was finally abolished in England in 1936. Today, people may give to collections during church services where the money is often used for charity work and for the upkeep and running of the church itself.

In recent years, the Christian churches have concerned themselves more with issues such as poverty and the fairer distribution of wealth in the world. The truth is that a few very rich nations hold most of the world's wealth and that resources of both money and food are not distributed equally.

Charities such as Christian Aid, CAFOD and Tearfund have been set up to try to co-ordinate the work of the churches and to try to ensure that millions of people are not left starving while the rest of the world is well fed and has a good standard of living.

In 1981, the General Synod of the Church of England said that:

the Synod [believes] that, as a matter of common humanity and of our mutual interest in survival, the world requires a new and more equitable system of economic relationships between nations.

Discussion

It has often been said that because of the National Lottery, people are now giving less to charities. Try to find out if there is any evidence for this. Do you think lotteries should be allowed if people are playing them rather than giving to charity?

Activity

Choose one Christian charity. Find out what it does and how it raises money for its work. Explain what particular religious teachings the charity is trying to put into practice.

Christian teaching about moral and immoral occupations

When it comes to business, Christians have a duty to ensure that they way in which they earn their living does not have a bad effect on other people. You could argue therefore that Christians should not be involved in the arms trade, in prostitution or pornography (the making and selling of sexually explicit material). Some people say that Christian doctors and nurses must never take part in an abortion. In the past, some Christians and some churches were involved in South Africa in a way which helped to strengthen the evil apartheid system which was in force there (see Unit 8).

Today, one of the most common areas of discussion about Christians and business relates to Sunday trading. In recent years, the law in the United Kingdom has been changed so that all shops can open on a Sunday. Some Christians have said that this breaks the fourth commandment:

Remember the Sabbath day by keeping it holy. Six days you shall labour and do all your work, but the seventh day is a Sabbath to the Lord your God. On it you shall not do any work, neither you, nor your son or daughter, nor your manservant or maidservant, nor your animals, nor the alien within your gates. For in six days the Lord made the heavens and the earth, the sea, and all that is in them, but he rested on the seventh day. Therefore the Lord blessed the Sabbath day and made it holy. (Exodus 20:8)

Christianity has no particular rules about what jobs people should or should not do. However, individual Christians might feel that they should choose work which is related to helping people, society or the environment, rather than work which might exploit other people or go against Christian teachings such as gambling or pornography.

Some Christians do take a different position in relation to some occupations. Methodists and the Salvation Army, for example, do not approve of the use of alcohol and many Christians are opposed to gambling. In both cases, this is because they see these activities as damaging families and individuals even though there are no specific biblical teachings about them.

Christians have different attitudes towards lending money at interest:

Here are two contrasting teachings, the first from the Old Testament and the second from the New Testament:

If you lend money to one of my people among you who is needy, do not be like a moneylender; charge him no interest.
(Exodus 22:25)

Again, it will be like a man going on a journey, who called his servants and entrusted his property to them. To one he gave

five talents of money, to another two talents, and to another one talent, each according to his ability. Then he went on his journey. The man who had received the five talents went at once and put his money to work and gained five more. So also, the one with the two talents gained two more. But the man who had received the one talent went off, dug a hole in the ground and hid his master's money.

After a long time the master of those servants returned and settled accounts with them. The man who had received the five talents brought the other five. 'Master,' he said, 'you entrusted me with five talents. See, I have gained five more.'

His master replied, 'Well done, good and faithful servant! You have been faithful with a few things; I will put you in charge of many things. Come and share your master's happiness!'

The man with the two talents also came. 'Master,' he said, 'you entrusted me with two talents; see, I have gained two more.'

His master replied, 'Well done, good and faithful servant! You have been faithful with a few things; I will put you in charge of many things. Come and share your master's happiness!'

Then the man who had received the one talent came. 'Master,' he said, 'I knew that you are a hard man, harvesting where you have not sown and gathering where you have not scattered seed. So I was afraid and went out and hid your talent in the ground. See, here is what belongs to you.'

His master replied, 'You wicked, lazy servant! So you knew that I harvest where I have not sown and gather where I have not scattered seed? Well then, you

should have put my money on deposit with the bankers, so that when I returned I would have received it back with interest.

'Take the talent from him and give it to the one who has the ten talents. For everyone who has will be given more, and he will have an abundance. Whoever does not have, even what he has will be taken from him. And throw that worthless servant outside, into the darkness, where there will be weeping and gnashing of teeth.'

(Matthew 25:14–30)

One modern development which is particularly concerned with the issues of equality for all people is liberation theology. This is a belief that people who follow Jesus' teachings must take positive action to fight against social injustice and the misuse of power by governments. This idea has followers from both the Protestant and Roman Catholic churches. Liberation theology is particularly strong amongst the priests in Latin America and parts of Asia and Africa. If the law acts against ordinary people in a way which is un-Christian, these people believe that they have a duty to oppose and, if necessary, break the law.

The Spirit of the Lord is on me, because he has anointed me to preach good news to the poor. He has sent me to proclaim freedom for the prisoners and recovery of sight for the blind, to release the oppressed,

(Luke 4:18)

Two famous Liberation Theology priests are Fr. Camillo Torres and Archbishop Oscar Romero:

- Camillo Torres was a Columbian who took part in armed uprisings and insisted that the Catholic who is not a revolutionary is living in mortal sin. He was shot dead in 1966 CE.
- Oscar Romero (1917–1980) was Bishop of El Savador. A close friend of Romero, Rutilo Grande was killed by government forces for his outspoken opposition to the country's politics. Romero preached sermons every Sunday on the radio. These were very critical of the way

in which the poor were treated. He opposed violence but encouraged poor people to organise in order to oppose the government. In March 1980 he himself was killed while celebrating mass.

In Latin America he is often referred to as 'St Romero of the Americas'.

Activity

Consider carefully whether there are any jobs that you would not do for moral reasons. Explain your reasons.

Archbishop Oscar Romero.

Islam

This topic looks at:
- Muslim teaching about concern for the poor and the right uses of money
- giving to charity in Islam
- Muslim teaching about moral and immoral occupations.

Muslim teaching about concern for the poor and the right uses of money

> Ye are the best of peoples, evolved for mankind, enjoining what is right, forbidding what is wrong, and believing in Allah.
> (Surah 3:110)

The greed and selfishness of the merchants in Makkah prompted Muhammad ﷺ to show that Islam had great concern for the poor. From the very beginning, he saw the practical, material world as part of Allah's creation and tried to combine spiritual ideals with daily living in the Islamic community. He wanted to fight the material concerns (thinking about money and possessions) of the merchants with the spiritual ideas of the Islamic community. He was able to do this when he moved to al-Madinah where there were many poor and suffering people, as well as the followers who had left everything, home and property, to follow him to al-Madinah.

Hoarding is forbidden in Islam. Wealth should be circulated because then everybody benefits. Making money by charging interest is forbidden so Muslims do not lend, borrow or invest money at interest.

Muslim teaching about poverty and zakah

To Muslims, all wealth and riches come from Allah and are for the benefit of all humanity. Central to Islamic belief in this matter is zakah (purification of wealth by payment of welfare due) which is one of the Five Pillars.

> And be steadfast in prayer and regular in charity: and whatever good ye send forth for your souls before you, ye shall find it with Allah: for Allah sees well all that ye do.
> (Surah 2:110)

Zakah is also central to the ummah, the worldwide brotherhood of Muslims. It is also an act of 'ibadah, duty and worship, and every Muslim must do it.

Zakah purifies the wealth that a Muslim has left so that no harm can come to them from it. Zakah itself is 2.5% of the income and savings of all Muslims after they have taken care of their families. It is not a charitable donation that people can choose to make, but an obligation (something they feel they have to do) on all Muslims. However, the rich pay more than the less well off and very poor people pay nothing at all.

The calculations for zakah are complex and made after all essential bills, personal expenses and family expenditure have been allowed for.

Zakah	
Money and savings	2%
Produce from naturally irrigated land	10%
Produce from artificially irrigated land	5%
Cattle	one per 30 animals
Goats and sheep	one per 40 animals
Five camels	one sheep or goat
Precious metals	7%
Mining produce	20%
Rent	2%

In an Islamic state zakah is a form of social security: it ensures that food, clothing, housing, medicine and education can be provided for every person.

> Alms are for the poor and the needy, and those employed to administer the (funds); for those whose hearts have been (recently) reconciled (to the Truth); for

those in bondage and in debt; in the cause of Allah; and for the wayfarer. (Surah 9:60)

> Bondage – slavery.
> Wayfarer – traveller.

Extra zakah is given at the festivals of Id-ul-Fitr and Id-ul-Adha. Additional voluntary charity called sadaqah can also be given when someone is in need.

> It is not righteousness that ye turn your faces towards East or West; but it is righteousness—to believe in Allah and the Last Day, and the Angels and the Book, and the Messengers; to spend of your substance, out of love for Him, for your kin, for orphans, for the needy, for the wayfarer, for those who ask, and for the ransom of slaves; to be steadfast in prayer, and practise regular charity, to fulfil their contracts which ye have made; and to be firm and patient, in pain (or suffering) and adversity, and throughout all periods of panic. Such are the people of truth, the God-fearing.
> (Surah 2:177)

> Adversity – trouble.

Charity should always be given privately:

> There is a man who gives charity and he conceals it so much that his left hand does not know what his right hand spends. (Hadith)

People should not boast about how much they give. The only exception to this would be when the giver is setting an example to encourage other people to give.

> Every day, each person has two angels near him who have descended from heaven. One says, 'O Allah!, compensate the person who gives to charity,' the other says, 'O Allah! Inflict a loss on the person who withholds his money.' (Hadith)

The poor do not see zakah as charity but as the right of the poor as members of the Muslim community to receive assistance. It purifies the poor because it frees them from the temptation to be jealous. When they accept zakah they too are worshipping Allah and accepting the wisdom of the will of Allah. The poor help the rich who give zakah to store up true riches with Allah.

> It is He Who hath made you (His) agents, inheritors of the earth: He hath raised you in ranks, some above others: that He may try you in the gifts He hath given you: for thy Lord is quick in punishment: yet He is indeed Oft-forgiving, Most Merciful. (Surah 6:165)

Some Muslims have started their own charity organisations to collect money to help people in need. There are many Muslim charities across the world:

Islamic Aid

Islamic Aid seeks to make immediate and lasting improvements to the lives of people affected by poverty, war and disaster.

Islamic Aid at work in a disaster area.

Islamic Relief Mission

Islamic Relief is an international relief and development charity, which aims to end the suffering of the world's poorest people. It is an independent Non-Governmental Organisation (NGO) founded in the United Kingdom in 1984 by Dr Hany El Banna. Islamic Relief is dedicated to alleviating the poverty and suffering of the world's poorest people.

> if any one saved a life, it would be as if he saved the life of the whole people (Surah 5:32)

Muslim Aid

Muslim Aid has helped save and improve the lives of millions of people in 50 of the poorest countries around the world. Muslim Aid provides relief to victims of natural disasters, wars and famine and, through long-term development programmes such as provision of clean water, shelter, education, income-generation and healthcare, Muslim Aid is tackling the root causes of poverty.

Discussion

Research the work of one Muslim charity. Find out what it does, how it raises its money and the particular Muslim teachings which it works to put into practice.

Activity

Explain why Muhammad ﷺ wanted to make social changes in al-Madinah.

Muslim teaching about moral and immoral occupations

Muslims are required to live according to the teachings of the Qur'an and therefore some occupations and activities are forbidden.

Money-lending where the lender benefits from **riba** (interest) is forbidden:

> That which ye lay out for increase through the property of (other) people, will have no increase with Allah. (Surah 30:39)

When people do owe money, Muslims are encouraged to be sympathetic to the debtor:

> If the debtor is in a difficulty, grant him time till it is easy for him to repay. But if ye remit it by way of charity, that is best for you if ye only knew. (Surah 2:280)

There are Muslim banks which have set up special facilities so that Muslims are able to borrow money without the bank making interest on the loan.

Along with not lending money at interest, all forms of gambling and activities such as lotteries are also forbidden in Islam:

> Satan's plan is (but) to excite enmity and hatred between you, with intoxicants and gambling, and hinder you from the remembrance of Allah, and from prayer: will ye not then abstain? (Surah 5:91)

This has sometimes led to problems in countries where there are lotteries and the money is given to charitable causes. Many Muslims feel that they cannot take charitable donations towards, for example, building a new mosque or school, if the money has come from gambling or a lottery.

Muslims in the United Kingdom take an active part in raising money for their mosque where it is distributed to the poor; many will send money to Muslim communities abroad. Muslim charities such as Muslim Aid and Islamic Relief work to help people in developing countries.

> The generous man is near God, near Paradise, near men and far from Hell, and the ignorant man who is generous is dearer to God than a worshipper who is miserly. (Hadith)

Work is an essential part of Islamic life. This is stressed in the Qur'an:

> But Allah has created you and your handiwork! (Surah 37:96)

The Qur'an also records the ways in which Muslims should not earn their living. Muslims cannot profit from alcohol or gambling, from brothels or prostitution:

> Women impure are for men impure, and men impure for women impure, and women of purity are for men of purity, and men of purity are for women of purity. (Surah 24:26)

nor from lying, fraud or burglary:

> **And do not eat up your property among yourselves for vanities, nor use it as bait for the judges, with intent that ye may eat up wrongfully and knowingly a little of (other) peoples' property.**
> (Surah 2:188)

The two pillars of salah (prayer) and sawm (fasting from sunrise to sunset through the month of Ramadan) are also important elements in Muslim teaching about work.

Praying five times a day at fixed times means that work is put into perspective when Muslims stop their normal activities to think about Allah. This is particularly true of Salat-ul-Jumu'ah, the weekly prayers at noon on Fridays. Islam does not have a day of rest but all Muslims should try to attend these prayers each Friday and hear the khutbah (talk) given by the imam. In a similar way, the fast of Ramadan brings people closer together in ummah (the world Islamic community) and helps them to focus on God when they are also controlling their bodies.

Discussion

There have been occasions when Muslims have been offered money from lotteries to help build a new mosque. Explain how Muslims might respond to this offer and why.

Activity

1 Explain Muslim teaching about zakah and how it helps the whole community.

2 Do you think that it would be a good idea if all religious believers were required to give 2.5% of their surplus income to the poor and the community? Explain your answer.

Summary

Although their practices may be different, both of these religions stress the importance of equality and they could both be said to be working towards the First Article of the Declaration of Human Rights:

All human beings are born free and equal in dignity and rights. They are endowed with reason and conscience and should act towards one another in a spirit of brotherhood.

Muslims and Christians both believe that wealth should be fairly distributed and that they should work not only to support their families but also to help those who are less fortunate. It is by doing this that they reflect God's love for them and for all humanity.

Questions

1 What do you understand by:
  (a) human rights
  (b) charity
  (c) materialism
  (d) interest
  (e) the developing world
  (f) liberation theology?

2 The Declaration of Human Rights was written in 1948. Do you think there are still things that religious believers can do to improve the way in which it works?

3 How far do you think religion should 'interfere' in the way in which business is done?

4 Explain how religious people might decide how much of their money they should keep and how much they should give to charity.

5 Explain why some religious people might say that it is wrong to take part in a public lottery.

6 Consider whether people should take a more active part in helping others as liberation theology proposes.

7 Some people say that being poor is a person's own fault and that they should solve their own problems. Explain how you would react to this idea.

Practice GCSE questions

Christianity

1 (a) Describe Christian teachings about concern for the poor. **[8 marks]**

(b) Explain why Christians might give money to charity. **[7 marks]**

(c) 'People must look after their family before they worry about the poor.' Do you agree? Give reasons to support your answer, and show that you have thought about different points of view. You must refer to Christianity in your answer. **[5 marks]**

2 (a) Describe Christian teachings about the use of money. **[8 marks]**

(b) Explain how Christian beliefs might affect a person's choice of career. **[7 marks]**

(c) 'It does not matter how you get your money, as long as you look after your family.' Do you agree? Give reasons to support your answer, and show that you have thought about different points of view. You must refer to Christianity in your answer. **[5 marks]**

Tips

In your answer you may write about Christian teachings from the New Testament, including those of Jesus and the ones found in the epistles. You could also describe the practical example set by Jesus and his disciples of caring for the poor.

It is important to remember that you are being asked 'why' Christians might give money and not 'how'. You could also explain that charity has always been part of Christianity since the time of the Deacons in Jerusalem and before. You might also talk about church tithing or collections as examples of helping the less fortunate.

There is no 'right' answer to this question. You might suggest that care for the family goes without saying as a first principle of life, regardless of religion. On the other hand, you might consider that concern for the poor is such an important aspect of Christian faith that it must override all other issues.

Here, you might consider Jesus' teachings about the right use of money and, in particular, the widow's mite, the rich young man and his teachings about charity in Matthew 5–7. You might also consider ideas of not wasting money on luxuries or unnecessary indulgence and stress the idea of moderation.

In your answer you might explain that some people will be drawn to work for the Church or their religion – this may be seen as a vocation. You might also consider moral and immoral occupations, such as prostitution, loan sharks, mercenaries, pornography, etc.

Building on your answer to (b) you might consider whether looking after a family is more important than considerations of morality. You might decide that concern for the family means that people will be prepared to make money in immoral ways if necessary. Remember that you must refer to specific Christian teachings in your answer.

Islam

1 (a) Describe Muslim teachings about
concern for the poor. [8 marks]

(b) Explain why Muslims might give money
to charity. [7 marks]

(c) 'People must look after their family
before they worry about the poor.'
Do you agree? Give reasons to support
your answer, and show that you have
thought about different points of view.
You must refer to Islam in your answer.
[5 marks]

2 (a) Describe Muslim teachings about the use
of money. [8 marks]

(b) Explain how Muslim beliefs might affect
a person's choice of career. [7 marks]

(c) 'It does not matter how you get your
money, as long as you look after your
family.'
Do you agree? Give reasons to support
your answer and show that you have
thought about different points of view.
You must refer to Islam in your answer.
[5 marks]

Tips

In your answer you may write about Muslim teachings from the Qur'an and, though not strictly charity, in the teaching about zakah. You should be able to describe zakah in detail and also mention sadaqah in your answer.

It is important to remember that you are being asked 'why' Muslims might give money and not 'how'. You might also explain that charity has always been part of Islam since the time of Muhammad ﷺ and is ordered in the Qur'an. You might refer to zakah as well as to specific Muslim charitable work and organisations.

There is no 'right' answer to this question. You might suggest that care for the family goes without saying as a first principle of life, regardless of religion. On the other hand, you might consider that concern for the poor is such an important aspect of Islam that it must override all other issues.

Here, you might consider general Muslim teachings about the use of money, responsibility and zakah. You might also consider ideas of not wasting money on luxuries or unnecessary indulgence and stress the idea of moderation.

In your answer you might explain that some people will be drawn to work for the mosque or for the wide Muslim community. You might also consider moral and immoral occupations, such as prostitution, loan sharks, mercenaries, pornography, etc.

Building on your answer to (b) you might consider whether looking after a family is more important than considerations of morality. You might decide that concern for the family means that people will be prepared to make money in immoral ways if necessary. You must remember to refer to specific Muslims teachings in your answer.

Introduction

This unit is concerned with religious responses to moral issues of war, peace, violence and justice. It looks at:

- attitudes towards war
- attitudes towards violence and pacifism
- issues of crime and punishment, government and justice.

Attitudes towards war

The most severe physical suffering and death can be a result of war. All war is an attempt by one power to defend itself against another or to try to take something, which may be as basic as freedom, from another group.

Most people would probably agree that war is wrong but religions have developed two theories which are sometimes used to defend or even support war.

Holy War

This is the idea that sometimes it is necessary to use physical violence in order to defend religion. The Crusades of a thousand years ago are one example of this, where Christian Europe claimed the Holy Land (the country which is now known as Israel) from the Muslims who governed it.

Just War

Sometimes a war is described as 'just' (fair). A **Just War** is one which is fought according to certain conditions. The first three conditions were developed by Thomas Aquinas (1224–1274):

1 It must be fought by a legal authority, e.g. a government.
2 The cause must be just.
3 There must be the intention to establish good or correct evil.

Later, four further conditions were added:

4 There must be a reasonable chance of success.
5 It must be the last resort.
6 Only sufficient force must be used and civilians should not be involved.
7 The benefits should outweigh the cost.

These conditions are designed to prevent war happening and to limit its effects. Some

wars can meet all of these conditions. For example, the Second World War 1939–1945 would appear to have been a Just War:

1 It was fought by Germany, Japan and the Allied countries (Britain, France, USSR, USA), who were legal authorities.
2 Germany was being attacked for invading other countries.
3 The intention was to correct the evil which Germany was doing.
4 The Allies felt that they had a reasonable chance of success and they did win.
5 All forms of negotiation with Hitler and the Third Reich had failed.
6 Most of the fighting was limited to the armies concerned and to harbours and munitions sites.

This looks as though it was a 'properly constituted' Just War. However, some of the actions within the war certainly broke condition 6. One of these was the Allied bombing of Dresden, a two-day raid by almost 2,400 bombers that destroyed the city and killed perhaps 135,000 civilians, to virtually no military purpose. During the 'Blitz', London was heavily bombed by the

Wars are fought every every year.

German Airforce and many civilians were killed and injured.

It is also necessary to consider the use by America of the first atom bombs during the Second World War. On 6 August, 1945 the first atomic bomb was dropped on the Japanese city of Hiroshima. It was reported that 129,558 people were killed, injured or missing and that a further 176,987 were made homeless by the bombing. The bombing flattened more than 60% of the city. Three days later on 9 August, another atomic bomb was dropped on the city of Nagasaki. This destroyed a third of the city and 66,000 people were killed or injured. Were these extreme actions really necessary to end the war?

Attitudes towards violence and pacifism

Many religious people believe that war and fighting is wrong, regardless of the outcome. Generally, pacifists do not approve of fighting, though some might permit action in terms of self-defence. During a war, people who will not fight because they believe that all fighting is wrong are called **conscientious objectors**. The best known of these are the Religious Society of Friends (Quakers). They will drive ambulances or provide any sort of support services but will not fight under any conditions.

Some religions, such as Hinduism, have particularly strong views on fighting. Hindus such as Gandhi, hold a belief called satyagraha, non-violent, non-co-operation which is a type of protest which does not involve physical violence. Other religions such as Baha'i are totally opposed to all forms of violence and discrimination and work actively to promote world peace and understanding.

Christianity and Islam have teachings about war and peace that may vary according to the situation in which believers find themselves.

The problems which can arise when someone does not want to become involved in other people's fights can be seen in this poem which was written by a Christian minister living in Nazi Germany:

First they came for
the Communists
and I did not speak out –
because I was not a Communist.
Then they came for the trade
unionists and I did not speak out –
because I was not a trade unionist.
Then they came for the Jews
and I did not speak out –
because I was not a Jew.
Then they came for me –
And there was no one left
to speak out for me.
(Pastor Niemöller)

Issues of crime and punishment, government and justice

Punishment theory

The punishment of criminals or wrongdoers can be said to have four possible aims. The specific aims may depend on the crime or the person being punished.

1 Deterrence – this may be individual: to deter the person from doing the same thing again, or general: to deter other people from doing the same thing.
2 Protection – to protect society and innocent people from harm.
3 Retribution – so that society and the victims of crime can see that the person has been punished.
4 Reformation – to give the criminal the chance to reform and live a better life.

Social injustice

The phrase 'social injustice' is used when some people are discriminated against in a society and have fewer rights or benefits than others.

Discussion

How far would you agree that there are some occasions when physical fighting is the only solution?

Activity

Although punishment theory has four different aims, consider whether most people just want people who have done wrong to suffer for their crimes.

Christianity

This topic is about:
- Christian attitudes towards war – the Just War
- Christian attitudes towards the use of violence and pacifism
- Christian beliefs about the treatment of criminals
- Christian responses to social injustice.

Christian attitudes towards war

Christianity is a religion which teaches that peace is what people should work for and fighting is always seen as essentially wrong. However, a war may be seen as justified if it is fought to overcome evil.

Many Christians believe that it is possible to fight a 'Just War', while some are very strict pacifists. During the two world wars many Christians, especially Quakers, were 'conscientious objectors', they refused to fight, but were often right at the front of the battle because they worked as medical orderlies or ambulance drivers. Pacifists believe that any response to war or conflict must be non-violent. Therefore they would agree with negotiations and sanctions (preventing a country from trading) but not physical fighting.

Some pacifists argue that the Christian principle of agape – love – means that violence is never acceptable. This is the principle of selfless love which Jesus taught:

> **Greater love has no one than this, that he lay down his life for his friends.** (John 15:13)

> **Dear friends, let us love one another, for love comes from God. Everyone who loves has been born of God and knows God.** (1 John 4:7)

Christians might also use non-violent protest such as boycotts and demonstrations to try to persuade other people not to go to war. A boycott is when people refuse to take part in something; you might boycott a certain brand of clothing by refusing to buy it or boycott a place by not going there.

Christian attitudes towards the use of violence and pacifism

There are many instances in the Old Testament of the Bible where violence is ordered by God and he commands the Israelites to fight wars against other peoples:

> **Then Moses went out and spoke these words to all Israel: 'I am now a hundred and twenty years old and I am no longer able to lead you. The Lord has said to me, "You shall not cross the Jordan." The Lord your God himself will cross over ahead of you. He will destroy these nations before you, and you will take possession of their land. Joshua also will cross over ahead of you, as the Lord said. And the Lord will do to them what he did to Sihon and Og, the kings of the Amorites, whom he destroyed along with their land. The Lord will deliver them to you, and you must do to them all that I have commanded you. Be strong and courageous. Do not be afraid or terrified because of**

An anti-war protest in London.

them, for the Lord your God goes with you; he will never leave you nor forsake you.'

(Deuteronomy 31:1–6)

People sometimes say that the Ten Commandments forbid killing but, in fact, the sixth commandment is:

You shall not commit murder.

(Exodus 20:13)

Christians believe that murder is different from killing. This can be seen in the next chapter of Exodus:

Anyone who attacks his father or his mother must be put to death.

Anyone who kidnaps another and either sells him or still has him when he is caught must be put to death.

Anyone who curses his father or mother must be put to death.

(Exodus 21:15–17)

However, the writers of the Old Testament looked forward to an era of peace:

'Come, let us go up to the mountain of the Lord, to the house of the God of Jacob. He will teach us his ways, so that we may walk in his paths.' The law will go out from Zion, the word of the Lord from Jerusalem. He will judge between many peoples and will settle disputes for strong nations far and wide. They will beat their swords into plowshares and their spears into pruning hooks. Nation will not take up sword against nation, nor will they train for war anymore. All the nations may walk in the name of their gods; we will walk in the name of the Lord our God for ever and ever.

(Micah 4:2–3, 5)

In the New Testament Jesus taught:

Blessed are the peacemakers, for they will be called children of God.

(Matthew 5.9)

You have heard that it was said, 'Love your neighbour and hate your enemy.' But I tell you: Love your enemies and pray for those who persecute you, that you may be sons of your Father in heaven. He causes his sun to rise on the evil and the good, and sends rain on the righteous and the unrighteous.

(Matthew 5:43–45)

There are only two occasions when Jesus appears to be angry and to take action himself: one was when he cursed a fig tree which was not bearing fruit:

Early in the morning, as he was on his way back to the city, he was hungry. Seeing a fig tree by the road, he went up to it but found nothing on it except leaves. Then he said to it, 'May you never bear fruit again!' Immediately the tree withered.

When the disciples saw this, they were amazed. 'How did the fig tree wither so quickly?' they asked.

Jesus replied, 'I tell you the truth, if you have faith and do not doubt, not only can you do what was done to the fig tree, but also you can say to this mountain, "Go, throw yourself into the sea," and it will be done. If you believe, you will receive whatever you ask for in prayer.

(Matthew 21:18–22)

The other time was when Jesus threw the money-changers out of the Temple in Jerusalem:

Jesus entered the temple area and drove out all who were buying and selling there. He overturned the tables of the money-changers and the benches of those selling doves. 'It is written,' he said to them, '"My house will be called a house of prayer," but you are making it a "den of robbers".'

(Matthew 21:12–13)

When Peter tries to stop Jesus being arrested in the Garden of Eden, Jesus prevents him:

> With that, one of Jesus'
> companions reached for his
> sword, drew it out and struck the
> servant of the high priest, cutting
> off his ear. 'Put your sword back
> in its place,' Jesus said to him, 'for
> all who draw the sword will die by
> the sword.'   (Matthew 26:51–2)

> And he touched the man's ear and
> healed him.   (Luke 22:51)

Many Christians have followed Jesus'
example and have refused to respond to
situations with violence.

Rustin Bayard was a black American
Christian born in 1910. He studied at
several universities but never took a
degree. From 1941–1953 he worked for
the Fellowship of Reconciliation, a non-
denominational religious organisation
and also organised the Congress on Racial
Equality in New York. He opposed racial
segregation but was a firm believer in
non-violent pacifist agitation. He became
a close adviser to Martin Luther King Jr,
Land organised the March on Washington
in 1963. He also organised a student
boycott of New York City's schools in
protest against racial discrimination. He
died in 1987.

Dietrich Bonhoeffer was a German
Christian who was killed by the Nazis for
helping Jews to escape from concentration
camps, and for his part in a plot to
assassinate (kill) Adolf Hitler. Although
Bonhoeffer was a Christian and a pacifist,
he believed the atrocities in Germany had
to be stopped at any cost.

He saw the treatment of the Jews by his
fellow Germans as an abomination. He
joined the Abwehr, a group which planned
to assassinate Hitler. The plan failed and in
1945 he was hung for treason. Although he
was planning to kill another human being,
he is still called a pacifist.

Even in the case of war, Christians believe
that they should forgive other people who
have injured them. It is therefore not right
to treat prisoners-of-war badly or to kill
anyone unnecessarily.

This is based on Jesus' instruction to Peter:

> Then Peter came to Jesus and
> asked, 'Lord, how many times
> shall I forgive my brother when
> he sins against me? Up to seven
> times?' Jesus answered, 'I tell
> you, not seven times, but seventy-
> seven times.'
> 　　　　　　　　(Matthew 18:21–22)

Activity

Is it correct to describe Dietrich
Bonhoeffer as a pacifist? Explain your
answer.

Christian beliefs about the treatment of criminals

Jesus' message could be seen as preaching
love and forgiveness and that therefore
criminals should not be punished.
However, what he was preaching was
true justice whereby people were not
judged and punished by people who were
themselves no better than the criminals.

This is seen in the story of the women
accused of adultery:

> 'If any one of you is without sin,
> let him be the first to throw a
> stone at her.' Again he stooped
> down and wrote on the ground.

> At this, those who heard began
> to go away one at a time, the
> older ones first, until only
> Jesus was left, with the woman
> still standing there. Jesus
> straightened up and asked her,
> 'Woman, where are they? Has no
> one condemned you?'

> 'No one, sir,' she said.

> 'Then neither do I condemn you,'
> Jesus declared. 'Go now and leave
> your life of sin.'   (John 8:7–11)

Jesus did not say that the woman had done
nothing wrong but that her accusers were
not fit to judge her.

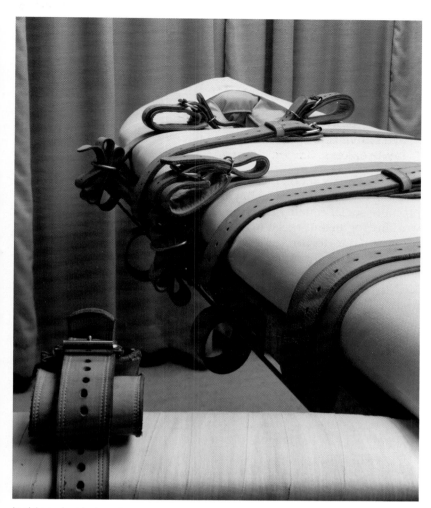
Inside a deathchamber.

Therefore, Christian teaching shows that people should be punished for their crimes but if they demonstrate that they truly regret what they have done then they should be forgiven. In addition, criminals must be tried by people who themselves are fair and honest.

The most severe punishment is capital punishment which is loss of life. Some Christians believe that capital punishment is still appropriate for very serious crimes, though others believe that it is never right to take a life because all human life is sacred and criminals must be punished justly but not executed.

Punishment by imprisonment is the most common way of dealing with people who break the law and are believed to be a risk to society. However, many Christians have been concerned about the way in which prisoners are treated. A Quaker, Elizabeth Fry (1780–1845), worked to improve the

conditions for prisoners and to ensure that they received their basic human rights both in prisons in the United Kingdom and when transported abroad, particularly to Australia. Many thousands of prisoners had died on these prison ships.

Today, this work is continued by the Howard League for Penal Reform. This was based on the work of a non-conformist, John Howard (1726–1790). Howard travelled all over Europe studying prisons and trying to find the best and most humane way of managing them.

Christians accept that criminals must be punished as without some form of punishment there can be no concept of justice. Similarly, although the criminal would be forgiven, the innocent need to be protected.

Christian responses to social injustice

Christians believe that social injustice is wrong because everyone was created by God and is therefore equally valuable to God.

Prophets of the Old Testament such as Amos urged people to fight social injustice:

> **This is what the Lord says:**
> **'For three sins of Israel,**
> **even for four, I will not turn back my wrath.**
> **They sell the righteous for silver, and the needy for a pair of sandals.**
> **They trample on the heads of the poor as upon the dust of the ground and deny justice to the oppressed.'**   (Amos 1:6–7a)

People are also told to have respect for foreigners:

> **When an alien (foreigner) lives with you in your land, do not mistreat him. The alien living with you must be treated as one of your native-born. Love him as yourself, for you were aliens in Egypt. I am the Lord your God.**
>   (Leviticus 19:33–34)

These teachings are repeated in the New Testament:

My brothers, as believers in our glorious Lord Jesus Christ, don't show favoritism. Suppose a man comes into your meeting wearing a gold ring and fine clothes, and a poor man in shabby clothes also comes in. If you show special attention to the man wearing fine clothes and say, 'Here's a good seat for you,' but say to the poor man, 'You stand there' or 'Sit on the floor by my feet,' have you not discriminated among yourselves and become judges with evil thoughts?

Listen, my dear brothers: Has not God chosen those who are poor in the eyes of the world to be rich in faith and to inherit the kingdom he promised those who love him? But you have insulted the poor. Is it not the rich who are exploiting (taking advantage of) you? Are they not the ones who are dragging you into court? Are they not the ones who are slandering (speaking badly of) the noble name of him to whom you belong?

If you really keep the royal law found in Scripture, 'Love your neighbour as yourself,' you are doing right. But if you show favoritism, you sin and are convicted by the law as lawbreakers. (James 2:1–9)

Many Christians act on these teachings and join organisations which work to promote social equality. This may be working for an anti-racist organisation, for prison reform, for Amnesty International or for organisations which support disadvantaged people such as MENCAP. Amnesty International was founded in 1961 by the British lawyer Peter Benenson who was a Christian.

Activity

Carry out some research into the work of Amnesty International and find out about some of the people whom they have managed to free from imprisonment.

This topic looks at:
- Muslim attitudes towards war – the concept of jihad
- Muslim attitudes towards the use of violence and pacifism
- Muslim beliefs about the treatment of criminals
- Muslim responses to social injustice.

Muslim attitudes towards war

The concept of jihad

The Arabic word **jihad** is often wrongly translated in the west as 'Holy War'. Jihad actually means 'to struggle in the way of Allah'. It is the personal effort made by every Muslim to devote his or her life to carrying out Allah's will and also means the fight against evil. This is greater jihad. A person who performs jihad is called **Mujahid.**

> The most excellent jihad is the uttering of truth in the presence of an unjust ruler. (Hadith)

Lesser jihad

Although jihad does not mean war, many Muslims believe that the fight against evil and the preservation of Islam may justify going into battle. This is then described as **Harb al-Muqadis**, which is technically a Holy War.

> The Prophet was asked about people fighting because they are brave, or in honour of a certain loyalty, or to show off: which of them fights for the cause of Allah? He replied, 'The person who struggles so that Allah's word is supreme is the one serving Allah's cause.' (Hadith)

Muhammad ﷺ himself led his followers into battle at the Battle of Badr in 624 CE, this was to defend the safety of the Muslims in al-Madinah. This was the first example of jihad being put into action on the battlefield.

Islam sees self-defence as a just cause for war, but Muslims are forbidden from being the first to attack.

> **Fight in the cause of Allah those who fight you, but do not transgress limits; for Allah loveth not transgressors.** (Surah 2:190)

A war cannot be described as jihad if:
- the war is started by a political leader rather than a religious leader
- an individual person declares war without the backing of the Muslim community
- the war is aggressive not defensive
- peaceful ways of solving the problem have not been tried first
- the purpose of the war is to force people to convert to Islam
- the purpose of the war is to gain land or power
- innocent women and children are put at physical risk
- trees, crops and animals have not been protected
- the war involves the destruction of homes or places of worship.

Muslims see jihad as a way to peace. The aim is to create a society where Muslims can worship Allah in peace, without other beliefs or politics being forced upon them. According to the Qur'an and the sayings of the Prophet (contained in the Hadith), Muslims are forbidden from starting a war. If the enemy offer peace, then Muslims too must put down their weapons.

In Muslim states where Islam governs politics as well as religion, fighting to protect your country and religion is seen as something that people should be prepared to do if necessary.

Muslim attitudes towards the use of violence and pacifism

As well as 'submission', the word 'Islam' can also mean 'peace'. Peace in Islam does not mean accepting a situation if it is unjust, but enemies and oppressors must be fought without hatred or vengeance, and once the battle is over, peace must be restored and differences reconciled.

> **Hate your enemy mildly; he may become your friend one day.**
> (Hadith)

The Qur'an teaches that all people are created by Allah and are therefore equal:

> **Of His Signs is the creation of the heavens and the earth, and the diversity of your tongues and colours.** (Surah 30:22)

Muslims must take these teachings about equality from the Qur'an and try to implement them in the world.

Islam aims to see an international order in the world which would enable people to live without the threat of attack or unjust rulers and without prejudice or discrimination on religious, cultural, social or economic grounds. The struggle to reach this world order is jihad. By working towards peaceful co-existence Muslims are living in obedience and submission to Allah and helping to save humanity from destruction.

Muslims are openly critical of any struggle or fighting between Muslim countries, as this goes against the whole concept of jihad.

Discussion

Consider how Muslims in a non-Muslim country might respond if they thought their religion was being threatened.

Activity

Give a full explanation of jihad and show how it might affect the life of a Muslim.

Muslim beliefs about the treatment of criminals

Islamic law, Shari'ah, is the basis for judgement and the treatment of criminals.

Shari'ah means the 'way to water', or the source of life. Living according to shari'ah is the way in which Muslims can reach Allah.

Islam recognises three types of sin: the first is shirk, associating someone or something with Allah; the second, zalim, consists of crimes such as murder, theft, suicide and illegal sexual relations; the third type covers lying, cursing and envy.

Punishment in Islam has nothing to do with the removal of sin, as only Allah can forgive and this only happens when someone is really repentant and asks God for forgiveness. Punishment is seen as a means of protecting and strengthening society.

It is believed that only Allah can know all the circumstances surrounding a particular person and their actions.

Penalties are known as hudu – 'boundaries' rather than punishments as they enforce boundaries between right and wrong that have been crossed.

Hudu applies to crimes which are dealt with in the Qur'an or Hadith. For example in a case of murder:

> **...if anyone slew a person—unless it be for murder or for spreading mischief in the land it—would be as if he slew the whole people**
> (Surah 5:32)

Soldiers outside a mosque in Najaf, Iraq.

This means that the only justification for murder is if the victim has committed a murder or if they are guilty of speaking against Allah and corrupting his teachings.

However, it is still not permitted to kill anyone except through legal means.

Adultery or fornication (sex outside of marriage):

> The woman and the man guilty of adultery or fornication—flog each of them with a hundred stripes: let not compassion move you in their case, in a matter prescribed by Allah, if ye believe in Allah and the Last Day: and let a party of the Believers witness their punishment. (Surah 24:2)

Defamation – destroying someone's character:

> And those who launch a charge against chaste women, and produce not four witnesses (to support their allegations)—flog them with eighty stripes; and reject their evidence ever after: for such men are wicked transgressors. (Surah 24:4)

Theft:

> As to the thief, male or female, cut off his or her hands: a punishment by way of example, from Allah, for their crime. (Surah 5:38)

Islam also allows for the person who has suffered from the crime to have recompense (compensation):

> O ye who believe! The law of equality is prescribed to you in cases of murder: the free for the free, the slave for the slave, the woman for the woman. But if any remission is made by the brother of the slain, then grant any reasonable demand, and compensate him with handsome gratitude. This is a concession and a Mercy from your Lord. After this, whoever exceeds the limits shall be in grave penalty. (Surah 2:178)

Concession – allowed by.

It is important to remember that once a person has been punished, repented and asked God for forgiveness, they must be treated normally – there is no further guilt and they must not be punished further in any way.

These punishments are those laid down by shari'ah but are not necessarily imposed, and much depends on the country in which the crimes are committed. The underlying principle here is that the laws are to protect society, not just to seek punishment of the criminal. Individual courts and countries may therefore interpret hudu in different ways. Allah is seen as forgiving and merciful and people are therefore urged to do likewise.

Muslim responses to social injustice

Islam sees three groups of people as being in need and requiring special care and attention: orphans; the needy; and travellers.

> What Allah has bestowed on His Messenger (and taken away) from the people of the townships—belongs to Allah—to his Messenger and to kindred and orphans, the needy and the wayfarer; in order that it may not (merely) make a circuit between the wealthy among you. (Surah 59:7)

Islam hopes that orphans can be brought up by relatives or family rather than in an institution. Orphans are entitled to know their family's history and background and to receive any inheritance that comes from their parents.

> To orphans restore their property (when they reach their age), nor substitute (your) worthless things for (their) good ones; and devour not their substance (by mixing it up) with your own. For this is indeed a great sin. (Surah 4:2)

The needy are the poor, disadvantaged or handicapped.

161

> It is not fault in the blind, nor in one born lame, nor in one afflicted with illness.
>
> (Surah 24:61)

Travellers in this sense are beggars or people who have lost all hope and Islam says they should be helped and encouraged to return to a stable and secure life.

Finally, there are the elderly. Elderly people are seen as the wealth of Islam because of all the work they have done in their lives and Muslims must show great respect to them:

> Thy Lord hath decreed that ye worship none but Him, and that ye be kind to parents. Whether one or both of them attain old age in thy life, say not to them a word of contempt, nor repel them, but

> address them in terms of honour. And, out of kindness, lower to them the wing of humility, and say: 'My Lord! Bestow on them thy Mercy even as they cherished me in childhood. (Surah 17:23–24)

The elderly are the wealth of Islam.

Discussion

Consider how Muslims might feel that they should respond to issues of social injustice and why they would act in certain ways.

Activity

Compare Muslim rules about the punishment of criminals with punishment theory.

Summary

This unit deals with the very serious issues of war, peace and justice. In different ways, all human beings are affected by these in some form during their lives.

It may be how people react to their own country, or another country going to war; it may be whether people think that any kind of violence is wrong or whether there are some instances where physical violence may be necessary.

It may be particular concerns about how criminals are treated. Some people may feel that all imprisonment is wrong; others may argue that people should be imprisoned until they have repented for their crimes. Some people, both Christians and Muslims, may feel that for some crimes capital punishment is the only suitable treatment.

Some people may also want to consider the treatment of prisoners such as those held by the USA in the Guantanamo Bay prison in Cuba.

Others may consider that for issues concerning both war and justice the best approach is prayer and to leave the resolution of the matter in the hands of God/Allah.

Whatever we do, it is likely to be a long time before we can really say that everyone is treated fairly and that there are no longer any wars being fought because people are living in peace. Nevertheless this is a goal which each of these religions believes we should try to reach so that everyone can have a better, happier and fairer life.

Questions

1 What do you understand by:
   (a) pacifism
   (b) retribution
   (c) deterrence
   (d) reformation
   (e) last resort?

2 Consider whether there really are occasions when we should take the life of another human being.

3 Do you think that it is possible for a member of one of these religions to be a pacifist and a true believer?

4 Consider whether religious people should involve themselves in political questions such as issues of war.

Practice GCSE questions

Christianity

1 (a) Describe Christian teachings about the treatment of criminals. [8 marks]

(b) Explain how Christians might respond to injustice. [7 marks]

(c) 'Religious people should never use violence.'
Do you agree? Give reasons to support your answer, and show that you have thought about different points of view. You must refer to Christianity in your answer. [5 marks]

2 (a) Describe Christian teachings about war. [8 marks]

(b) Explain why Christians might work for peace. [7 marks]

(c) 'Violence is sometimes necessary.'
Do you agree? Give reasons to support your answer, and show that you have thought about different points of view. You must refer to Christianity in your answer. [5 marks]

Tips

In your answer you should consider the way in which criminals should be treated and you may also wish to look at the aims of punishment. However, you also need to deal with specific Christian teachings about punishment and forgiveness.

You might explain Christian attitudes to injustice. You could suggest possible responses such as the use of the vote, protests, petitions, letter campaigns, etc. You might also want to discuss Christians working for organisations that campaign against injustice. You may consider the need for non-violent or, perhaps, violent protest.

In answering this you might consider what exactly are the circumstances of the possible violence and if this means physical fighting, etc. You may put forward a pacifist, non-violent protest view, whilst also considering that violence may sometimes be necessary as in a Holy War for example.

In answering this question you may take a number of routes. You might consider that murder is forbidden in the Ten Commandments, that Just War is permitted, that Jesus may, or may not, have been a pacifist.

In your answer you will probably explain that Christians are generally opposed to violence but you might also explain the occasions when violence may be necessary. You might consider whether Jesus was a pacifist or taught pacific ideals. You might also write about specific Christian groups such as the Religious Society of Friends (Quakers).

You might decide that, from an absolute pacifist perspective the statement is wrong. On the other hand, you may consider that there are positions when most people might be pushed to violence as a last resort. You must remember to refer to Christian teaching in your answer.

Islam

1 (a) Describe Muslim teachings about the treatment of criminals. [8 marks]

(b) Explain how Muslims might respond to injustice. [7 marks]

(c) 'Religious people should never use violence.'
Do you agree? Give reasons to support your answer, and show that you have thought about different points of view. You must refer to Islam in your answer. [5 marks]

2 (a) Describe Muslim teachings about war. [8 marks]

(b) Explain why Muslims might work for peace. [7 marks]

(c) 'Violence is sometimes necessary.'
Do you agree? Give reasons to support your answer, and show that you have thought about different points of view. You must refer to Islam in your answer. [5 marks]

Tips

In your answer you should consider the way in which criminals should be treated and you may also wish to look at the aims of punishment. However, you also need to deal with specific Muslim teachings about punishment and forgiveness and you could also look at the aims of punishment in shar'iah.

You might explain Muslim attitudes to injustice and the commitment to justice, for example the belief that everyone accused of crime has a right to a fair trial, that everyone has the right to freedom of expression, and so on. You could suggest possible responses such as the use of the vote, protests, petitions, letter campaigns, etc. You might also want to discuss Muslims working for organisations that campaign against injustice. You may consider the need for non-violent or, perhaps, violent protest.

In answering this you might consider what exactly are the circumstances of the possible violence and if this means physical fighting, etc. You may put forward a pacifist, non-violent protest view, whilst also considering that violence may sometimes be necessary as in lesser jihad for example.

In answering this question you may take a number of routes. You might consider that murder is forbidden, that Holy War (lesser jihad) is permitted in certain circumstances, and that Islam is essentially a pacific (peace-loving) religion.

In your answer you will probably explain that Muslims are generally opposed to violence but you might also explain the occasions when violence may be necessary. You might consider whether Islam is essentially pacifist and to what extent lesser jihad overrides this consideration.

You might decide that, from an absolute pacifist perspective the statement is wrong. On the other hand, you may consider that there are positions when most people might be pushed to violence as a last resort. You must remember to refer to Muslim teaching in your answer.

Glossary

General

abortion when a pregnancy ends before a baby is born, either by accident (miscarriage) or deliberately (procured abortion)

active euthanasia when steps are taken to bring death more quickly. This is against the law

Amnesty International an organisation that helps people who have been sent to prison unfairly

apartheid a system of government in which people of different races are kept apart

Big Bang a massive explosion which many scientists believe marked the beginning of the universe

conscience a sense of knowing that something is right or wrong

conscientious objectors people whose consciences lead them to object to fight wars

cosmology the science which includes study of the origins of the universe

developing countries the poorer countries of the world

ethical monotheists people who believe that there is one God who gives them moral rules

euthanasia a 'good death'; mercy-killing; the deliberate ending of a life

evolution the process by which living things change through natural selection

hospice a place where terminally ill people can go for nursing and respite care

in vitro fertilisation (IVF) a form of fertility treatment where an egg is fertilised outside the womb

involuntary euthanasia a form of euthanasia where the patient cannot or does not give consent

medical ethics questions of morality which are raised by medical situations

monogamy remaining faithful to only one sexual partner for life

monotheists people who believe that there is only one God

moral evil the kind of evil and suffering that is caused by people doing wrong

natural evil the kind of evil and suffering that is caused by natural events such as earthquakes and floods

natural selection the process by which the fittest creatures best suited to their environment survive and the weaker ones die out

non-violent protest a way of making a point without fighting. Such a protest could be in the form of a march, making a speech, or using a vote

North–South divide the difference between rich countries (which are mostly in the northern half of the world) and the poorer countries (which are mostly in the southern half of the world). *See* developing countries

omnipotent all-powerful; able to do anything

omniscient all-knowing; able to know everything that can be known

pacifists people who believe that violence is never justified

palliative care medical care which involves pain control

passive euthanasia a form of euthanasia where no action is taken to postpone death. This is not against the law

prayer communication between God and humanity

sanctity of life the belief that human life is special to God

segregation the physical separation of different groups of people, especially black and white people. *See* apartheid

voluntary euthanasia a form of euthanasia known as 'assisted suicide', where someone asks for help to bring death more quickly

Christianity

agape a Greek word for unconditional love

altar a table used for sacrifice; in Christianity, it is the table where the Eucharist is celebrated

annulled dissolved – when a marriage is annulled, it means that it is not considered to have been a real marriage from the beginning

Apostles' creed a statement of Christian beliefs

Ascension when Jesus went into heaven after his resurrection

Church of England the Anglican Church, founded by Henry VIII

creationist a person who believes that the biblical story of creation, as described in the book of Genesis, is literally true

Desmond Tutu a black South African Christian who has campaigned against racism

Devil a supernatural power of evil

doctrine of the Trinity the belief that God is 'three persons'; the Father, the Son and the Holy Spirit

double effect the argument that actions such as euthanasia can be allowed if they are a side-effect of a good action such as pain relief

ecumenical movement the work done by some Christians who work to bring peace between the different Christian groups.

ensoulment the time at which a person is believed to receive a soul from God

Eucharist another name for Holy Communion; the sacrament of the sacrifice of Jesus and the unity of Christians

evangelical a kind of believer who emphasises the need to share the Christian faith, and who often takes a more literal view of the Bible

font a basin used for holding water for baptisms

Gospels the four books which tell the story of the life, death and resurrection of Jesus

Holy Communion *See* Eucharist

hymns prayers set to music, for use in worship

Just War theory a theory which outlines the conditions necessary for it to be right to go to war or continue to fight a war

Kingdom of God/Kingdom of heaven a time when humanity is ruled by God and behaves according to agape (unconditional love)

lectern a raised desk on which the Bible is rested when it is being read in church

liberation theology a way of thinking which says that Christians should fight against injustice on behalf of the weak

Lord's Prayer the prayer that Jesus taught. It is used regularly by Christians

Lord's Supper *See* Eucharist

Martin Luther King Jr. a black Christian civil rights activist

Mass the name given to the Eucharist by Roman Catholics (*see* Eucharist)

New Testament the part of the Bible which contains stories of the life of Jesus and teachings about Christian living

Old Testament the part of the Christian Bible which also forms the Jewish scriptures, and was written before Jesus was born

parables stories told by Jesus and by others, which illustrate a moral or religious message

pulpit a raised platform on which a speaker stands in church to be more easily seen and heard

resurrection being raised from the dead to new life

Roman Catholic Church the Christian Church which accepts the authority of the Pope as a successor of Peter

sacrament a symbolic way of acknowledging the grace of God

Sermon on the Mount a collection of Jesus' teachings about the right way to live, found in Matthew 5–7

sermon a speech in which religious and moral ideas are explained, usually in church

stoup a container for holy water, placed near the entrance of some churches

Taizé a Christian ecumenical centre

Trevor Huddleston a white priest who campaigned against apartheid in South Africa

Islam

'al-Janna paradise

Adhan call to prayer. From the same root, Mu'adhin (one who makes the call to prayer)

Akhirah everlasting life after death – the hereafter

al-Fatihah the Opener. Surah 1 of the Qu'ran. Recited at least 17 times daily during the five times of salah. Also known as 'The Essence' of the Qur'an

Al-Mi'ra j the ascent through the heavens of the Prophet Muhammad ﷺ

Al-Qadr the belief that Allah has already decided what will happen to everyone in the world

Din-ul-Fitrah a description of Islam as the natural way of life

fitrah being born without sin

Hadith saying; report; account. The sayings of the Prophet Muhammad ﷺ, as recounted by his household, progeny and companions. These are a major source of Islamic law. Some Hadith are referred to as Hadith Qudsi (sacred Hadith) having been divinely communicated to the Prophet Muhammad ﷺ

Hajj annual pilgrimage to Makkah, which each Muslim must undertake at least once in a lifetime if he or she has the health and wealth. A Muslim male who has completed Hajj is called Hajji, and a female, Hajjah.

Harb al-Muqadis Holy War

Hudu boundaries or penalties

Ibadah all acts of worship. Any permissible action performed with the intention to obey Allah

'Iblis the Jinn who defied Allah by refusing to bow to Adam (peace be upon him), and later became the tempter of all human beings

'Iddah a three month period of reconciliation before a divorce may take place

iman faith

Islam peace attained through willing obedience to Allah's divine guidance

Jahannam the fires of Hell

Jihad personal individual struggle against evil in the way of Allah. It can also be collective defence of the Muslim community

Jinn being created by Allah from fire

Ka'bah a cube-shaped structure in the centre of the grand mosque in Makkah. The first house built for the worship of the One True God

Khalifah successor; inheritor; custodian; vice-regent

Khutbah speech. Talk delivered on special occasions such as the Jum'uah and Id prayers

Laylat-ul-Qadr the Night of Power, when the first revelation of the Qur'an was made to Prophet Muhammad ﷺ. It is believed to be one of the last 10 nights of Ramadan

Makkah city where the Prophet Muhammad ﷺ was born, and where the Ka'bah is located

mala'ikah angels

mihrab niche or alcove in a mosque wall, indicating the Qiblah – the direction of Makkah, towards which all Muslims face to perform salah

minaret a tower on a mosque from which the Adhan or call to prayer is made

minbar rostrum; platform; dais. The stand from which the Imam delivers the khutbah or speech in the mosque or praying ground

Mujahid the name given to a person who completes jihad

Qur'an that which is read or recited. The Divine Book revealed to the Prophet Muhammad ﷺ. Allah's final revelation to humankind

Ramadan the ninth month of the Islamic calendar, during which fasting is required from just before dawn until sunset, as ordered by Allah in the Qur'an

riba interest made on money

Risalah Prophets

Sabians an ancient race of people referred to in the Qu'ran

sadaqah additional voluntary charity which can be given when someone is in need

Salah prescribed communication with, and worship of Allah, performed under specific conditions, in the manner taught by the Prophet Muhammad ﷺ, and recited in the Arabic language. The five daily times of salah are fixed by Allah

Salat-ul-Jumu'ah Friday prayers at the mosque

Sawm the time of fasting, from just before dawn until sunset, during the month of Ramadan

Shahadah declaration of faith, which consists of the statement; 'There is no god except Allah, Muhammad ﷺ is the Messenger of Allah'

Shari'ah Muslim law, which all Muslims should follow. In countries where the government is Muslim, the legal system in based on Shari'ah

Shaytan rebellious; proud. The devil

shirk association. Regarding anything as equal or partner to Allah. Shirk is forbidden in Islam

Surah division of the Qur'an (114 in all)

tawhid the belief that there is only one god, Allah. Allah created and looks after the universe, and he rules and controls everything that happens

Ummah community. The world-wide community of Muslims; the nation of Islam

wudu the ritual washing of hands, mouth, nose, face, arms, head, ears and feet before prayer

Yawmuddin The Day of Judgement

zakah the payment of money to the Muslim community, which purifies the remainder of a person's wealth

Zalim wrongdoing against Allah, other people, or yourself